# Winner Takes All

Exceptional People
Teach Us How to Find
Career and Personal Success
in the 21st Century

# Winner Takes All

---

## Exceptional People
## Teach Us How to Find
## Career and Personal Success
## in the 21st Century

---

Noelle Nelson

INSIGHT BOOKS

PLENUM PRESS • NEW YORK AND LONDON

Library of Congress Cataloging-in-Publication Data

Nelson, Noelle C.
   Winner takes all : exceptional people teach us how to find career
and personal success in the 21st century / Noelle Nelson.
      p.    cm.
   Includes bibliographical references and index.
   ISBN 0-306-46005-X
   1. Success--Psychological aspects.  2. Success in business.
I. Title.
BF637.S8N425   1999
158.1--dc21                                                99-12706
                                                              CIP

ISBN 0-306-46005-X

© 1999 Noelle Nelson

Insight Books is a Division of Plenum Publishing Corporation
233 Spring Street, New York, N.Y. 10013

10 9 8 7 6 5 4 3 2 1

A C.I.P. record for this book is available from the Library of Congress

Printed in the United States of America

To Suzy and Frank Cross,
the original Winners in my life

# Contents

# PREFACE

When I was all of 6 or 7 years old, my parents took me to see my first opera—*Madame Butterfly*. At the climax of the performance, the desperate Cio-Cio-San fully realizes the extent of her supposed husband Pinkerton's abandonment, and sees no way out of the shame brought on by his betrayal. Just as Cio-Cio-San takes her father's ceremonial dagger and is about to impale herself, I jumped up from my seat and screamed at the top of my lungs, "No! No! Don't do that!" My astounded parents tried their best to calm my anguished sobs, explaining that it was just make-believe, but I wasn't fooled. I knew better. Even when Cio-Cio-San came to take her bow at the final curtain, I was convinced this was some other person wearing poor dead Cio-Cio-San's clothes.

Since then, I've stubbornly refused to believe that there was no way out, and have always looked for positive solutions to the difficulties, challenges, and uncertainties that we all face at one time or another, each in our own unique way. I am profoundly convinced that "There's got to be a better way!" than giving up on ourselves or on life. *Winner Takes All* is yet another step on my continuing journey toward that better way. Human beings are so very valuable and life so very precious that it deserves to be lived happily and successfully. I pray I may contribute in some small way to that happiness and success.

*Encino, California*

# ACKNOWLEDGMENTS

I wish to thank first and foremost all the Winners in the world who are the shining lights for the rest of us. My thanks also go to the journalists of *Time, U.S. News & World Report,* the *Los Angeles Times, Parade, People, New Age, Reader's Digest,* the electronic media, and the many others who report on Winners' challenges and successes so that all of us can know about them and be inspired. Despite what is often said, I have found the media to be rich with accounts of positive, uplifting examples of the human experience.

I thank my editor, Frank Darmstadt, who somehow manages, despite all his other obligations, to be always available to me, and whose unerring instincts and professionalism have helped me write a better book than I could on my own. My thanks to Alan Young and all the other fine staff at Insight Books, who make my job easy. Special thanks go to Diane Rumbaugh, whose patience, good humor, terrific research skills, and unflagging enthusiasm I value beyond words. My deepest gratitude to Mitchell Taubman, Ph.D., who was kind enough to read the original manuscript and whose wise words helped it become a "for real" book.

For permission to quote copyrighted materials, I am grateful for the excerpt from *Love, Medicine & Miracles: Lessons Learned about Self-Healing from a Surgeon's Experience with Exceptional Patients* by Bernie S. Siegel, M.D. Copyright © 1986 by B. S. Siegel, S. Korman, and A. Schiff, Trustees of the Bernard D. Siegel, M.D., Children's Trust. Reprinted by permission of HarperCollins Publishers Inc.

I value your thoughts and comments, and can be reached via E-mail at nnelson@dr.noellenelson.com, fax at (310) 392-0747, or voice mail at (310) 859-4604. Thank you!

# Winner Takes All

Exceptional People
Teach Us How to Find
Career and Personal Success
in the 21st Century

# QUIZ

## ARE YOU A 21ST CENTURY WINNER?

Here is a quiz to help you determine your personal "Winner Quotient"—how closely your attitudes and beliefs resemble those of Winners.

Answer the following by circling *True* for the statements you agree with, and *False* for those you disagree with.

| | | | |
|---|---|---|---|
| 1. | The Future is wide open, it is whatever you make of it. | True | False |
| 2. | Whatever happens, happens. You have no control over your Future. | True | False |
| 3. | We live in a frightening world and the best thing you can do is just try to get by. | True | False |
| 4. | The world can be a scary place, but there's still plenty of room for happiness and success. | True | False |
| 5. | Success is all about luck—either you've got it or you don't. | True | False |
| 6. | You're never too old to learn. | True | False |
| 7. | You can't teach an old dog new tricks. | True | False |
| 8. | Man is inherently good. | True | False |
| 9. | Man is inherently evil. | True | False |
| 10. | Give people an inch, they'll take a mile. | True | False |

1

| | | | |
|---|---|---|---|
| 11. | People are generally trustworthy. | True | False |
| 12. | People will take advantage of you every chance they get. | True | False |
| 13. | Life's a grand adventure, with all its ups and downs. | True | False |
| 14. | Life's a struggle, then you die. | True | False |
| 15. | Where there's a will there's a way. | True | False |
| 16. | Every cloud has a silver lining. | True | False |
| 17. | As one door shuts, another door opens. | True | False |
| 18. | My past does not determine my future. | True | False |
| 19. | I am a product of my past. My future is already set. | True | False |
| 20. | Who I am is up to me. | True | False |
| 21. | No matter how hard I try, or how hard I work, I'll never end up on top. | True | False |
| 22. | Who I am is what my parents, society, schools, and other people have made me. | True | False |
| 23. | Who I am inside matters more to my ability to succeed than any specific skill I have or don't have. | True | False |
| 24. | The only thing that matters is the packaging: how you package yourself determines your success. | True | False |
| 25. | If you're not computer literate and technologically minded, forget it—you'll never make it in the Future. | True | False |
| 26. | If you're over 40, it's almost impossible to have a successful Future. | True | False |
| 27. | Age carries with it a wealth of experience, a broadening of abilities, and a sense of perspective, which can be put to good use in a successful Future. | True | False |
| 28. | Everybody has within them what it takes to be a Winner. | True | False |
| 29. | Some people are born Winners, others aren't. You can't fight your fate. | True | False |
| 30. | Dreaming is for children and fools. | True | False |
| 31. | Dreaming is the very stuff of which reality is made. | True | False |
| 32. | There is nothing like a Dream to create the Future. | True | False |
| 33. | Dreams are a waste of time. | True | False |
| 34. | Dreams come in all shapes and sizes. | True | False |

| | | | |
|---|---|---|---|
| 35. | The only dreams worth having are big dreams | True | False |
| 36. | Dream all you want, but it's still just fantasy. | True | False |
| 37. | Commit yourself to making your Dream come true, and you're halfway there. | True | False |
| 38. | When you dream a Dream, you can also dream the means and opportunities to get you there. | True | False |
| 39. | Choice is scary. If you make a wrong choice, you're stuck with it. | True | False |
| 40. | Choice is the way you focus your attention and energy on something. If you don't like the results, make a new choice! | True | False |
| 41. | The ability to accomplish my Dreams lies within me, in my inner qualities. | True | False |
| 42. | Success is all about timing—you have to be in the right place at the right time, that's the only thing that matters. | True | False |
| 43. | Success is continuous: continually reborn, renewed, rechosen, and ever changing. | True | False |
| 44. | Money is the greatest resource of all. With it, you can do anything. Without it, you can do nothing. | True | False |
| 45. | Imagination is the greatest resource of all. It is the magic key that opens the door to all other resources. | True | False |
| 46. | Whatever resources I need to accomplish my Dream are out there—all I need to do is search creatively for them. | True | False |
| 47. | Once you're successful, hold on with all your might to what you've got and how you got it. You have to stand firm to weather any storm. | True | False |
| 48. | Once you're successful, be fluid and flexible enough to change when change will move you in the direction of continued success, including changing your dreams when they become outdated. | True | False |
| 49. | If it ain't broke, don't fix it. | True | False |
| 50. | If it ain't broke, make sure it still contributes to your success, for otherwise it may be an impediment. | True | False |

To determine your Winner quotient, add up the number of *True*s you circled on the following statements: 1, 4, 6, 8, 11, 13, 15, 16, 17, 18, 20, 23, 27, 28, 31, 32, 34, 37, 38, 40, 41, 43, 45, 46, 48, 50.

If you circled between 21–26 of these statements *True*, congratulations! You're already a Winner, showing your true colors by wanting to learn even more about becoming increasingly successful.

If you circled between 13–20 of these statements *True*, you're doing great! You're well on your way to becoming the truly successful Winner you always secretly suspected you could be. Use the information given in this book to help you fully get there.

If you circled between 6–12 of these statements *True*, keep up the good work! You know some of what it takes to be a Winner and are ready to learn more. You will find much of value in this book to develop your Winner's potential more fully.

If you circled between 0–5 of these statements *True*, welcome to a new and different adventure! You'll find much in this book to open your mind to a new way of thinking, which you can put to good use for your success in the Future.

Now that you know where you stand, read on to discover why these beliefs and attitudes are characteristic of Winners and how they will benefit you in the pursuit of *your* 21st century success.

# INTRODUCTION

What do you do . . .

- when you're 52 and all dressed up with nowhere to go, a casualty of "downsizing"?
- when you're in complete remission after the mastectomy and your doctor happily announces that you can look forward to another 50 years . . . that you didn't plan for?
- when you realize that second family you started at 45 is going to be your responsibility for the next 30 years and you haven't a clue how you're going to handle it?
- when what you've been trained to do and loved all your life goes not just out of business, but also out of existence?
- when you are 20 years old and it seems there is no way out: no one wants to hire you, no one wants to know your problems, and the world is in a mess?
- when you finally get out of that battering relationship, and find yourself happily single, yet terrified you won't make it on your own?
- when it seems your field of endeavor is full of younger, sharper, hipper contenders and your years of acquired expertise no longer mean much?

- when you've worked hard all your life, looking forward to retirement and get ousted at 60, with a pension just big enough to feed the dog?
- when you've been the homemaker, and your partner dies unexpectedly leaving insurance too negligible to matter, debts neither of you anticipated, and a future that looks unutterably bleak?
- When everything you thought was sure and solid suddenly slips away, when all you expected to happen doesn't, and what you didn't expect does, when your well-laid plans for your future become irrelevant overnight?

## WHAT DO YOU DO?

Everything is different now. The old rules no longer apply. What used to spell success, doesn't. "Work hard, keep your nose to the grindstone" may just mean you get your nose ground. Loyalty to a company may only mean goodbye to that golden parachute (or watch) as you sink with the corporate ship. We're living to ripe old ages and who's ready for it? Our world has become amazingly unpredictable. The rate of change in all areas—work, social, technological, biological, communications, political—is geometric.

Life expectancy alone has radically altered how we view our lives. We are living longer—much longer. Diseases and injuries that would have killed us or greatly shortened our lives are now treatable, good health is being sustained way beyond what we had anticipated, and we have no maps for this part of the journey. We have no idea what is in front of us, of how to thrive in those extra 30–40 years most of us seem to have been granted.

In the work world, you can no longer expect your company to last (mergers, acquisitions, failures) or your job to last (downsizing, replacement of jobs with computers and temps, disappearance of many middle management positions). For that matter the skills you have relied upon valiantly for your entire work life may be completely outdated by next week! A young man, for example, trained as a graphic artist, painstakingly created labels and other such commercial graphics by hand. He left to do a year of volunteer work abroad; when he returned, commercial graphics were now being done completely on computer, and he had to retrain from scratch. You may or may not stay long enough with the company to receive your pension, which, given the sudden leap in longevity, will probably not be enough to take care of you anyway. Your wife may decide to have a child postmenopausally; those children you thought were out of your home for good may return. The list goes on and on.

What was once a known and therefore predictable future for most people has become an unknown and therefore unpredictable future. Too many of us confronted with years of living yet to do find ourselves terrified of being unable to cope. Traditional problem-solving approaches do not seem to apply. "Go back to school" yes, but to do what? "Get another job" yes, but how and what? Everywhere you look, life seems so chaotic, unpredictable, unstable, and getting more so. The result is depression (a disorder of hope, the inability to see a positive future) and anxiety (panic and fear of the future), the levels of which we have never seen before.

Why? What is it that makes this particular time, the eve of a new millennium, so different? What is revolutionary about the times we are living, and will continue to live as we enter the 21st century, is the changing proportion of what is Known to what is Unknown. It used to be that when an individual looked into his or her Future, most of it was "known" in that most of it could be predicted on the basis of the past, on how other people had lived, and on the nature of the world. Up until about 10 years ago, you would have felt secure, for example, in predicting that as a 50-year-old man, you'd probably be in the same job until retirement at 65, and have a modest pension through your company. With that, your savings, and Social Security, you could live comfortably—although watching your budget—in the house you live in now, until about 72 or 75 years of age, when you'd probably quietly leave this life in your sleep. This was pretty much what people around you were doing, and there was no apparent reason to think you'd be doing anything all that different. To that extent, your Future was "known."

In the last 10 years or so, all that has changed. The Unknown has taken precedence over the Known. There is far more Unknown now in our Future than there is Known. This is not a passing trend. Given the continuing advances in technology (mechanical and biological), which alter not only the way we live and the number of healthy years available to us, but also the way we communicate and relate to one another, the Unknown will continue to grow relative to the Known with each passing year. This is why traditional means and methods of dealing with one's Future are not sufficient. Traditional means and methods attempt to deal with the Known. Getting a good education, learning job-related skills, working hard, doing your best—all these are wonderfully valuable steps to success, but they don't begin to address the unpredictable and changeable nature of the Future we are now facing.

In order to deal with the increasingly large portions of Unknown that will compose our Future, we need new ways of approaching our individual and collective Future if we are to be successful. Abraham Maslow, a visionary pioneer in the area of human growth and potential, was already aware in the late '60s of the phenomenal rate of change and what it implied. Maslow talked about the need for a new type of human being, "people who don't need to staticize the world, who don't need to freeze it and make it stable, who don't need to do what their daddies did, who are able confidently to face tomorrow not knowing what's going to come, not knowing what will happen, with confidence enough in ourselves that we will be able to improvise in that situation which has never existed before."[1] Where are we to find these new ways of being, of going about our lives? *From those who, in their own way, have already faced a similar unpredictable Future composed more of Unknowns than of Knowns—and been successful.*

In my practice as both a psychologist and a trial consultant, I have worked with literally hundreds of individuals who have experienced life-altering events that dramatically changed the nature of their lives from one moment to the next. Some lost their lifelong jobs to downsizing or new technology, some were faced with obligatory retirement at a relatively young age (athletes, people engaged in physical activities), some were struck by illness or injury, and some were surprised by unexpected wealth, children, or fame. Of these people, some have been able to refashion their lives in highly successful and innovative ways. Others seem to be "stuck," as it were, in the time and place of the event, unable to create new lives for themselves. Both types of individuals faced the same disruption of life as they knew it; both types were faced with a Future that no longer had any predictability or resemblance to the Future they had assumed would be theirs. Yet for some reason, one group of individuals constructed new and often very successful lives for themselves, and the other did not. This seemed to be as true for people in the public eye as for those leading more private lives. As I worked with and observed the individuals who were successful in refashioning their lives, the reasons why came to light. Successful individuals, whom I came to refer to as "Winners," had an entirely different way of dealing with an unpredictable and uncertain Future than those who were less successful. I realized that these Winners could help us learn much needed new ways to approach our Future. All of us, as we go into the 21st century, face a largely Unknown, highly unpredictable, and uncertain Future. From these exceptional people, we can learn how to be successful in the Unknown of our personal Future.

What is it that Winners know, that we don't? Well, it has little to do with their age, sex, ethnicity, education, or bank account. The many examples of exceptional people throughout this book show the universality of Winners, for Winners come in all shapes and sizes, representing a wide range of ages, ethnicities, physical abilities/disabilities, intellectual levels, occupations, and socioeconomic status. The difference is not in Winners' outward appearance or abilities, but in their inner traits and qualities, qualities we all have in abundance, but whose power we fail to recognize or use. The ability to create success in the face of an Unknown Future has to do with *who you are*, not the specifics of what you do or have. Winners share certain beliefs, attitudes, and ways of dealing with the Future, which I have come to think of as a *winning mindset*. That mindset appears to be a tendency to reach into the Future for answers, rather than into the past. Winners are unusually good at leaving the past behind them and turning their focus clearly toward the Future. Not only do Winners spend little time looking into the past for the reasons why a life-changing event happened to them, but in addition, Winners don't turn to the past to find how to respond to the event. Winners look to the Future for how to succeed in the Future. Until I investigated how they did that, it seemed impossible. How could you look to the Unknown for answers? Yet I have witnessed, time and time again, that looking to the Future for Future success is indeed a powerful solution to the uncertainties of the Unknown, and that is what led to my writing this book.

Why does this matter to you? Because like it or not, the years ahead will be turbulent, tumultuous ones. New skills will be required to succeed in the face of rapid change and constant innovation. People who learn these new skills will be better able to navigate successfully through what otherwise would be a perilous Unknown. People who use this knowledge will have the means to lead happier, more prosperous lives than those who don't. It's as simple as that. However, you don't need to wait for a crisis, or to have your Future yanked from under you, to use these skills. On the contrary, using the skills described in this book will help you deal successfully with the Future so you *don't* find yourself in crisis situations. And if, unfortunately, you do, then knowing these skills will help you resolve your crisis more swiftly and successfully. Either way, you'll come out—a Winner.

## How to Use This Book

Described in this book are eight steps to your success in the Future, each step represented by a chapter. These steps are the ways I have observed that Winners use to approach the Future successfully, and that I have in turn shared with my clients to help them assure their Future. The steps constitute an *approach* to the Future, so it doesn't matter whether you want to create a successful Future for yourself in the area of work, relationships, sports, or other pursuits; these steps will provide you with a sure and steady path to success. The examples in the book are primarily work and career oriented, since for many people, that's the area of most concern in the upcoming century.

Each step builds upon the preceding ones, so it's best to read the chapters in sequence. You might want to read the book quickly through a first time to get an overview of the approach and how the steps fit together, then come back to each chapter and apply the recommended steps to your desired Future.

In Chapter One, you'll learn about the power of belief, and how a certain type of belief will open the Future up to you in a positive and dynamic way.

In Chapter Two, you'll find out how you are far more equipped to succeed in the Future than you ever realized, as you explore the value of your inner qualities.

In Chapter Three, you'll discover the impact Dreams have on your ability to succeed in the Future and how to dream a very special Dream for yourself.

In Chapter Four, you'll learn to harness the power of your Dream so that it is no longer "just a Dream" but a vibrant choice that will pull you firmly into your success.

In Chapter Five, you'll realize how to empower your Dream with your own inner qualities, and how to choose and commit to it so you are securely anchored in a positive Future.

In Chapter Six, you'll realize how many valuable resources you have at your immediate disposal, and how to use them to transform your Dream of success into a reality you actually live day by day.

In Chapter Seven, you'll see how you can develop a Winner's attitude, which will give you the emotional and psychological muscle to succeed, even when the going gets rough.

In Chapter Eight, you'll find out how important flexibility is to your success in the Future, and how to make the adaptations and adjustments that will keep you steady on your success track, over and over and over again.

To help you better understand how to use the steps in creating a successful Future for yourself, I've used the example of how four very different individuals—Paul, May, Kathy, and Jim (names and other details changed to protect their privacy)—from completely different backgrounds and situations, were introduced to and learned to use the eight steps in creating their Futures. As you read their stories, think about your situation and how the solutions Paul, May, Kathy, and Jim came up with as they faced challenges, problems, and difficulties might help you in the development of your success.

At the end of each chapter there is a section called "Personal Success Log" that will guide you in step-by-step fashion to the development of your own Winner's traits. You'll be creating your personal "Manual for Success in the 21st Century" as you think about and answer the questions asked of you in each of the eight Personal Success Logs.

The Future is a vast Unknown, exciting and mysterious. Use the eight steps as Winners do, to help you go confidently into that Future, creating the success, love, joy, and abundance you truly deserve, the life of a Winner!

## NOTES

1.  Abraham H. Maslow, *The Farther Reaches of Human Nature* (New York: Viking Press, 1972), p. 59.

# CHAPTER ONE

---

## BELIEVE IN A POSITIVE FUTURE

*When I Look into the Future, What Do I See?*

Beliefs are the bedrock upon which all experience is built. Your success depends on the beliefs you hold. What you believe determines how you go about things, whether you seek out one type of situation or another, and what you are or are not willing to try. Beliefs that in the past wouldn't have held you back, nowadays will.

For example, you may believe that "you can't teach an old dog new tricks." As long as our world was relatively stable, you didn't have to learn many "new tricks" once you were an adult and functioning comfortably in society. For generations, if you were a typesetter for example, you could work for a newspaper your whole life without altering how you did your typesetting hardly at all. Your belief that "you can't teach an old dog new tricks" didn't affect your success. But with the explosion of change in every area, it's no longer possible to be successful without being willing to learn new skills. Beliefs that mattered little before, now take on critical importance.

So, for example, given your belief that "you can't teach an old dog new tricks," you believe you're too old, at all of 54 years of age, to learn how to work with computers—even though you're well aware of the growing importance of computers in virtually all businesses. So you don't seek out people-friendly computer courses or schools, you don't try to

13

find a support group for the computer-challenged, you walk right past the "Computers for Dummies" section of your local bookstore; in short, you don't even try to find out if there is a way for you to learn computers. As far as you're concerned, it won't work, so why bother. Meanwhile, you are closing yourself off from umpteen opportunities for your advancement and future success. You are enslaved by your limiting belief.

Winners hold beliefs that free them to seek maximum benefit from their world. Let's say, for example, you have a 62-year-old brother, who believes "you're never too old to learn." Truly a Winner's belief. Your brother, guided by his belief, has somehow managed to find himself a subsidized program for "seniors learning computers" at the local high school. It's not costing him a dime to learn as much as he wants to about computers, he's managed to buy a rebuilt computer for a ridiculously small sum from the company that supplies the school, and, to boot, he has a new social set composed of like-minded seniors. They're considering designing their own Web page as soon as they can figure out which one of the local servers will give them the best deal. Just as your belief ("old dog") enslaves you, your brother's ("never too old") has set him free to pursue a new and potentially profitable arena. Your brother's belief is typical of a Winner. It is open, expansive, and encourages personal growth.

All of your beliefs, about yourself, your abilities, your potential, your "place" in the world, and so forth, affect how you live your life. In fact, beliefs are so powerful that they can even affect whether you live or die. Dr. Bernie Siegel, the well-known surgeon who works primarily with cancer patients, discusses how critical beliefs are to one's survival. One of his patients, Edith, a frail woman who weighs only 85 pounds, told Dr. Siegel she didn't need him or his "Exceptional Cancer Patients," a group Dr. Siegel started to help patients deal with emotional and psychological issues underlying their cancer. Edith said, "I don't need you and your group. My mother always told me when I was a youngster, 'You're scrawny, but whatever happens, you'll always get over it. You'll live to be 93, and then they'll have to run you over with a steamroller.'" Edith, Dr. Siegel reports, "has survived a heart attack, a bleeding duodenal ulcer, the death of her husband, and breast cancer invading the chest wall. She is now alive more than half a dozen years after her surgery. Every time something happens, she hears her mother's words." Edith believes her mother's words. By all rights, Edith shouldn't be alive, given what she has gone through! Yet, because of the power of belief, what Edith holds as truth directly impacts even something as basic as her health. "If we all programmed our children this way," Dr. Siegel goes on to say, "we'd be creating survivors."[1]

Your beliefs about the Future will determine how you live your Future. The good news is that if you find you have beliefs that limit your ability to create the Future you want for yourself, you can change them. One of the major foci of Dr. Siegel's Exceptional Cancer Patients Group is the changing of patients' beliefs, so he can help them become "survivors." By changing your beliefs, you take the first step toward changing the way you live your life. No matter how difficult or wonderful your past has been, no matter what your life is like now—good, bad or indifferent—by changing your beliefs about the Future, your Future life can be better. That's how important beliefs are. The bad news is you can't change your beliefs unless you know what they are. Even though our beliefs run our lives, most of us have little if any conscious awareness of what those beliefs are. Because the Future is something few of us look at until it is upon us, our beliefs about the Future tend to be even more unconscious. So the first thing to look at in creating a successful Future for yourself is "What are my beliefs about the Future?"

## DISCOVER YOUR BELIEFS ABOUT THE FUTURE

In going about discovering your beliefs about the Future, start by looking for your "core beliefs." These are beliefs that make broad, sweeping statements about life. Core beliefs have the greatest impact on your life because one core belief will generate a whole host of secondary beliefs. For example, "Man is inherently good" is a core belief. If you believe that "Man is inherently good," then you will hold a number of secondary beliefs consistent with your core belief, such as "People are generally trustworthy," or "When you give people the benefit of the doubt, they'll usually rise to the occasion." If you have a core belief stating that "Man is inherently evil," your secondary beliefs will be quite different, for example: "If you give people an inch, they'll take a mile," or "People will take advantage of you every chance they get." These secondary beliefs are what determine how you see life and how you live it on a day-to-day basis.

If you hold a core belief that "The Future is a wonderful realm of immense opportunity," your secondary beliefs will be positive and attract the kinds of experience that support your vision of a joyous and success-filled Future. "The Future is wide open, it is whatever you make of it," for example, is a typical Winner's core belief. It is a core belief that stresses the enormity of possibilities available in the future, and the degree to which an individual is in charge of his or her own future. From this belief, Winners will generate secondary beliefs such as "Where there's a will, there's a way," "Every cloud has a silver lining," and "As one door shuts another one opens." These secondary beliefs determine how Winners evaluate their experiences and what they are willing to do or not do. Winners' beliefs imply a Future full of positive possibilities, and support Winners' ability to go into the Unknown with confidence and hope.

Your core beliefs about the Future directly impact how you will or will not go forward successfully into the Unknown. Unfortunately, many of us do not have such positive core beliefs. Most people's core beliefs about the Future tend to fall into one of the following four categories, all of which will potentially hamper your ability to create a successful Future for yourself.

- The Future is a great big yawning pit of nothingness.
- The Future is a terrifying and fearful place.
- The Future is all rosy and wonderful.
- The Future is controlled by forces outside yourself.

The easiest way to find out what your core beliefs are about the Future is to ask yourself:

"When I look out there, in the Future, what do I see?"

This was the first question I asked of four individuals—Paul, May, Kathy, and Jim—whose lives had been disrupted for various reasons, and who suddenly had to create new Futures for themselves. Each of them was facing the Unknown. Each of them came to me to help them through this unexpected and often frightening life change.

PAUL, a middle manager for the past 30 years with a small company specializing in business supplies and office copiers, had been squeezed out of his job when his company merged with a larger company. He felt lost, a fish out of water, confounded by the lack of available jobs and worried that his age (midfifties) meant he would stay jobless.

MAY, a 32-year-old single mom, had survived her cancer despite all predictions to the contrary. Although this was great news, May was overwhelmed by the debts she'd incurred and the total change of lifestyle required if she was to continue to survive.

KATHY had been successful all her life, yet now at 50 found that as much as she wanted to keep working as a hair stylist in television and movies, the "biz" no longer wanted her. Wanting with all her heart to deny the reality of what was happening to her, Kathy nonetheless had eventually to come to grips with the question: "What am I going to do for the rest of my days? Am I now just a throwaway person forever stuck on the sidelines of life?"

JIM, 44 years old and proud owner of his own rig, lived by the phrase "Once a trucker, always a trucker"—until his ailing back made it clear that something was going to have to change. Jim had no idea where to start creating a different life for himself; as far as he was concerned, life was something that just fell in your lap and you dealt with it.

Paul, May, Kathy, and Jim's names, of course, have been changed, as well as other details to protect their confidentiality. However, Paul, May, Kathy, and Jim's stories are very similar to many other people's stories, and can help us a great deal by serving as examples through each of the eight steps of becoming a Winner.

Paul, May, Kathy, and Jim each had different core beliefs about the Future, which in turn impacted their vision of what was and wasn't possible for them.

Paul's vision was of an empty Future, one that held no hope.

## The Future Is a Great Big Yawning Pit of Nothingness

When Paul came to see me, he was profoundly depressed. At 57 years of age, Paul was out in the marketplace, beating the pavement, but he couldn't seem to find a job. "There are just too many middle managers out there," Paul told me, angrily. He was morose about the direction his life would take from here on. In addition, Paul felt betrayed and abandoned. He couldn't believe that the company where he had spent his entire working life would boot him out, just like that, regardless of his years of service.

Recruited straight out of business college, Paul had started as a junior assistant, rising steadily until he achieved his middle management position, where he expected to stay until he retired at age 65—a typical career path in his line of work. Paul loved his job, and he was good at it. Becoming a "casualty of the merger" was something he never expected.

When I asked Paul, "When you look out there, in the Future, what do you see?" he replied despondently: "Nothing. A great big nothing. Up until a year ago, I knew what life was about, I knew what my future held: keep my nose to the grindstone, tow the line, work steadily until retirement and then enjoy the rest. But since I got laid off, I don't see a future. No one's hiring middle managers, my retirement fund is just enough to cover the basics, and that's if I do everybody a favor and die by the time I'm 70. What's to enjoy? Frankly, I don't see anything when I try to see ahead. Just a great big empty hole."

I nodded. I was only too familiar with this story, having heard similar tales from so many others. To see the Future as a great big pit of yawning emptiness is tragic. Paul cannot conceive of a positive Future for himself; his beliefs preclude that. Seeing nothing, only emptiness, in the Future gives Paul nothing with which to guide him to success. The very living of life becomes a burden.

"It makes doing everything so hard," Paul said, getting up from his chair, pacing restlesly as he continued. "You have no idea. It's all I can do to get up in the morning—if you can call it morning. Some days I don't make it out of bed until 10:00, 11:00—me! Who always used to rise with the birds and made fun of anybody who was still in bed at 7:00 A.M. Well I'm eating my words now. My wife complains that I drag around all day, and she's right. I shuffle to the kitchen, shuffle to the living room, shuffle back to the bedroom, I feel 102 years old, and I'm only 57! Oh, I do all the "right" things—I comb the paper for ads, send in resumes, I even worked with a headhunter for a while. Doesn't matter, nothing works—and nobody cares. They should cart me off to the glue factory. There's nothing left for me to live for, nothing." Paul sat heavily back down in his chair, his energy spent.

Paul's depression is profound because he has lost all hope, and it is the loss of hope, more than any other single aspect, that keeps us from moving forward into the Future. We need something in that vast darkness of the Unknown, something to light our way into the Future, and that "something" is hope.

Hope is the ability, among all possible outcomes, to see glimmers of positive possibility. If you don't see the glimmer of a positive possibility ahead, you won't move forward. It just won't happen. Winners' beliefs are hopeful beliefs that affirm the continually renewed opportunities for happiness, growth, transformation, meaning, abundance, and success life offers. Winners are capable of holding such beliefs in the face of the most horrific-appearing Futures.

Viktor Frankl, for example, well-known psychologist and survivor of the German concentration camps, realized that the individuals who did the best in the face of the unspeakable horror of the camps were those who were constantly reaching out for a meaning to fulfill, for something that would allow them to transcend themselves.[2] Seeking for meaning is only possible if you first have a belief that meaning exists, that there is a reason to reach out. That reason is called "hope." Hope is very much what keeps human beings alive and seeking a better Future, for themselves as well as for succeeding generations.

The Future becomes empty, as it has for Paul, when you cease to believe there are any positive possibilities "out there." He cannot even begin to create a successful future for himself with such a belief as his foundation.

Unlike Paul's, May's vision was of a well-filled Future. The only problem was that May's Future was full of fear.

## The Future Is a Terrifying and Fearful Place

When May first started coming to see me, she was suffering from anxiety and panic attacks. May had been diagnosed with breast cancer two years earlier. Despite the mastectomy, her cancer had metastasized, and May wasn't expected to survive. Lo and behold, after more surgery, chemotherapy, radiation, rigorous changes in diet and lifestyle, and all sorts of alternative health modalities, May did survive and her cancer is in remission. Her doctor not only pronounced her well, but more than likely able to live a long and healthy life.

"Which is great," May said, "And I'm tremendously grateful, but what am I supposed to do now?!" As pleased as she was with her astonishing recovery, May was in a state of complete panic. A 32-year-old single mom, May was raising her 11-year-old son on her own. Her ex-husband was unfortunately a "deadbeat dad," and neither she nor her son, Thomas, had seen hide nor hair of his dad for over five years. "I'm it," May said. She was the only means of support for herself and her son, whom she loved dearly.

May had done financially well as a pattern maker, but she couldn't go back to pattern-making because of the demanding hours and constant pressure characteristic of the garment industry. "My doctor says I just wouldn't survive it, but what else can I do?" May asked. "I have to work, or we won't eat!" May had spent all her savings, insurance, and what little pension she had accumulated on medical bills. She'd taken out loans wherever she could. May still owed lots of money and had barely enough to live on for a couple of months. She couldn't get disability anymore because she was no longer really disabled. May was desperate. She knew she had to do something, but had no idea what.

When I asked May, "When you look out there, in the Future, what do you see?" "What do I see?" May replied. "Starvation! Me and Thomas, ending up homeless somewhere. Horrible images." May stopped a moment, trying to keep her already rapidly beating heart from speeding up on her. "Take your time," I said. "Breathe. It will help." "I'm OK," May replied, "I just get so upset every time I think about the Future. I'm scared to death. I mean, I wasn't expected to survive, I've spent my life's savings—and I'm here! I'm alive. And it looks like I'm going to live, knock on wood, for a long time. I mean, let's face it, I'm only 32. Which is great, except I don't know what I'm gonna do. I can't go back to work as a pattern maker, I don't have any other skills. The best I can probably do is a burger-flipping job, but that'll hardly pay the rent and besides, they'll probably say I'm overqualified." May shook her head, her brow furrowed with worry as she continued. "I'm at my wit's end. I can go on welfare for a while, but then that'll stop; I'm not really disabled, so I can't get disability. No matter where I turn, the Future looks awful! I'm worried sick all the time, and then I get these panic attacks. The Future? I'm petrified!"

It is awful when all you see in the Future is a collection of life-threatening, terrifying possibilities. No wonder anxiety kicks in at that point. Anxiety, which usually starts with worry, can eventually progress to full-blown panic attacks, such as May's, agoraphobia, where you're too scared even to leave your home, or a variety of other debilitating responses. When you believe that the only possibilities in the Future are frightening ones, it is very difficult to build toward a positive Future. You have no basis from which to do so. Your beliefs freeze you in place, limiting your ability to see beyond the negatives to a possible positive. A fearful Future is no better than an empty one.

If, for example, you believe that the Future is a nightmarish place, where crime, terrorism, and random violence abound, your beliefs will lead you to closing your doors, restricting your ventures into the Unknown or the new, for fear of your life. "But Dr. Noelle," you say, "there are already lots of criminals, terrorists, and violence in our world. I can't make myself believe that tomorrow I'll wake up, and presto! no more violence. It's just not going to happen." I agree. It would be foolhardy to believe such a thing, and that's not how Winners operate. A Winner, fully aware that there are criminals, terrorists, and violent people in our world, will hold beliefs that *despite* such people there is plenty of room for goodness and joy in the Future, and therefore will remain open to a positive Unknown.

There is a world of difference between *acknowledging* the existence of violence in the world, and *holding the belief* that the world is a dangerous and violent place. Acknowledging the existence of violence in the world can lead to many positive acts, which in turn can lead to many successes: leading a neighborhood watch, becoming a police officer, becoming a spiritual healer, being a teacher to disadvantaged youngsters, being a prison counselor, to name but a very few possibilities. Holding the belief that the world is a dangerous and violent place just makes people want to hole themselves up somewhere safe and try to last it out as best they can. You will not venture out into the Unknown if your beliefs make it too fearful to do so. Holing yourself up is the opposite of moving forward into the Future.

But what about those who see a rosy Future? Wouldn't it seem that believing in a rosy Future would guarantee safe and successful passage into the Unknown? Well, it depends what that "rose" is based on, as Kathy found out.

## The Future Is All Rosy and Wonderful

"When you look out there into the Future," I asked Kathy, "what do you see?" Kathy, a bright, vivacious 50-year-old, was grappling with an uncertain sense of identity and self-esteem. When she came to see me, she hadn't been hired at her chosen profession, hairstylist to performers on television shows and movie sets, for quite a while. Given her age, Kathy felt a true change of life coming on, not just hormonally, but also in other ways. As much as she didn't want to think about it, and often denied it, Kathy had an underlying fear that her age made her a "has-been" in the TV and movie business and that she would soon have to create a totally different life for herself. Given her level of denial, I wasn't surprised by her answer.

"Oh, I never think about things like that," Kathy laughed. "The Future? Everything always turns out just fine, it always does. I'll get hired on a film, something will turn up, and everything will be fine." I point out, as gently as I can, that Kathy hasn't been hired on a film, a series, or even had a "day call" for over 18 months, and that despite a wonderful resume she is regularly being passed over for hair stylists who have far less experience but are 20 years her junior." "Oh, that's a phase, just a phase, you'll see!" she explains. "Nothing to worry about."

As tempting as it is to say that Kathy's beliefs about the Future are those of a Winner, they aren't. First of all, her "rose" is based on denial, not reality. You can no more build a positive Future for yourself by believing that the Future is full of only positive possibilities than you can by believing that the Future is loaded with only the ghastly negatives. Winners are uncommonly good at seeing *both* the positive and negative possibilities in their Futures and then making choices that are clearly focused on the positive, thus firmly supporting their likelihood of success. Believing, for example, that "Every cloud has a silver lining" acknowledges that there are clouds *and* that there is a benefit to be derived from every mishap. Believing that "Life is a grand adventure" expresses a willingness to see the whole of life, ups *and* downs, as an experience worth living. Winners are realists in their ability to acknowledge all aspects of life, and they are optimists in their choice of beliefs to guide and direct them.

Secondly, Kathy's assumption that everything will turn out fine *because it always has* is fallacious. The last thing we can expect the Future to be is whatever was true in the past. The very thing that makes our individual and collective Futures so different than the futures of previous generations is the far greater proportion of Unknown that lies before us. Our grandparents could look ahead into their Future and be quite confident that what they foresaw, based on past experience, was what would come to pass. Your parents thought that they could do the same. And until fairly recently, they could. But as of the 1990s and from here on in, your past is no longer a reliable predictor of your Future. "Oh, that's terrific," you say sarcastically. "So if I've had a good track record in the past, that means I won't in the future?" you ask. No, that's not what it means. It means that your track record in the past, in and of itself, is irrelevant to your success in the Future. You may have fantastic success in the Future—indeed, this book is dedicated to helping you achieve such success—but it won't be because you've been successful (or unsuccessful!) in your past.

Resting your Future on the belief that "things will turn out fine because they always have in the past" is foolhardy at best and likely to lead to disaster. This is not to say that the belief "Things will turn out fine" is problematic, it's resting that belief on *past history* that is the problem. Winners often believe that "Things will turn out fine," and such a belief is frequently what sustains them through long periods of challenge and difficulty. However, their belief is based on seeing the positive possibilities that lie in the *Future*, not in their past.

If seeing the Future through the rose-colored glasses of denial won't help you create the Future you ardently desire, neither will giving that Future away to someone or something other than yourself. Jim's vision of the Future was virtually nonexistent, since he didn't see himself as having much if anything to do with the creation of that Future.

## The Future Is Controlled by Forces Outside Yourself

At 44 years of age, Jim had been a long-distance truck driver for over 20 years, proud of having bought his own rig before he was 30. Trucking had served Jim well over the years, but it was time to quit. When he began his sessions with me, Jim had been having back problems and various stress-related ailments for over two years. Jim would say to me, "I've got to get out of trucking, Doc, it's going to be the death of me." The problem was, Jim couldn't retire because he didn't have any savings. "I never really thought about it," he told me. "I thought I'd be trucking all my life, like most truckers." He didn't belong to a union, so he had no pension plan, and what little he could claim from workmen's compensation didn't even "feed the dog," according to Jim. "So I guess I'll just keep on trucking," Jim said. "There isn't much else for me to do."

"Well, maybe, maybe not," I said. "Let me start by asking you, Jim, when you look out there, in the Future, what do you see?" I ask. "I dunno" says Jim. "What do I see—umm, I guess I'll be doing pretty much what I'm doing, unless something comes along and I get to do something different." "Get to do something different?" I ask, not understanding. "Yeah, you know if the economy changes and maybe someone offers me a good job, you know. The Future is just what happens to you tomorrow, and you know, whatever happens is whatever is going to happen. Why sweat it?"

Why, indeed? Because if you don't direct your Future, if you don't actively take charge of it, "whatever happens" is indeed what you will get. When you believe that the Future is just "what happens to you tomorrow" you're no longer in charge of your life. You can't create the Future you desire unless you're willing to be in charge of it. Believing, as Jim does, that the Future happens *to* you, rather than the Future being something you create, is very disempowering. It limits your ability to be proactive, to seek out and thus actualize your chosen Future. With this type of belief as the foundation to your Future, you will only see those possibilities that *others* open up to you—and that is a very limiting set of possibles, indeed. Your Future happiness and success then become dependent on the whim of others. That's a chancy road to personal success, at best.

Your Future is going to be created for you by someone or something. When we're young, by default it's our parents or other caretaker. At 10 years old, you don't get to make decisions such as "I'm not going to school next year," or "I'm moving to Omaha to make a better life for myself." Kids don't have much choice in such matters. But by the time you're grown, it's your decision, or whoever/whatever you're allowing to do the job for you. Winners are adamant in their belief that they are in charge of their Futures, regardless of how dependent they may be on others. Winners firmly believe that it is up to them to run their own show, even if they need a great deal of help and support to do that.

## CHALLENGE YOUR BELIEFS

Once you know what your beliefs are about the Future, then you can start taking charge of the success in your Future by deliberately looking at those beliefs. In other words, *challenge your beliefs.*

How do you do that? First of all, by understanding the nature of a belief.

## *A Belief Is Not a Fact*

A belief is a statement about something, a conclusion we reach about how life works, based on what we've observed, or what we've been told about how life works by parents, primarily, as well as by schools, churches, friends, and society at large. A belief is not a fact. Yet belief is what we act upon, and more often than not, what we assume is fact. If you believe that all dogs are dangerous, you're not likely to have one as a pet. If you believe people are basically dishonest, you'll count your change very carefully and eye any stranger with great wariness. If you believe that you have to be very intelligent to be a chiropractor, and you believe you are of limited intelligence, you won't try to get into chiropractic school, even if that's your heart's desire. The possibility that a number of fine chi-

WINNER'S CIRCLE

Beliefs come in all shapes and sizes. Thomas Rollerson's "Dalmatian Dreams" was born out of a single belief: that every human being, regardless of age, deserved to realize one final wish. Frustrated when his lover, dying of AIDS, was told he was too old to have his final wish fulfilled, Rollerson, then 29 years old, created "Dalmatian Dreams," the only national wish-granting foundation for adults. As of 1998, the foundation had, in its short four-year existence, granted some 700 final wishes to terminally ill people. It is utterly amazing what Winners can accomplish when fueled by positive belief.[3]

ropractors are of average intelligence, or that you are intelligent enough to make it into chiropractic school, never occurs to you. You don't even try. Your actions are dictated *by your belief.*

You use your beliefs as you would an instruction manual, your personal "How to go about living life." What you believe is what will determine what you are and are not willing to do. "Fact" has little to do with it. Most "facts," as scientists long ago discovered, are variable and change as we are better able to measure, explore, observe, and discover. The world was flat, until we discovered it was round. Man can't fly, until the Wright brothers did. Women can't bear children after menopause, until medical science found a way for women to do so. There was no life on Mars, until scientists found traces of the elements that are the basis for life. For a very long time, it was believed that it was impossible to run a four-minute mile. Now athletes do it all the time. There are very few "facts" that do not change. Rather than assume that something you believe is fact, question it. You will radically alter your concept of what is possible for you in the Future with that one simple change. Knowing how beliefs work will allow you to choose beliefs that work for you.

## Beliefs Attract Experience

The second life-altering realization about beliefs is that beliefs attract experience. What does that mean? That what you believe directly impacts the experiences you will have in life. Your experiences are a result of the information you receive in any given situation, and how you respond to that information. For example, you're walking along, and you see a big burly man waving his fists and muttering to himself. Based on this information, which you receive as evidence of an angry and therefore potentially dangerous man, you respond to the situation by crossing over to the other side of the street to avoid a confrontation. Another individual might receive the same information as evidence of a slightly mentally disturbed man, caught up in his own private turmoil and unlikely to harm anyone, and respond to the situation by feeling compassionate toward the man and just walking on by.

How you received that information and how you responded to it was determined by your beliefs. Beliefs determine what you will be open to, what you will pay attention to, what you will pick up from among all the environmental stimuli bombarding you at any given moment. This happens through a process known as "selective perception." You couldn't possibly pay attention to everything going on around you all day long, so you "selectively perceive" what is relevant to you, what is of interest to you. The beliefs you hold directly influence the kinds of information and stimuli you will pay attention to.

We all have a sort of radar, a scanning system that helps us select what we will pay attention to. Your beliefs behave much like radar, which lets in certain information that crosses its screen, and rejects other information as being unworthy of attention. If, for example, you have a belief that "The world is out to get me," your "radar" will scan the environment for "proof" that that is the case. You will interpret the various events of your day in a way that upholds and supports the belief "The world is out to get me." For example, when a car cuts in front of you on the freeway, you will ascribe it to "They are out to get me."

Another individual, who believes "I'm a lucky person," looks for "proof" that substantiates a "lucky" belief, and will interpret the same event as "Wow, was I lucky that car didn't hit me." Your beliefs directly influence how you experience your world.

Beliefs are enormously powerful. How you experience your world dictates much of how you respond to that world. If your beliefs about the Future are limiting and constricting, you will respond to your Future accordingly. By challenging your beliefs, you will see whether you are setting yourself up for a successful Future, one full of joy and abundance, or a miserable Future, one filled with despair and scarcity. From there you can choose beliefs that work for you in your pursuit of Future success rather than against you.

## WINNER'S CIRCLE

Lani Guinier, 48 years old, believes that power comes from moving on, from choosing to move forward even when life hits you upside the head. Such a belief empowers winners like Guinier to succeed where others might fail. In 1993, Guinier, who was teaching law at the University of Pennsylvania, was nominated by President Clinton to be in charge of the Justice Department's civil rights division. A heated battle ensued over her nomination, spurred by some of her academic writings. Guinier was not allowed to answer the criticism, and soon thereafter Clinton abruptly withdrew her nomination. Despite enduring humiliation and public embarrassment, Guinier chose to move forward, and in July of 1998 became the first black woman ever named to a tenured professorship at Harvard Law School. Her belief in the possibility of a positive Future is what enabled her to move forward and create that Future for herself.[4]

As I helped Paul challenge his beliefs, he came to see how much he had confused belief with fact, which both depressed him and stunted his ability to create the Future he wanted. Our starting point was examining Paul's conviction that "there is nothing out there."

PAUL

I asked Paul to look a little deeper and see what possibilities other than complete emptiness might be "out there" in the Future for him. "OK, so I'm looking. And what I see is—there's nothing out there for me. That's really all I see," Paul said, despairing. "That's a belief, Paul," I said gently. "It is not a fact. It is a statement about something, and that statement may be true or false—or anything in between." "Semantics!" Paul cried out. "I'm in hell here and you're playing semantics with me!" "No, I'm not, Paul," I replied. "If I'm playing anything at all, it's the truth game." "What do you mean?" Paul asks.

"You believe that there is nothing out there for you," I reply. "But the truth is that there is an infinity of things out there for you." "Like what?" Paul asked. "Like finding some kind of work that totally enthralls you," I replied. "Work that fulfills you in ways your previous work never did, perhaps whole new areas of interest, ways of contributing to society while doing good for yourself that you've never thought of." "OK," Paul said slowly, "All right, that might be out there, but for me? I don't have any marketable skills, apparently, and I don't know where I'd even begin to look for new areas of interest." "I can appreciate that, Paul," I said, "but you see, it isn't your Future that is bleak. It's your *beliefs* that are making it seem bleak. Your beliefs are limiting your view of what is out there. And beliefs can be changed." "I don't get it" Paul said.

"OK," I said, continuing, "you concede that you might be able to conceive of positive possibilities in the Future, but you don't have any marketable skills with which to make those happen, right?" "Right," said Paul. "That's a belief, Paul, that's not a fact," I continued. "The fact is, you don't know if you have marketable skills. You believe that you don't. You may fear that you don't. But in truth, you don't know. The same with areas of interest. As it stands right now, you don't see any that attract you. You may fear that there aren't any. But the only true statement is—you don't right this minute see any other interesting areas of interest. That doesn't mean they don't exist."

"So what do I do now?" asked Paul, somewhat sarcastically. "Just say to myself 'I believe I have marketable skills' and that's it, my Future is now magical?" "No," I replied, smiling. "What you do now is open yourself to the *possibility* that you don't have all the answers, that there may be many as yet unknown joyous possibilities in your Future, and be willing to start with that belief as your foundation, rather than clang the door shut on future happiness by choosing to believe there's none out there. The truth is, there's none out there that you can see right this minute. That doesn't mean it isn't out there."

The Future is the Unknown. The Unknown is just that—unknown joys, woes, happinesses, failures, successes, highs, and lows. Unfortunately, our tendency is to think of the Unknown in terms of the negatives. Quite frankly, if babies thought of the Unknown as solely filled with negatives, they'd never leave the bassinet! We fear the Unknown greatly, yet at one time everything was Unknown. Your next breath is unknown, until you've breathed it and then it is known. Being willing for the Unknown to be at least as full of positives as it might be of negatives, as Winners are, is simply a more realistic view of life, and a far more empowering belief with which to go into the Future. Once you open that door for yourself, positive Futures become possible.

Sometimes, however, it is difficult to see how a positive Future could possibly exist. May's fears were so overwhelming, she had difficulty seeing past them to a better life.

MAY

When I introduced May to the concept of positive and negative possibles equally available in the Future, she sighed and said, "It sounds real good to me intellectually, Dr. Noelle, but I just don't buy it." "Why not?" I asked. "Because when I look out there, it's pretty dismal," May replied, unhappy with this whole conversation. "When you say 'dismal,' May, what do you mean?" I asked. "I mean dismal, as in scary. I'm afraid I won't get a job, and if I do, I'm afraid it won't pay nearly enough to take care of us. I'm afraid we'll have to live in some awful cramped place, just eking out enough to live day to day, and that life will be reduced to outrunning the cockroaches. Not a pretty sight," May concluded.

"So basically, fear is running your Future," I said. May nodded her head. "I hate to admit it," she said ruefully, "but in a word—yes." "And you could be right about every single one of your fears," I said. May looked shocked. "Oh please don't say that, Dr. Noelle, I'm terrified as it is," May pleaded. "You could also be completely wrong," I continued. "It is possible, after all that you could get a job. It is possible that you could get a job which would pay more than your last job. It is possible that you could get a job which would enable you to easily afford a comfortable home for you and your son. The problem is that by letting your fearful beliefs run the show, you're not even allowing in the possibility of a bright and hope-filled Future, which means you are highly unlikely to attract positive experiences into your life."

No matter how grim your present seems, no matter how despairing your Future appears to you, be willing to accept the belief that the Future holds positive possibilities. Fear isn't the only human reality. As difficult as it may be sometimes to believe that you'll ever get to a satisfying and happy Future, it is critical to allow the possibility that such a Future exists. Once you've admitted the possible existence of a positive Future, no matter how impossible the way there looks, you open the door to the possibility of manifesting success for yourself.

The wonderful thing about possibilities is that they can be turned into probabilities, and from there into actuality. If, however, you remain unwilling even to conceive of a positive Future, then indeed, you are in all likelihood condemning yourself to a negative Future. Don't do that to yourself. Be willing to believe in the possibility of a bright Future as your first step to getting there.

## WINNER'S CIRCLE

Lithuania's current president, 71-year-old Valdas Adamkus, was forced to flee his homeland when the Soviet Union seized it after World War II. Adamkus emigrated to the United States and lived here 50 years, all the while dreaming of the day his homeland would be free and he could return. Little did Adamkus know he would return as its president! Yet his profound belief that one day his country would be free is what led Adamkus to take the steps that would make him president. Adamkus began by joining the Lithuanian independence movement. Then, during his 30 years with the Environmental Protection Agency, Adamkus visited his homeland as often as possible on environmental projects, addressing fellow Lithuanians over the Voice of America radio broadcasts. When the Soviet Union collapsed, the impossible became possible, and not only could Adamkus return, but his frequent visits to his homeland were judged sufficient to establish residency. Adamkus's work with the independence movement and Voice of America made him well known in his country so he could successfully run for president. All this, starting with Adamkus's simple belief—contrary to all evidence at the time—that one day Lithuania would be free. He then built on that belief by taking concrete steps that led to its realization.[5]

The reverse is also true. Being a "cock-eyed optimist" will not serve you. Seeing the Future as *only* full of bright promises is setting yourself up for a giant fall. If you don't allow for negative possibilities, then you have no protection, no way of dealing with such possibilities should they arise. Then you're suddenly at the mercy of these negative events: having never considered that you might lose your job, that your spouse might up and run away with the local beautician (of either sex), or that your skills might be totally worthless in today's job market, you have no way of dealing with these events should they occur.

Kathy's denial of any negative possibilities in the Future became clear as we examined her beliefs.

KATHY

"Are you telling me I'm in trouble?" Kathy said, aghast. "Are you telling me I'm headed for some awful Future I know nothing about?" "No," I said, "I'm telling you you're headed for a Future you know nothing about. And that if you want it to be a wonderful Future, then you have to be willing to entertain the possibility that your Future could hold negative situations, and therefore it is necessary to create your Future actively, purposefully, rather than leaving it up to "everything always turns out." Leaving "luck" or "chance" or "fate" in charge of your Future is what is scary.

Too often, we choose the belief "Everything always turns out just fine" because we're terrified of looking at what the Future might actually hold. Kathy was scared that if she really looked into the Unknown ahead, all she'd find was loneliness, unhappiness, and poverty. Her belief in a "rosy" Future had no real basis, it was just her way of pushing away the monsters. I spent some time with Kathy helping her look into what she feared would be a miserable Future. As she did so, to her great surprise, Kathy found that she saw much hope and genuine brightness in the Unknown as well as pockets of potential misery and unhappiness. With the two possibilities in mind, Kathy was able to return to her original belief, "Everything always turns out just fine," but from a very different perspective.

"I can see the way things might turn out badly," Kathy said, "and I can choose to believe that even if there are bumps in the road, things still do turn out just fine." Her belief was no longer based on denial. Pretending that the Future will be great by closing your eyes to reality isn't the same as having a grounded belief that the Future holds lots of possibilities for success. Winners aren't afraid of looking at negative possibilities. They know that a realistic assessment of possible dangers and pitfalls is how you avoid those. Kathy's belief was now capable of guiding her to success.

You can't get to a positive Future with beliefs that deny positive or negative possibilities, nor can you get to a positive Future with beliefs that deny your power, the part you play in creating your Future. In challenging Jim's beliefs, the first thing that came to light was Jim's profound conviction that he played no part in creating his Future.

## JIM

I started by asking Jim directly if he believed he was in charge of his Future. "In charge of my Future?" Jim asked, shaking his head. "I don't know where you get such ideas, Doc," he said. "The Future is one big political–economic–social mess—and there ain't nothing you or me can do about it." "So what you're telling me, Jim, is that no matter what you do, you have no impact. You aren't running the show. Someone or something outside of you is responsible for how your life goes," I commented in return. "Well, maybe not how my whole life goes every minute of every day," Jim replied, "but certainly for the Future." "What's the difference?" I asked, curious. "What's the difference between how your life goes every day and your Future?" "Well," Jim said slowly, "the Future is out there somewhere—I can't see it, taste it, smell it, or touch it. My day to day is in front of my nose, thank you very much." "But the breath you breathe now was in your Future just a minute ago," I said, "so how is that different today than next year?" "Well, I'm talking about the big things, you know like getting a decent job outside of trucking, making something of my life, things like that." Jim continued, "I have no impact on the big things. Whoever has the money or the guns has the power, and that's who runs the show. They'll decide if I get a job or whatever. It's that simple. It's out of my hands." "So you see your personal Future as something you have very little control over," I said. "You're darn right I do. No matter how hard I try or how hard I work I'll never end up on top," Jim stated flatly.

With that belief in place, I dreaded to think what Jim's Future would look like. One thing was for sure, he'd never end up on top. His selective perception, his "radar," would never pick up the opportunities for him to get ahead regardless of his efforts, no matter how present those opportunities might be. He would be systematically guided away from such possibilities by his own belief. The thought appalled me. I continued working with Jim.

"Have you ever known anyone to end up on top?" I asked, challenging Jim's belief that he was taking for fact. "What do you mean?" he asked, warily. "Well, did you ever know a trucker, for example, who started out as a trucker and ended up owning a trucking company?" I asked. Jim thought briefly, "Sure, my first boss," he said. "But what does that have to do with me?" "Did your first boss come to own that trucking company because somebody gave it to him?" I asked, ignoring Jim's question for the moment. "No," Jim said slowly, "But the bank gave him the loan he needed." "Did he have any particular leverage with the bank? I mean did his wife work there or his dad own the bank or anything?" Jim laughed. "Not exactly," he replied. " My boss's dad was a migrant farmer and his wife worked with him, doing his books and such." "So he put his trucking company together pretty much on his own," I said. "Yeah, I guess so," Jim said, eyeing me strangely. "What are you getting at?" he asked.

"Well, Jim," I replied, "If one person can do something, anybody can do it. You say your Future is out of your hands, that no matter how hard you work or how hard you try, you'll never come out on top. But here's your old boss, someone you know well, who did come out on top, and who didn't get there by having all the money or guns to do it with. Anything he did, you can do. Your statement 'Whoever has the money or the guns has the power, and that's who runs the show' is just a belief. It isn't fact. If it were fact, your boss couldn't have owned his own company. It would never have happened." "So what you're saying is because he did what he wanted to do for himself, I can accomplish what I want for me," Jim said. "In a nutshell," I said, "yes."

Observing how other people have done things that are contrary to whatever belief it is that you hold is a compelling way to challenge your beliefs. It also demonstrates clearly how a belief is something you choose to accept, not a fact.

The belief that the Future is controlled by others takes away your power. It is a defeatist attitude toward the Future. When you believe you are not in charge of your life, you lose the ability to create an abundant and successful life for yourself. All doors look closed to you, and thus, they are. Challenge such disabling beliefs and take back your power. In the process you will also claim your rightful success in the Future.

## HOW TO DEVELOP BELIEFS THAT WORK FOR YOU

"So how do I do this? What's the solution?" you ask. "I'm not sure what my beliefs are about the Future. What if they're awful? Surely you're not just going to leave me here with a bunch of imprisoning beliefs?" No, not if I can help it! Start, as I did with Paul, May, Kathy, and Jim, by asking yourself the following questions, as you begin your first Personal Success Log.

Answer the questions in the Log to the best of your ability. Think of the Personal Success Logs at the end of each chapter as an opportunity to get to know yourself better. This knowledge will then give you the key elements to creating a successful Future for yourself. You may find that your answers to these questions change over time. That's great! Come back to your Personal Success Logs as often as you like, to help you grow and change in the direction of continual success.

## Personal Success Log 1: Your Beliefs

### Step #1: What Are My Beliefs about the Future?

Most of us go through life without ever asking ourselves what those beliefs are, and thus are powerless to work with them. Ask yourself, what do I believe lies "out there" in the Future? Do I see the Future as a void, a big empty pit of nothingness? What kind of nothing? Be descriptive with yourself.

Do you believe the Future is scary, full of hazards and dangers? And if so, what are those hazards and dangers? Be specific. Is it that the economy will just get worse and worse? That crime will be increasingly rampant? That getting a decent education will be impossible for all but the very wealthy and thus not for your children? What specifically are your fearful beliefs about the Future?

Do you believe that "luck" or "fate" determines your Future? That as long as you work hard and keep your nose to the grindstone you'll be fine? Do you believe that if you just "follow the rules" you'll be OK? These are disempowering beliefs, because they don't take into account that if you're working hard at something that's going out of date, you won't be successful. If you're following the rules, what happens to you when the rules change?

Do you believe someone or something else is in charge of your success? Is it the economy, or the politicians, or your crummy family that never gave you anything in life that stands in your way? Do you believe that the unpredictability of the world stands in the way of your success?

An easy way to discover your beliefs about the future is to write a stream of consciousness starting with the words "I believe the Future is . . ." and then writing anything and everything that comes to mind. Don't censor yourself, just keep writing. Whenever you get "stuck,"repeat your beginning prompt, "I believe the Future is . . ." until you've written about two pages worth. More is fine, just try to get at least two pages written. Then go back, and pinpoint what your different beliefs are. You may surprise yourself! Make a list of your beliefs, without judging or censoring them as "Oh that's a terrible belief." Just make your list. It will become the basis of your power.

*Step #2: Transform Your Disempowering Beliefs into Empowering Beliefs*

Now it's time to transform your disempowering beliefs into empowering beliefs. Beliefs aren't set in cement. Beliefs are simply habits, ways you are used to thinking about things. You can change your beliefs, just like you can change your habits, any time you want.

First, sort out your empowering beliefs about the Future from your disempowering beliefs. Empowering beliefs are those that support your growth into a positive Future. Disempowering beliefs are those that either limit your growth, or support a negative view of the Future. An empowering belief, for example, is one that says "Money is the root of much good." Such a belief supports your desire for abundance in a positive Future. "Money is the root of all evil," is a disempowering belief. It limits your monetary growth if you wish to be a good person, and thus supports a negative view of the Future (you'll be poor). The empowering belief that "The Future is wide open, full of opportunities" clearly supports growth (opportunities) in a positive Future. The belief that "The Future is dark, scary, and full of pitfalls" is a constricting one. It both limits your growth—people tend to advance very cautiously in dark scary places full of pitfalls—and fosters the perception that the Future holds only negative experiences.

Take the list you created in Step #1 and pull out the disempowering beliefs. Write those down separately. Then next to each disempowering belief, write out what might be the empowering belief you could replace it with. For example, replace "The economy is only going to get worse" with"No matter what the economy does, some people always make money, and I intend to be one of them." Replace "I'll never get anywhere, I have no marketable skills" with "I have all the marketable skills I need to get wherever I want to, I just don't know what those are yet—and what I don't have, I can acquire." Then make a list out of all your empowering beliefs, put it up on your bathroom mirror (or the fridge!) so you can see your list frequently, and read your list several times every morning and every night, until your new empowering beliefs are as much a part of you as your old disempowering beliefs were. Habits are formed out of repetition. Use repetition to form new habits—new beliefs—which serve you well. You will start to *perceive* your world differently, and as you do so, you will *experience* your world differently. Eventually, you will begin to *act* differently, in line with your new beliefs.

Let the Unknown of the Future work for you rather than against you. Accept the belief that there are at least as many positive possibilities in the Unknown as there are negative ones, and choose, as Winners do, to hold those beliefs that open you to those positive possibilities.

Once you've opened yourself to positive possibilities about the Future, you're ready to open yourself to positive possibilities about yourself. For if you are to create a new Future, there is first the creation of a new you.

## NOTES

1. Bernie S. Siegel, *Love, Medicine & Miracles: Lessons Learned about Self-Healing from a Surgeon's Experience with Exceptional Patients* (New York: Harper & Row, 1986), p. 87.
2. Viktor Frankl, *Man's Search for Meaning* (New York: Pocket Books, 1959, 1980).
3. Alex Tresniowski, Ron Arias, "Wishful Thinker," *People Magazine,* July 6, 1998, pp. 117–118.
4. Christina Cheakalos, Elizabeth McNeil, "Talking Back," *People Magazine,* July 13, 1998, pp. 115–117.
5. Anne-Marie O'Neill, Craig Mellow, Barbara Sandler, "Prodigal President," *People Magazine,* June 29, 1998, pp. 129–132.

# CHAPTER TWO

## CREATE A NEW FOUNDATION FOR SUCCESS

### Who Am I? What Do I See in Me?

We used to say "I'm a sales rep, a teacher, a lawyer, a secretary, a convenience store manager, an orderly, a housewife, a school janitor," or whatever our occupation was, and base our sense of "Who I am" on our ability to *do* that specific thing. You'd learn how to do something, and you could legitimately expect that with a few adjustments and adaptations to new technology or ways of doing things, you could do pretty much the same thing your whole life. New technology didn't get implemented all that quickly and certainly not industry-wide overnight.

All that has changed dramatically. Basing your ability to go forward successfully into your Future on a specific set of skills is a death sentence. Too rarely are those skills going to remain constant, and if they do, then the context or the form in which those skills are used will change dramatically. Take doctors, for example. Doctors with the degree "M.D." have been the primary recognized and accepted health care givers in our society for generations. The medical profession seemed to be one that would never change, at least not in terms of their secure status, economic power, or the way the profession was run. In the past 10 years, however, the rise of alternative health care givers and the numbers of people who treat with them has been astonishing. Not only do many people prefer alternative health care, but traditional M.D.'s now have to take into account and frequently work with such disciplines as acupuncture, chiropractic, and homeopathy if they are to satisfy patient preferences.

Not only have M.D.'s been displaced as the primary health care givers, the setting in which they practice has also undergone tremendous changes. Traditionally, M.D.'s have practiced as "sole practitioners" or in small groups. In both settings, physicians managed their practices by themselves in the way that pleased them. Since the advent of H.M.O.'s and other such "managed care" plans, managing one's practice has vastly changed. Being a successful M.D. now frequently requires an ability to work within the administrative guidelines of managed care, insurance company regulations, and in other such situations where the doctor's recommendations are but one factor in a patient's overall treatment plan. These changes in how practices are run require administrative, management, and communication skills that were rarely before part and parcel of "becoming a doctor."

Such radical change is true in many different professions. A receptionist, for example, used to need to be able to answer phones (later, work a switchboard), take messages, greet visitors, and perhaps do some filing. Now receptionists have been largely replaced by automated phone systems, and whoever is sitting at the front desk to greet visitors is also working on a computer, with virtually no filing to be done, given the status of the paperless office.

Even in our personal lives, "What I do" used to be quite stable. "I'm a wife and mom, I'm a husband, I'm a dad, I'm a grandma or granddad," for example, reflected a predictable set of expectations as to what that meant. You knew what would be expected of you as a wife, mom, husband, dad,

## WINNER'S CIRCLE

Football Hall of Famer Mel Blount, athlete par excellence, now 50 years of age, could certainly have defined himself only as a football player, being the Pittsburgh Steelers' top cornerback and pass interceptor in the 1970s. But Winner that he is, Blount never considered himself fundamentally a football player. He saw football as terrific practice for life, but not his life's work. That work involved kids, and his job was to be "shepherd." For now, Blount "shepherds" kids at his two farms, where courts and social agencies place troubled or "at risk" inner-city children for varying lengths of stay. On the farms, children learn responsibility and gain a sense of accomplishment—inner qualities typical of Winners. The children can take back these newfound qualities to their "real" lives when their stay is over.[1]

or grandparent; you knew "what to do." For the most part, you felt competent at being able to fulfill your roles in these various capacities. Nowadays being a mom may mean some of your children move back in when you're 55—a Future you had never anticipated. Being a granddad may mean adopting your granddaughter, addicted at birth to crack cocaine, because your daughter, never able to free herself of her own addiction, died shortly after the child was born and no father was around to take over. You can no longer expect the "doing" of "parent" to follow as predictable a path as it has for so many years.

## SUCCESS RELIES ON YOUR INNER QUALITIES

So how does this impact your ability to create a successful future for yourself? Basing your sense of competence on "What I do" will not work anymore. "What I do" is too unreliable, too changeable to provide you with a solid ground of being from which to go safely forward. Your occupation, job, or profession is likely to undergo radical transformations in the years ahead, few of which we can foresee, making your "What I do" of little value. "But if what I know how to do has little value," you say, "How am I going to cope? I can't just go into the Future without skills, that would be

---

### WINNER'S CIRCLE

Richard Elizondo, a veteran police officer, was paralyzed from the neck down when he and his son were ambushed by a gunman in early 1998. Despite the struggles of coping physically with the ordinary tasks of day-to-day life, the 35-year-old Elizondo focuses determinedly on the future. He never considered law enforcement a "job." To him it was a calling, something he always knew he would do since he was 6 years old. And continues to do. Winner that he is, Elizondo didn't give up who he is—a law enforcement person. If Elizondo defined being a law enforcement person solely as someone who walks a beat or physically chases down wrongdoers, he'd have bowed out the day he got shot. Instead, he is now seeking different ways to be involved in law enforcement, ways that are adapted to what he can now do. For example, Elizondo gave his first guest lecture to a crime science class just seven months after the shooting. He plans to finish his bachelor's degree in psychology, and looks to return to law enforcement as a crime scene analyst.[2]

disastrous." You're right, that would be disastrous, and absolutely you need skills with which to go into the Future. What is different about the times we are living, is that you need skills, but those skills may change many times over your lifetime. Therefore, you create as the foundation to your ability to function and succeed in the Future not a set of skills, but a profound understanding and appreciation of your *inner* qualities. You stand upon a ground of being called "Who I am," not "What I do." Defining yourself by what you do limits your potential for success.

## Grounding Yourself in "Who I Am"

Grounding is essential. Grounding is the basis, the foundation that makes it possible for you to do something, no matter how many times that something changes form. For example, an individual in the hands on healing professions—nurse, rehabilitation expert, physical therapist—usually has a ground of being of caring for others, willingness to take responsibility, and an ability to learn. These inner qualities hold true no matter how many changes occur within the fields of nursing, rehabilitation, or physical therapy. These *inner qualities* are what give the nurse, rehabilitation expert, and physical therapist the ability to continually learn new and different skills and ways of relating to patients and their care as these occur in the Future. Grounding yourself solidly in "Who I am" is the key to competence in the Future.

This is true even when all evidence seems to point to the contrary.

---

### WINNER'S CIRCLE

During World War II, when the war was not going well for the United States, Sgt. J. Cameron Wade volunteered and accepted a reduction in rank so he could fight with other African-American soldiers alongside white infantrymen. At the time, the U.S. armed forces was racially segregated. Despite receiving the Purple Heart, Wade and many other volunteers never had their ranks restored. Their discharge papers made no mention of their combat service, even though the volunteers fought bravely and well. That same bravery and willingness to do for others—Winner traits indeed—are what Wade used in lobbying to restore appropriate rank and status to himself and his fellow servicemen. He was successful, and in 1998, at 74 years of age, along with four of his comrades in arms, became the proud recipient of a Bronze Star.[3]

WINNER'S CIRCLE

Christopher Reeve, the celebrated actor ("Superman") who was rendered quadriplegic in a freak accident where he fell from a horse, has since sought to make the world more aware of the need for spinal cord injury research and funding. Reeve's "just cause" is his profound conviction that he and others like him deserve the best life they can create for themselves. Reeve's perseverance, courage, ability to communicate well, and caring are the inner qualities Reeve brings to his task, his "good grounding" that makes it safe for him to go after his cause. Reeve is thus well equipped to do the "doing" involved.

Who you are is what carries a Winner to success through very different experiences.

## Good Grounding Equals Competence Plus Safety

Good grounding makes it not only possible, but safe for you to do something. For example, a hero goes forth for a just cause, whatever the specifics of that cause may be. A hero has good grounding when the hero goes forth knowing he or she is *well equipped* to deal with the obstacles and challenges ahead, and therefore, is safe. Winners go into the Unknown with the profound conviction that they deserve the best life they can create for themselves or others (their "just cause"), and the "good grounding" Winners have is the perseverance, openness to learning, courage, and flexibility, for example, that they bring to the task.

Unless you have some sense of safety, you will not risk going off into the Unknown of your Future. Given that the world around us is in a state of chaos, constant change, uncertainty, and instability, it is difficult to rely on what you know how to do for that safety. Increasingly, we must somehow find grounding elsewhere, and the surest place to ground ourselves is in our inner worlds, in who we *are*.

## Competence

The most basic form of inner grounding is the feeling of competence, a "gut" feeling that whatever is needed to accomplish the task at hand, "I can do this." The Winners I have worked with almost invariably tell me

## WINNER'S CIRCLE

Interestingly enough, Christopher Reeve was greatly helped by his wife in understanding that who he was, was far more important than what he could do. Reeve had to make a critical decision regarding whether or not to have surgery just five days after his tragic fall. He recounts how he could easily have let go of life at that point, after realizing the full consequences of his injury. But his wife told him that he was still himself, and that she loved him—period, just as he was. Being reminded that he was still himself, and lovable as such, was enough to galvanize the Winner within Reeve. His recognition of just how valuable it is to remember the "who I am" is reflected in the name of his book, *Still Me.*[4]

that they had no idea how they were going to accomplish building a new life for themselves, after the event occurred that now obliged them to do so. All their former skills were usually of little help to them, or worthless in their present form, and more often than not the task before them seemed daunting, if not downright insurmountable, yet somehow from deep within, Winners know "I can do this." Often their "I can do this" defies all logic, makes no sense viewed from the outside, yet it is that "I can do this" upon which they figuratively stand, and from there figure out everything else.

For example, a Winner I worked with had been horribly damaged in an automobile accident. He had permanently lost the use of arms and legs so that his previous modes of employment were out of the question, yet he found a way to maneuver about sufficiently well in a wheelchair, supported his ability to speak and think with voice-activated technology to replace his nonfunctioning arms and hands, and successfully created gainful employment for himself, all of which started with his profound conviction that "I can do this." "I faltered many a time," this Winner told me, "but every time, somehow, I'd climb back up on my mental rock, that feeling of 'I can do this, somehow I know I can do this,' and that would give me the strength to keep going." Such reliance on an inner sense of competence is typical of Winners. Regardless of the enormity of the task at hand, of their lack of skills with which to undertake that task, Winners find a way to do what it takes by relying on their inner sense of competence.

You need a basic sense of competence, an inner knowing that "I can do this," regardless of whatever skills you may or may not have, in order to continually create and re-create a successful Future for yourself. As your current skills become outdated or no longer useful to you, a solid ground of being is what will give you the confidence to go successfully into the Unknown.

## BUILDING COMPETENCE

Competence is built from the inside out. Contrary to popular opinion, a solid ground of being is established when your competence comes from within yourself, as a recognition of your inner qualities, which then spreads to a confidence that given those qualities, you can do whatever it is you need to do. Realizing this changed Paul's initial perception of himself as an incompetent person.

PAUL

When I asked Paul, the middle manager who was "mergered out" if he generally felt that he could cope with life, if he felt "competent," he laughed. Then Paul said: "I used to, I used to feel that I'd get up in the morning, and yeah, I had what it took to do pretty much whatever needed doing. But since the merger, since I haven't been able to get hired again, no—if anything, I feel increasingly less competent, like I can barely cope with putting the garbage out. By next week I probably won't feel competent to do even that." Paul shook his head, "It's awful." "So what do you do about it?" I asked. "Do about it? Nothing." Paul replied. "I mean, what can I do about it? I'm not working, so I'm hardly competent in that area, and I don't know—that just seems to bleed into the other parts of my life. I don't feel competent, that's all. Maybe once I get work again—that's gotta happen eventually, doesn't it? Maybe then, I'll feel competent."

What Paul didn't realize at this point was how upside down his thinking was, given the tumultuous state of our world. If Paul waited for work to give him a feeling of competency, he might wait forever. The way to success, as demonstrated by the Winners I have worked with, is exactly the reverse: Winners feel competent *first*, and then use that *feeling* to support learning the specific skills that will make them competent at a particular job or project.

"But what do I base my competency on?" Paul asked. "Clearly I'm good for nothing, I have no marketable skills. How in the world can I be competent?" "But you are competent, Paul, as a human being." I responded. "You do human being great." "Sure," Paul replied, "So does everyone else on the planet. How does that help me?" "Because the *way* you do human being 'great,' Paul, is specific to you," I replied. "You have qualities and abilities that are uniquely yours, which you can use to form your personal ground of being, your ground of 'I can do this. I can cope.'"

Paul was silent. "I do?" he asked finally. "You do," I replied. "Why is this important?" Paul said, challenging me. I smiled. "Because image precedes reality," I replied, then continued, explaining, "because how you view yourself, what you see yourself as capable of, will influence your willingness or lack of willingness to create a positive Future for yourself." "We're back to that," Paul said, "the 'creating my Future' part." "Yes we are," I answered. "As long as you see yourself as barely capable of taking out the garbage, you're not likely to open your mind to think in creative terms of what fulfilling and satisfying work you might generate for yourself. You can't see yourself as inept, outdated, or outmoded and at the same time see yourself as successfully venturing into the Unknown. You won't feel safe enough. You have no grounding, no basis from which to venture forth. With such a negative self-evaluation, you'll get slaughtered, at least that's your vision." "Heck, that's my reality, right now," Paul said. "All right," I said. "So let's work on changing that."

## *Who Am I? When I Look Inside, What Do I See in Me?*

"Paul," I asked, "when you look inside, what do you see inside yourself, who's home?" "Boy," Paul sighed. "I don't know—not much of anyone." "Well, someone's there," I said, "because you're still breathing. So let's break it down. Take a look at the following list and tell me which of these descriptors might apply to you." I handed Paul a list containing the following descriptors:

| | |
|---|---|
| honest | thinker |
| trustworthy | feeler |
| hard-working | doer |
| apply myself | visionary |
| troubleshooter | practical person |
| problem solver | hands-on type |
| communicator | flexible |
| conflict resolver | good at "rolling with the punches" |
| negotiator | reliable |

good with details                     information seeker
good with follow-through              good listener
conceptually oriented                 good with visuals
patient                               advocate
teacher                               good at selling
motivator                             good at representing self
healer                                good at representing others
artist                                persevering
information gatherer                  persistent

"Wow," said Paul, "that's quite a list. OK—I'd say I'm honest, trust-worthy, hard-working, and yeah, I apply myself. I'm not a troubleshooter, but I am a pretty good problem solver." As he continued down the list, Paul started to get excited. He was finding a number of other words that he felt applied to himself: negotiator, doer, reliable, good with follow-through, patient, good listener, good at representing others, persistent.

"Those are your inner qualities, Paul," I said. "And you have un-doubtedly many more that I just don't happen to have included on this list. These qualities have nothing to do with a specific job, project, or task. They are the qualities you bring to whatever specific task you undertake. You may have developed them as the result of working on or with a spe-cific whatever, but now they exist independently of that specific task. They are yours, to apply however and whenever you wish." "Huh," Paul com-mented. Then he sat silent a moment, thinking. "That's not so bad," Paul said. "No, it's not," I replied. "You see, with these, you can cope. You are competent. These qualities are what make up your 'I can do this.' They form your ground of being. Knowing that you have these qualities, you can venture forth. You have something of substance to go out there with."

## "Who I Am" versus "What I Do"

Qualities relate to "who I am" rather than to "what I do." "Who I am" is then applied to "what I do" now, in the present and into the evolving present that is your Future. Since the "what I do" is likely to change radi-cally throughout your lifetime, the "who I am" becomes much more im-portant to develop as your ground of being. "Who I am" is something you can continually develop throughout your lifetime and apply to different tasks, projects, jobs, and pursuits, as needed. This is a much more reliable and solid ground of being than "what I do." It is under your control and puts you in charge. That feels good. That feels like "I can cope."

What Winners seem to be particularly good at is pulling out the broad qualities that underlie a particular task-specific skill (the "who I am") and using these for a new and different sort of task (the "what I do"). For example, patience is something that a Winner I worked with learned as a part of her job, which consisted of putting radio components together. As she put radio components together, this Winner not only learned patience, she also learned how components work together to create a whole greater than the sum of the parts; the end result of all the radio parts put together is sound transmissions, words and music, that no one of the components by itself can produce. This Winner was subsequently severely injured when a poorly constructed scaffolding loaded with crates of heavy equipment fell on top of her at work. She applied the patience and her understanding of how components fit together, both inner qualities acquired as a result of doing her job, to a new "job"—rehabilitating her broken body, at which she was remarkably successful.

For those of us who don't have the intuitive ability to apply underlying qualities to new demands that this Winner had, it is very helpful to learn what your qualities are and then use that knowledge purposefully to assist you in meeting the changing demands of your Future. Sometimes, as May found out, your qualities are hidden underneath what appear at first blush to be negative traits.

MAY

"So you want me to tell you what my qualities are, is that right?" May asked, in answer to my suggestion that we help her construct a solid ground of being for herself. May's forehead was all twisted up in concentration as she looked up at me, waiting anxiously for my reply. I was coming to know that look very well. I nodded. "Yes, I do," I said. "Gosh, I don't know," May continued, thinking hard. She sat silently for a moment. Then May said, "Well, I don't know if I can talk in terms of qualities, but I can tell you what my personality is. Can we do it that way?" "Sure," I replied, "That'll be a good start." "Well," May said, "if there's anything I know about myself, who I am inside, is that I'm a worrier. I worry all the time. I worry better than anyone I know. Even when I was at my busiest, doing really well as a pattern maker, I was always worried. Would I get the job done on time? Was my work precise enough? Would I have time to drop Thomas off at the sitter before delivering the job? Or would he enjoy coming along with me instead? Gosh, isn't that awful, Dr. Noelle?" "Actually, no, it's not awful at all," I replied. "You really have a lot of good qualities buried in there underneath all that worrying." May looked at me puzzled.

## Finding the Positive Value of Your "Negative" Traits

"Let me explain," I continued. "Your worrying is actually an expression of your conscientiousness. You were worried about whether or not you would do your work and your parenting 'good enough.' So let's put 'conscientiousness' down as one of your qualities. Something you are, in everything you do." May stared at me for a long moment. "I never thought about it that way," she said. "I always thought worrying was a bad thing." "Worrying," I said, "is only a bad thing when it runs the show. When you are stressed out by your worrying rather than seeing it for the positive quality underlying it." "I see," May said, "so you're looking for my positive qualities—who the real me is, the one inside." "Yes, absolutely," I replied. "Knowing who you are inside will help you determine what you can do successfully in the Future. No matter how often that Future changes, you can apply your inner qualities to help you thrive." "Hey, I like this," May said, getting excited.

"OK, so I know one thing for sure—I'm a survivor," she said. "That you are," I replied, "What else?" "Let's see, I'm a nice person—well, that doesn't help much," May said, peremptorily dismissing her niceness. "Why do you say that?" I asked. "Because nice doesn't have anything to do with being successful, getting a job, that sort of thing," May replied. "Oh really?" I said, "and what underlies your being nice? Caring about people, perhaps? Or is your 'being nice' just a phony act?" May looked at me, shocked, "No, it's not phony! I really am nice. I mean, yes, I care about people and I think people like it when you're nice to them." "All right," I said, "So stop dismissing your qualities, and let's keep 'being nice'—only I'll rephrase it as 'caring about people' because that's more specific and underlies the behavior you call 'being nice.'"

As we continued our work together, May, much to her surprise, found that her sensitivity to others reflected an ability to tune in to other people easily, that her "survivor" quality contained within it many other qualities—persistence, patience, perseverance, courage, hopefulness, to name but a few, and that overall, she had a whole host of qualities she had never considered valuable before. These were the qualities May could use as her ground of being in forging a new and successful Future for herself. "Wow," May said. "Discovering that I have all these qualities makes me feel real different about myself. It gives me a lot of confidence! I am capable, I can do things, I'm not just a bowl of quivering jelly-nerves." "No, you're not," I said, smiling at her analogy. "Practice thinking about yourself in this new light," I said. "I think you'll find your anxiety starts to decrease." May nodded, happily. "I think you're right," she said. "I already feel different. I'll keep working on it."

I did not invent May's qualities. They all were there, within her, simply unidentified, unappreciated, and therefore unusable as the valuable assets that they are. Too many of us fail to achieve the successes we deserve, because our focus on "what I can do" ignores the more crucial, underlying "who I am." Knowing who you are, your inner qualities, greatly expands what is possible for you in your world, and gives you safe and sure ground of being from which to create a successful Future, however daunting, however Unknown.

Winners excel at finding the positive value of what could be perceived as "negative" traits.

---

### WINNER'S CIRCLE

Tom Whittaker is one such example. Climbing Mount Everest is daunting for those in the peak of physical condition. Well, Whittaker dreams of being the first amputee to climb Mount Everest. He's already tried twice, and is going for a lucky third. Whittaker's belief is that his climb will inspire and motivate people to becoming more empathic toward people with disabilities. Disabled at age 30 when a drunk driver slammed into his van, 49-year-old Whittaker flat out states, "I wouldn't take my foot back if you gave it to me. This is who I am." After the accident, which resulted in the amputation of Whittaker's right foot and removal of his left kneecap, Whittaker not only learned to walk again, but then founded the Cooperative Wilderness Handicapped Outdoor Group. The group instills confidence in disabled people by encouraging and helping them to engage in rugged physical activity. By his belief, his obvious inner qualities of courage, determination, imagination, and resourcefulness, as well as his actions, Whittaker is truly a Winner.[5]

---

Sometimes there is an overriding trait that seems to pull the plug on all the rest of your inner qualities and make them worthless. Kathy, who felt she had numerous qualities, was nonetheless plagued by what she considered an irremediable flaw in her ground of being—her age.

KATHY

Kathy's first response to my question asking her what she felt her qualities to be was a blithe "Oh, I'm very competent, Dr. Noelle—I'm gifted, I'm talented, people like me, I do good work, nothing wrong in that department." "Yes," I replied, "I'm sure you are, but do you feel secure with your inner qualities. Do you feel safe, like 'yes, I can create a successful Future in the Unknown with what I've got'?" Kathy cast her eyes down, quiet. She looked up at me and said, without her usual verve: "I'm growing old. Older, anyway. I'm not 20—or 30 or 40—anymore. It doesn't seem to matter how talented or wonderful I think I am—I'm getting old. And no one wants old people around. No I don't feel safe. And old is a lousy ground of being."

## The Bugaboo of Getting Older

How you regard age and aging is tremendously important to your ability and willingness to go into the Future successfully. After all, if you think that any age after 60 is "old" and have negative associations to "old," as does Kathy, how can you possibly create a vibrant thriving Future for yourself from 60 to 90 or older?

"Old" is not the problem, it's our all-too-common assumptions of what "old" means that is. This is not to say that "old" doesn't matter. It does! As we live into healthy older years, we are different. Some activities and pursuits are less attractive to us, some more. This is true of any age-related developmental stage. For example, showing off to giggling girlfriends or telling wild (mostly made-up) sexual tales to the locker room crowd generally drops off after our early 20s. Wanting to give back to the community usually increases in one's 50s. But for most of us, our image of "old" is in fact our image of poor health and ill old age, not good health and well old age.

These realities are changing, and with them, so must our self-image of "old." "No one wants old people around," says Kathy. For many, that seems to ring true. But let's put it another way: no one wants cranky, mean, self-centered, boring, closed off, obstinate, authoritarian, demanding, critical people around. And a lot of older people we have known have been ornery and cantankerous because of little known nutritional imbalances, poorly fitting hearing aids, dentures (among others), and undiagnosed depression. As we age without becoming ill or unhealthy, as medical science and technology provide aging individuals with the correct support their bodies and minds need, "old" is taking on a whole different

---

### WINNER'S CIRCLE

There are many Winners who show us how age can be a plus in succeeding, but no one more so than astronaut 77-year-old John Glenn. After Glenn orbited Earth in 1962, he had every reason to believe he'd be flying much more, yet he didn't. Time after time, Glenn's requests to go back up were denied. Finally, in 1964, he resigned, and pursued other careers, both private and public. In 1995, in the course of reviewing materials as a member of the Senate Special Committee on Aging, Glenn realized that many of the changes people go through as they age parallel the experience of astronauts during weightlessness. From that single realization, Glenn investigated, enrolled others in his idea, and eventually succeeded in landing an historic place for himself as a crew member on the Discovery space shuttle launched in October 1998. And indeed, Glenn conducted numerous scientific experiments on aging while up in space. Glenn's age is what he used explicitly, overtly, and deliberately as his reason for going back up into space. Age can be a tremendous plus! As Glenn has demonstrated brilliantly, Winners aren't afraid to use it as such.[6]

---

meaning. "Old" will come to define an important and valuable developmental stage (probably a number of them) rather than the unvenerated and generally useless tag end of a life.

## The Benefits of Getting Older

"If for a moment, Kathy," I said, continuing our discussion, "you set aside all the bad things you think getting older are about, what would you say is different about you now, as you go into your 50s?" Kathy thought for a while. "Well," she said slowly, "I guess the first thing I'd say is I don't react as quickly to things. I mean if someone says something I don't like, I'm not as quick to judge them or get defensive about it." "So would you say you're more tolerant of others, perhaps?" I asked. "Yes, that would be true." She paused, thinking again. "Let's see. I don't like doing 15 things at once, any more. I'm much happier when I can do just one thing, take my time, and really do it in depth. And I'd say I listen better, I'm not so hasty to get my own two cents worth across. But the biggest difference, Dr. Noelle," Kathy said, looking up at me, "is that I think I have a better sense of perspective. I'm better able to see how things will fit or work in the long run, without losing sight of what's going on in front of my nose." Kathy laughed. "Not that I seem to be applying any of this to my own current situation!" "Well, you are and you aren't, Kathy," I replied. "You are applying it unconsciously to a degree. You'll find you'd get better results now that you are more consciously aware of your qualities and thus can begin to apply them purposefully to creating your Future."

Now what's interesting is that some of what Kathy related as differences she sees in herself as she grows older could be regarded as "negative." For example, Kathy mentioned that she was less quick to react. She described this as a plus, meaning that she gets less defensive and judgmental. Too many people see slower reactions as purely a downside—and indeed, if you want to be a race car driver, it is a downside. But for many other of life's activities, a slower reaction time can be used to advantage, as in Kathy's case. Kathy also mentioned not liking to do "15 things at once" any more. Too many people see this as "I can't do as much as I used to be able to do" and stop with that self-image, rather than appreciating the increased attention to detail and deeper focus they bring to their activities by doing one thing at a time.

Winners provide inspiring examples of how to appreciate yourself and value your qualities to give you the wherewithal to accomplish your goals when in the eyes of others, you may appear vastly diminished.

To a Winner, becoming incapacitated in any way, via illness or injury or the aging process, just means it's time to rely on other qualities for their sense of competence. Getting older simply means it's time to find a new ground of being, a different choice of qualities that will form the basis for a positive self-image. "I get it," Kathy exclaimed happily. "I can say to myself I am more tolerant, a better listener, able to see the big and little picture, and all these qualities make me valuable. My age has nothing to do with anything. I just need to seek out situations where these qualities are

---

WINNER'S CIRCLE

Professor Stephen Hawking, for example, is a well-known and highly regarded theoretical physicist, considered by his fellow scientists to be one of the most brilliant human beings on earth. Hawking has been trapped in a wheelchair by Lou Gehrig's disease since the age of 26. Despite an increasingly incapacitated physical condition, Hawking continues to give to the world via his lectures, books, and seminars. He demonstrates by how he lives that he has confidence that he still has value in the world.

---

## WINNER'S CIRCLE

Muhammad Ali, the world-famous boxer, now 56 years old, has Parkinson's disease, a debilitating illness which among other things restricts his ability to speak and to move well. Yet Muhammad feels he has a mission, and that is to love. His confidence in his ability to love, and the value that love has, is what keeps him on the road nine months out of the year, visiting hospitals, hugging the sick and infirm, giving them love as best he can.

---

valued." "Exactly," I said. "Now you have a positive self-image, one that supports your competence and gives you the grounding for success, with which you can go confidently into your Future."

Sometimes it's hard to see that positive self-image because your inner qualities are hidden behind what you don't like about life and other people. Then you need to do some mental detective work to figure out, as Jim did, what those inner qualities are.

JIM

I explained to Jim the difference between doing and being, and after a few false starts, Jim began to come up with aspects of his inner self. "I don't fuss much," Jim said. "I don't get myself into a snit over things—seen too much on the road to do that," Jim said. "I'd be dead by now if I took every little thing seriously." Jim stopped for a moment. "OK, what else," he said, continuing. "I don't like a lot of complications, you know? I don't like people telling me what to do." Before Jim could go on, I stopped him. "Jim, you're giving me a terrific list of who you aren't, what you aren't like, but you're not giving me who you are, or what you are like. So how about if for starters, we look at what you said a little differently."

"OK," Jim said, eyeing me warily, "so how do you want to tell it?" "Well, for example," I replied, "If you say you don't fuss much, and don't get yourself into a snit over little things, that tells me you can tolerate a fair number of hassles without getting upset, and that you're pretty patient with the ongoing 'stuff' of life. Would that be true?" "Yeah," Jim replied, "you could put it that way." "And telling me you don't like complications," I continued, "really tells me you like things to be straightforward. Saying you don't like people telling you what to do tells me you deal well with being on your own, with setting your own guidelines and rules." "Why, I sound like a pretty smart fellow!" Jim said, smiling for the first time.

*Let Your Inner Qualities Give You a Winner's Confidence*

"You are a pretty smart fellow," I grinned, agreeing, "but more importantly, how does reframing your 'what I'm not's' into 'What I am' make you feel?" "Like I'm smart, like I'm OK, like I'm a lot better than I thought I was," Jim said, surprised. "That's what identifying your qualities in a positive way does," I said. "When you discover what your inner qualities really are, suddenly you have the basis, the raw material, the platform on which to stand. You become confident."

It's important to identify your qualities in a positive fashion. As you can see from the above, what frequently seems like a negative statement— for example, Jim's "I don't like complications"—may in truth contain a positive attribute, once you turn it around. So don't let negative statements or what seem like negative traits stop you from considering the positive that may lie just underneath. Confidence cannot be built on a foundation of negatives. That just doesn't work. Be sure to seek out the positive that lies within all of us. As I explained to Jim, a ground of being is the sum of who you are, not who you *are not*.

"Huh," said Jim, intrigued. "Can you see how identifying your inner qualities in a positive way helps you be successful in the world?" I asked, knowing that Jim's primary concern was getting out of trucking and into something better for himself as quickly as possible. "Yes," Jim said slowly, "I think so. Knowing that I deal well with being on my own, setting my own rules like you say, kinda helps me think differently about what I might do. I realize I just might be able to create my own work for myself, rather than relying on someone to give it to me. Seems like a start, anyway." And it was a very good start indeed.

Your inner qualities will support any number of occupations, skills, projects, causes. You are no longer limited by what you happen to know how to do.

How to Create and Develop Your Personal "Who I Am" as a Solid Foundation for Your Success in the Future

"Who I am" is timeless and ageless, although the specific qualities of "who I am" change over time and with age. Developing your ground of being from "who I am" rather than from "what I do" gives you a solid foundation for "I can cope, I am competent" which readily leads to "I can succeed."

## *Personal Success Log 2: Your Inner Qualities*

*Step #1*

Make your list of qualities. Don't worry about "I should be different, I should be this other way"—that's not who you are! Make *your* list. Regardless of your gender, ethnic background, age, upbringing, life experiences, or special circumstances, you have inner qualities, and you have enough of them to ground yourself solidly in your "who I am." There are many more qualities than those given as an example in working with Paul. Use that list as a "starter kit" and complement it with other qualities. If you're unsure as to your qualities, ask friends and family to tell you what they think your qualities are. Often we are blind to our own value.

Look at what you've considered your "downsides" and see if in fact, those aren't positive qualities turned upside down. "I'm impatient," for example, may in fact be "I'm eager to get things done," which reflects enthusiasm, a valuable quality. "I'm a slow learner" may be more accurately stated as "It may take me a while to learn something, but once I've learned it, it's with me for life." Don't, of course, delude yourself. If your "I'm impatient" actually stems from "I think all other people are stupid and inept," don't falsify that as a positive attribute! Instead, recognize that your "I'm impatient" isn't a quality, and go look for something within yourself that is.

Beyond that, if you feel that you have some glaring lacks or too few qualities, then work on that. Humans are not an inert substance, like cement, which can't grow. On the contrary, humans are among the most consciously changeable organisms on earth. If you don't think you have enough qualities, develop some. Find someone you admire and figure out what are their qualities. Learn by observing these individuals how those qualities play out in their lives. Read self-help books on the subject. Take classes in personal development. Read biographies of people you respect, or watch documentary movies. There are many many ways to develop those qualities you feel you lack or are underdeveloped in you.

Most of us have numerous qualities that can contribute to a strong and vital sense of competency, but these are unrecognized, underdeveloped, or underused. Learning what your qualities are will encourage you to "pump them up" as it were, so they are strong and in good shape, readily available for your use.

*Step #2*

Put your list of qualities and qualities-in-the-making by that list of positive beliefs about the Future you have up on your bathroom mirror. Do the same drill with this new list as with your "positive beliefs about the Future" list. Read your list of qualities daily, not to puff yourself up, but to remind yourself of the assets you have going for yourself, your personal ground of being.

*Step #3*

Start seeing yourself and thinking of yourself in terms of this new image. Actively think of yourself as a "caring, honest, persevering, reliable, good-sense-of-humor" individual, for example, rather than as an "I'm an OK person, I'm sort of average, I get along" individual. Although there is nothing inherently "wrong" with this description, it simply does not provide you with a firm ground of being with which to go confidently into the Unknown of your Future. The self-image you develop for that purpose needs to be a springboard from which you can soar, not a plank to walk off of and drown.

*Step #4*

Your qualities are worth nothing if you aren't using them. Knowing you are a caring individual, for example, is useless information (in the context of this book) if that caring isn't expressed in your everyday life. "Caring" will not serve as part of your ground of being if it just lies there dormant. The whole idea of having a ground of being is to have something solid from which to move forward, not something just to stand on.

Start responding to situations in your life deliberately using these qualities. When something comes up, ask yourself, "All right, which of my qualities could I use here? My listening quality, my patience, my 'stand up for what's right' quality? Which would best serve me?" Then try one. You may not always make the perfect choice, but more often than not, the quality with which you choose to respond will work well for you.

So when your boss is critical of your work, for example, choose your listening quality, rather than falling into your usual defensiveness. When you're frustrated by a project you're working on, choose to persevere, rather than drop it and go on to a new project. Qualities are like a muscle, they strengthen with use.

## Step #5

Start visualizing yourself using your qualities as your new ground of being. Visualizing means to close your eyes, preferably in some quiet place where you won't be disturbed, and see the scene you've chosen unfold in your mind. Another description of visualizing, in the context of this book, might be "purposeful daydreaming." For example, pick one or two of your qualities, close your eyes, and now see yourself going through an average day deliberately using those qualities. See how they work—or don't work, in which case just pick a different quality to work with. You're mentally rehearsing using your qualities, which again, makes them stronger.

Visualize using different qualities from your list. Then visualize using various qualities in all sorts of different situations. This exercise, done over time, will open your mind to the value your qualities have, and to the many possible uses for your qualities that you hadn't thought of before.

Your ground of being is your foundation. It's what allows you to take off. Where to? Into a Future pulled by a Dream. For Dreams are the stuff of which, surprisingly enough, reality is made.

## NOTES

1. Tom Callahan, "I Consider Chipmunks Therapy," *U.S. News & World Report,* August 26/September 2, 1991, pp. 86–87.
2. Lindsey M. Arent, "Amid Daily Struggle, a Focus on the Future," *Los Angeles Times,* August 16, 1998, Metro B3.
3. "Just Rewards," *People Magazine,* August 17, 1998, p. 89.
4. Elizabeth McNeil, "Man of Steel," *People Magazine,* May 11, 1998, pp. 215–222.
5. Christina Cheakalos, Johnny Dodd, "Higher Purpose," *People Magazine,* May 11, 1998, pp. 60–62.
6. Jeffrey Kluger, "Back to the Future," *Time Magazine,* August 17, 1998, pp. 41–50.

# CHAPTER THREE

## BE WILLING TO DREAM

*What Inspires Me? What Future Calls to Me?*

Victor Hugo is quoted as saying, "There is nothing like a Dream to create the Future." How right he was! Dreams are what anchor you to the Future. Dreams are what pull you forward. Dreams, after all, live in the Future. Once you've fulfilled a Dream, it's an accomplishment, now in your past. It is no longer a hope or aspiration calling you to your Future. A Dream is only a Dream as long as it is in front of you, ahead of you.

### YOU GOTTA HAVE A DREAM

Although you may have no idea of how you are going to get there, if you have a Dream, you know what you are aiming for, and you therefore can go about the process of making that Dream come true. The song from the classic Broadway musical "South Pacific" says it well: "You gotta have a Dream, if you don't have a Dream, how you gonna make a Dream come true?"

### *A Dream Pulls You into the Future*

Dreams are fundamental to your success in the Future. Given that the Future is Unknown, it is just as full of potential misery as joy. What you project into the Future determines how you will use your energies and the time that is your life. If you project a nightmare, it will drive you away from the Future. If you project a Dream, it will pull you toward and into the Future.

For example, the cult projected that the Future on Earth would be a nightmare, and thus, driven away from the Future, put their energies into escaping the nightmare by joining an alien race. Fear of their projected nightmare is what pushed the members of the Heaven's Gate cult into mass suicide in 1997. In a very different example, the researchers working on the AIDS virus projected their Dream of a cure onto the Unknown of the Future, and put their energies into fulfilling that dream. Although a cure has not yet been found, the researchers were pulled by their Dream into developing a "cocktail" of protease inhibitors allowing those suffering from AIDS to live longer and enjoy a better quality of life. And researchers are still actively pursuing their Dream of a cure.

## Dreams Project a Piece of Known into the Unknown

When you dream a Dream for yourself, you are actually projecting a piece of Known into the Unknown. It is the Known of your wishes and ardent desires, which you now cast out into the vastness of the Unknown. A Dream provides a certain security in a world seemingly fraught with insecurities, of certainty in an era full of uncertainties. You may not have any idea of how you'll get there, but one thing you know for sure is, "This is my Dream."

This is why a Dream is an anchor into the Future. A Dream, as intangible as it may seem, is steady and true. A Dream will draw you to it across time and space. It is a powerful motivator for success.

## Dreams versus Nightmares

Psychologists have long recognized that all of us need a motive, a reason, to do anything in life. At the most basic level, you're motivated to do something because it satisfies a need. That need is either to get away from something you don't like (pain, loneliness, a sense of inferiority), something Erich Fromm called "freedom from," as in "freedom from fear," or to move toward something you do like (enjoyment, fulfillment, acheivement), what Fromm called "freedom to," as in "freedom to love."[1]

In terms of creating your Future, there appear to be two fundamental motivators. One is to push yourself away from a Future you fear (the nightmare); the other is to pull yourself toward a Future you love (the Dream). Some people achieve great wealth because they are afraid of being poor and starving (nightmare); other people achieve great wealth because they love what they do and have fun making money (Dream). Some people marry because they are afraid of being alone (nightmare); other people marry because they love sharing their lives with another person (Dream). Human beings have been driven by fear for eons, and have been equally pulled by the love of work, family, humankind, challenge, knowledge, adventure, and so much more, for just as long. Both motivators have been effective in assuring basic human survival.

However, if what you want to do is create a positive, successful, and fulfilling Future for yourself, fear is a poor motivator. Fear is a constricting emotion, it tends to motivate people into hoarding whatever they have, choosing safety and low risk over happiness and satisfaction. It carries with it a profound resistance to change, which leads to stagnation at best, or a continually deteriorating condition at worst. As we go into the 21st century, an unwillingness to change in and of itself is the sure road to failure. Fear is an increasingly less viable motivation.

Certainly, all of us have a basic instinct to survive that carries with it elements of fear. And sometimes, fear is a powerful and useful *short-term* motivator. For example, you're afraid you won't make the rent this month, so out of that fear, you take a side job. In the short term, you experience relief—now you can pay the rent. That feels good. Taking side jobs month after month out of fear however will soon cease to yield any kind of positive feelings. Choosing to deal with your fear by allowing yourself to be *pulled by what you love*—for example, you find a certain type of side job personally rewarding and therefore build it up into a steady business—is gratifying and fulfilling in the long term.

So how do you motivate yourself to reach for a positive Future? How do you find that which will pull you into a successful and happy Future? You dream, as Winners do: consciously, creatively, purposefully. You reach for the hope or aspiration that a Dream is: that something you hope for, want to have happen, and aspire to.

## Dreams Are for Winners

Too often, people think that dreams are for the simpleminded, or for artists, or for children, not realizing how incredibly powerful dreams are in motivating human behavior. Most successful people are tremendous dreamers. I remember a client of mine telling me how when he was a construction worker, he used to walk by a famous restaurant every day, on his way to the job site. There was no way he could afford a meal at that restaurant, much less the clothes that would be considered appropriate to even walk in the place. Carrying his lunch in a brown paper bag, day in day out, the man would dream of eating lunch in that restaurant one day. That dream symbolized for him what wealth meant, and motivated him until 20 years later, he not only ate at the famous restaurant regularly, but could have bought the restaurant had he wanted to.

Winners allow themselves their dreams, no matter how outlandish or impossible those dreams may seem to others.

You dream in order to motivate, inspire, and guide yourself into a successful Future that speaks to *you*—regardless of anybody else's opinion on the matter.

"But Dr. Noelle," you say, "I can't dream! If I sit down and try to dream up something grand for myself in the Future, all I come up with is stupid stuff, like 'Win the lottery,' or 'Be a race-car driver.' I have no idea what I really want, what I really hope for." "Patience," I say. You ab-

---

### WINNER'S CIRCLE

Elvis Stojko, for example, many times World Champion skater, had a Dream of incorporating martial arts artistry into his skating routines. When the 25-year-old Stojko first began to incorporate martial arts into his skating, his unusual style caused much furor in the international skating community, where grace and balletic style have long reigned uncontested. Stojko's style was hotly debated and he was encouraged to drop it—to take ballet, get in touch with his feminine side, in short, cease to dream his Dream in order to become a champion. Elvis Stojko didn't care. He had a Dream—his Dream, nobody else's—and that Dream motivated him to continue developing his martial-arts skating style, even as his technique and physical prowess on the ice grew. Finally the skating world couldn't deny the brilliance of Elvis's skating and took his unique style seriously. Since then Elvis has won skating championships time and time again.

solutely can dream. You just don't know how yet. Keep reading, and you'll see how dreaming a Dream isn't mysterious. You can learn to dream, like you can learn to do anything else. You just need to take it step by step. And the first step is to find your Dream.

## FINDING YOUR DREAM

Finding your Dream can be thought of as a treasure hunt, for indeed, a Dream found is a treasure trove. For some, finding their Dream is easy, for others a challenge. Paul found his Dream in the rich experiences of his past, in what he'd always loved to do. To find his Dream, however, first Paul had to let go of his resistance to the very idea of dreaming.

PAUL

"Dream!" exclaimed Paul, still suffering from his joblessness, in response to my question, "Do you dream of a Future for yourself?" "You must be kidding. Dream what?" Paul asked. "How can I dream, I don't even have a job yet," Paul said, continuing. "And that's why I want you to dream," I replied, "to help you get that job." "Yeesh, this really seems the long way around," Paul complained. "Why can't I just stick with the want ads? Heck, maybe I should just take a job as a sales clerk." "Is that what you want to do?" I asked. "No," Paul said. "I want my old life back!" "Well, you're not going to get your old life back, Paul, that's the whole problem," I said. "Your 'old' life is in the past—dead, gone, and irrecoverable. You need to create a Dream in order to have a new life that will please you as much if not more than your 'old' life." "That's not even possible," Paul said, looking down glumly at his shoes. "How do you know?" I asked, gently. "I don't know," Paul sighed, "It's just not." "All right," I answered. "Indulge me—how about I help you dream a little, and let's see if maybe something is possible, some kind of new life you might enjoy."

## The Gold Mine of Your Past

"OK, fine. You're not going to let up until we go through this exercise anyway, are you?" asked Paul wryly. "No, I'm not," I said, smiling. "So here goes. Think back over your life before the merger. What are some of the things you loved to do?" I asked. "They don't have to have anything to do with work, just things you loved to do." Paul sat thinking silently for a while. Then he looked up at me, "You know, I think one of the happiest times of my life was when my kids were growing up. I really loved helping them learn, showing them the ropes." Paul's face grew soft at the memory. "I remember how much fun I had teaching my boys how to tie their shoes—I haven't thought of that in years! And how much I enjoyed teaching them how to play ball, and fish—and even how to schedule their time so they could do homework and play too." Paul grew silent, reminiscing. "I remember," he said, continuing, "I taught them how to budget their allowances and figure out a savings plan before they hardly had anything worth budgeting or saving! I don't know—it was fun for me, showing them the ropes. I loved doing it, and the boys responded to it great. They never seemed to resent it, if anything, it's what made us so close." Paul stopped talking as he sat there, remembering good times.

"However, Dr. Noelle," Paul said continuing, "I don't see myself creating a career out of raising more kids! I'm still putting the last one of mine through college." I laughed. "I agree, Paul, and I promise you that's not what I had in mind. But let's look at what you just told me in terms of creating a dream for yourself," I said. "You like to help people learn 'the ropes.' You like to teach people skills you've learned through your experience that will be valuable for them as they grow. Would you say that's accurate?" "Yeah," Paul said slowly, "But why did you say 'people'—I mean, I've really only shown my sons 'the ropes.'" "Really?" I asked. "What about the employees you managed while you were a middle manager? Weren't you showing them the ropes?" "Well, yes, I guess so, among other things," Paul replied. "Did you enjoy that part of your job?" I asked. "Yes," Paul said, smiling, "actually I did. Probably more than any other part, come to think of it." "OK," I said, "So what I'd like to challenge you to do is to daydream: to sit with yourself and dream up situations in which you could teach people skills you've learned through your experience, skills which would be valuable to them. And having more kids doesn't count."

If you don't know what a dream might be for you, look to what you love—past and present. Think about the activities you've done and the experiences you've had that have brought you the most enjoyment, the most satisfaction. Then look to what has excited you, stimulated you, stirred your soul through the years, and what does so now. Somewhere in there, as improbable as it may seem, is the germ of a Dream that could pull you forward into a successful and fulfilling Future.

---

WINNER'S CIRCLE

In 1987, Julie Alban, then 21 years old, was shot in the back by her boyfriend when she was trying to break up with him. Striking her in the waist, the bullet paralyzed Alban from the waist down. Her life, as she had known it, was over. Nonetheless, two years later, Alban entered the Western State University College of Law in Fullerton, California. For as long as she could remember, Alban's Dream had been to go to law school, and she refused to let her ex-boyfriend take that dream away from her. Today, she is highly valued as a prosecutor with the District Attorney's office in Long Beach, California. Her expertise? Prosecuting misdemeanor domestic violence cases. A Winner through and through, Alban has not only succeeded in living her Dream of being a lawyer, but is actively using her knowledge of the type of violence that shattered her body—domestic violence—to help others.[1]

---

Sometimes a Dream found in your past is the only thing that will pull you into the Future.

## *Look to What Inspires You*

Sometimes you will find your Dream by looking to what inspires you. Such was the case with May, although at first, she couldn't see how what inspired her could possibly become a Dream that would lead her into a successful Future.

MAY

"What inspires me?" asked May, the cancer survivor, repeating my opening question to her as we met, once again. "Gee, at this point, just getting a paycheck would be inspirational," she said. "I understand," I said, "but I'm talking about a different kind of inspirational. What in your life has uplifted you, made you feel just terrific, what have you been really excited about?" May sat quietly, thinking. "My recovery," she said. "The fact that I actually got through it. I mean, I know it sounds trite, but I really am different now. I know I can do things I never dreamt I could do." May smiled, "There's that word—dream! That's funny." "Anything else about your recovery that excited you?" I asked. "Outside of the obvious, which is that you did recover." "Um, yes," May replied. "It surprised me actually. I've never been a very physical person, but as part of my healing, I learned an awful lot about my body, and I really enjoyed that. I liked the learning part, plus I liked all the stretching and physical exercises I did to help my body out."

"How did that come about?" I asked. May explained: "Well, I'd be in bed for so long after the surgeries, between that and the chemo, my body just ached something fierce. I had to do something to ease the pain, and what I discovered was that stretching and certain kinds of gentle exercise really made a difference. I became very aware of my body, and what I could and couldn't do with it. I still do some of the exercises and stretches."

"Now, given just those elements—the fact of your recovery, that you did get through it, and your enjoyment of the physical awareness and working with your body to ease pain—what Dream might come out of that?" I asked. May smiled, "You know, I have sort of thought of that—I know it sounds hokey but I would like to help people, share with them my experience; that would really be exciting. But I can't write, Dr. Noelle," May said, frustrated, "that's just not my thing." "Who ever said writing was the only way to share an experience?" I asked. "Well, how else? I'm not a movie star or someone who could talk about it on TV," May said. "Don't limit yourself," I replied. "Dream. Dream about the different ways you might be able to help people by sharing your experience and your knowledge. Meditate on it. Think about it. Spend some time on this. Dream. And then we'll go on to how to make that Dream come true."

Our society doesn't encourage dreaming. We tend to value "doers" over "dreamers." However, to expect to leap in a single bound from what you love to translating that into a successful and meaningful Future is unrealistic. The time for "doing" will come soon enough. Be patient with

## WINNER'S CIRCLE

Ruth Fertel was a 38-year-old divorced mom back in 1965. She was faced with the challenge of paying college tuition for her two sons while making only $4,800 a year as a lab assistant at Tulane University School of Medicine. Fertel racked her brains for ways to make more money, diligently combed the classifieds, and one day, saw a little ad that said "Steakhouse for Sale." That inspired her! She just knew she could do it. Fertel mortgaged her house to raise the funds to buy the steakhouse, invented a new way to cook steaks, and became the proud owner of Ruth's Chris Steak House chain. Fertel still runs her $177 million dollar a year empire at 71 years of age.[2]

---

WINNER'S CIRCLE

Sixty-seven-year-old retired banker Elbert Loewenstein was inspired to walk to his 50th high school reunion to generate scholarship funds for his high school. And walk Loewenstein did—from Pinetop, Arizona, to Gibbon, Nebraska, in 51 days, raising $50,000 in pledges along the way.[3]

---

yourself! Start by exploring what you love, what inspires you, and be willing to spend some time dreaming of possibilities. As the song says, "If you don't have a Dream, how you gonna make a dream come true." The first part of that equation is—to Dream.

Winners' dreams are often highly personal and specific. What inspires one person can be very different from what inspires another.

Winners allow themselves to be pulled forward by what inspires them—however common or uncommon that inspiration may be.

## A Dream Is Whatever Pulls You into the Future

Too often, we expect our Dreams to be lofty and serious. Dreams come in all shapes and sizes, from quiet Dreams of having a home with a yard for your family, to all-encompassing Dreams such as world peace or ending world hunger, with every conceivable type of Dream in between. What matters is not the "loftiness" of your Dream, but whether it works for you. A Dream works for you when it is strong enough to pull you into the Future. That's it. That's all that is required.

Don't put down or ignore what you love to do because it doesn't seem "important" enough. When you look for a Dream to dream, let what you love to do, what you enjoy, be your guide to finding that special Dream that is yours alone. Kathy was ready to dismiss what she loved to do as "trivial." It's only as we worked with it that Kathy realized what she considered "trivial" actually contained the beginnings of a wonderful Dream.

KATHY

"What do you love to do?" I asked Kathy, the out-of-work hair stylist, as we began her 'let's go hunting for a Dream' session. "Go shopping, of course!" she laughed as she responded, great peals of merriment ringing out. "You're not laughing," Kathy said, looking over at me, and indeed, I wasn't. "I'm taking you at your word," I said. "Didn't you mean what you said?" Kathy grew silent. "Actually, yes, I do. But everybody loves to go shopping, Dr. Noelle; that doesn't exactly qualify as the ingredient for a dream." "Maybe, maybe not," I replied. "What is it about shopping that you love?" "Hum," Kathy said, "I never thought about that. Well, let me see, I love choosing clothes for people, not just me. Girlfriends will take me shopping with them often, to help. I love the feel of textures and fabrics. I really get into color—what colors go with what, what colors look good on different people. I like to assort outfits and accessories. Figure out a whole look. I really love making people feel good by helping them look good."

"Actually," Kathy continued, looking away shyly, "I have always had this dream of owning a little dress shop, very trendy, very upscale. Somewhere women would come to get 'outfitted'—the whole nine yards, you know: the dress, the shoes, the earrings, the works. But how am I going to get the money to get a shop, Dr. Noelle? I mean, that's too ridiculous for words. I can't even get a job!" "Hang on, Kathy," I said, stopping her before her dismay could get out of hand. "We're talking about dreams here, not how to make them come true. That comes later, OK? For now, just be

---

### WINNER'S CIRCLE

Curtis Mayfield, 55 years old, a famous composer of soulful music, became quadriplegic after a freak onstage accident. He was so weak he couldn't cough, much less belt out a song. The beloved guitar on which he had worked out so many melodies was useless to him now. And yet, Mayfield had his Dream—to compose once again. Had Mayfield let the apparent impossibility of his Dream stop him, that would have been the end of it. After all, how does a man compose who has neither arms, hands, nor voice available to him? Inspired by his Dream, Mayfield used his imagination mightily. With the aid of voice-activated recorders to capture song ideas, the innovative use of computers to write music, and the collaboration of friends, with patience and despite blacking out during several recording sessions, he did it. In 1997, Mayfield released his first original album since the accident, "New World Order," which was received so enthusiastically that not only did it sell well, but director Spike Lee used its title track in his movie "Get on the Bus." Had Mayfield not allowed himself to Dream, that never would have happened.[4]

willing to dream. And it sounds like you already have a dream that is near and dear to your heart." "I do," Kathy nodded, "I've had it for years—I just have never thought it would do any good to dream it. I mean, after all, what are the odds of my getting there?"

Dream the impossible dream. Winners are willing to let their imaginations roam freely. Winners trust that no matter what the Dream, big or small, they'll get there.

## A Dream Built Purposefully Is Still a Dream

Sometimes finding your Dream doesn't come quickly or easily. That doesn't matter. As you look at what you loved in the past, what inspires you and what you enjoy, you can quite purposefully build a Dream that will work for you. Just because a Dream doesn't appear spontaneously to you doesn't diminish its value. Jim found that discovering his Dream took effort and deliberate thinking. In the end, however, his Dream pulled him into success every bit as effectively as the more "spontaneous" Dreams others have come up with.

Jim had to get accustomed to the very idea of Dreams, however, before we could get started on helping him find his.

JIM

"Dreams!" Jim, the soon to be ex-trucker snorted, responding to my request that he tell me about his dreams. "Dreams are for kids. I don't have time for that foolishness. I thought you were supposed to help me through this mess into some kind of plan for my life." "And that's exactly what I'm doing, Jim," I said. "Dreaming is a critical part of figuring out the 'plan for your life' as you call it." "I really don't see how," Jim continued. "All dreams are is indigestion, anyway." I smiled, "I'm not talking about that kind of dream, Jim, I'm talking more about the 'what do you want to be when you grow up' type of dream."

"Oh," Jim said. "Well, I never wanted to be anything much when I grew up. I never gave it much thought. Maybe a fireman or something." "So how did you become a trucker?" I asked. "I don't know, I just did," Jim replied. "Friend of mine was trying to start a trucking business, and he'd ask me to spell him when he got sick or something, and when he got his second truck, he said I was pretty good at it and would I like to come on board. Heck, I was 18, doing grease monkey stuff at the local gas station. Trucking sounded pretty exciting. Been with it ever since."

"Do you love it?" I asked. Jim sighed. "Love trucking? No. Hurts my back and gives me leg cramps and stomach problems and my sleep is all messed up. I did enjoy it in the beginning—I was real proud when I got my own rig, but that was many years ago. Trucking hasn't been much fun for a long time." "Then why did you keep doing it?" I asked. "Man's gotta eat," Jim replied. "I don't have an education, and trucking sure seemed better than digging ditches." "Oh?" I asked, looking for elements of a Dream no matter how well hidden, "How is it better than digging ditches?" Jim frowned, "Well, I like to drive. I mean at least with trucking, you keep moving."

"Did you ever drive just for pleasure—when you weren't driving on a job?" I asked. "Oh sure," Jim replied, brightening up, "we used to drive a lot. My wife and me, we'd drive all over the countryside on my days off, before she passed away, that is. She knew everything about the history of all the local places, and I could listen to her talk about that all day. It was real interesting! She used to tease me that I drove more on my days off as I did in the truck. She was probably right." "Did you mind doing all that driving?" I asked. "Oh no, cars don't bother me as much, plus it was always short hops. You know, we'd drive some, and then stop for a while, drive some more, and then stop again. No, I didn't have trouble with that," Jim replied. "Is driving around to historical sites something you might enjoy doing on your own?" I asked. Jim thought about it for a while. "Not totally by myself, no. I'd like it if I were doing it with other people, yes. I mean I know an awful lot about those places now, and I can really get into talking about them. It's fun. I still don't see how any of this is going to help me get a job," Jim complained. "Patience," I replied. "Stay with me on this."

I sat thinking for a moment. It's easier to create a Dream if you have a number of ingredients to play with and I wanted to help Jim uncover more of those. Then I remembered, "Jim, you said you were a grease monkey before you hired on as a trucker. Can you tell me a little more about that?" "Hmm," Jim said, musing, "well, being a grease monkey was kind of a natural for me. I pretty much was born able to tinker. My mom used to tell stories of me being 2 years old, taking her toaster apart and trying to figure out how to get it back together." He laughed, "Seems I didn't do such a hot job—damn thing never did work after that." Jim paused, then continued, "But I could fix most anything, from the time I was a boy. Still can. It's fun for me, you know, a challenge. And I get real satisfaction from when I can get the thing to work again. But that ain't no dream, Doc," Jim said, "that's just tinkering."

"Oh, I'm not so sure, Jim," I said. "Dreams aren't necessarily big things. Dreams are anything that motivates you, pulls you forward. It doesn't matter if someone's dream is to climb the Himalayas or to see their kids through college. A dream is something in the Future you truly desire, with all your heart and soul, and that you are willing to steadily move toward. And as you accomplish one Dream, you need to project another, so you keep pulling yourself into the Future."

"OK," Jim said slowly, "I hear what you're saying, Doc, but I don't know how to do that. All I keep coming back to is I need some money, I need a job." "We'll get to that part, Jim," I said, "but for now, I want you to spend some time thinking about what you could do with either driving around the countryside, your enjoyment of historical places, and/or your tinkering abilities." "In other words," Jim said, "You're asking me to dream on purpose." "Yes," I said, "that's exactly it. Dream on purpose." "Just make it up?" Jim asked. "Just make it up," I replied, "and don't worry about whether it could make money for you or if you could really make it happen or anything else like that. Just make up a dream for yourself—something that you'd have fun accomplishing, something that could pull you forward."

"OK," said Jim, still dubious. "I'll give it a try."

Just because you haven't had a Dream since birth doesn't mean you can't have one now. Like Jim said, you can Dream on purpose—not all of us have wonderful spontaneous Dreams. Some of us do have to work on it. That's OK. Divinely inspired, or worked through with grit and determination, a Dream is a Dream is a Dream and either kind will pull you just as surely into a viable Future.

## Four Dreams

After Paul, May, Kathy, and Jim had all worked through their musings and mulling and thinking and imaginings, here are the Dreams they came up with. I asked each of them to start the Dream with the words "I would love . . ." just to make sure they got off on the right foot.

PAUL

"I would love to bring my middle-management expertise to young and growing companies—small companies, partnerships, professional businesses, maybe even small stores, mom-and-pop operations, that kind of thing. I'd love to spend some time with them, create hand-tailored programs that fit their needs and their budgets, and maybe have a kind of maintenance arrangement so I could help them along until they were really on their feet. That would be a nice Dream."

MAY

"I would love to develop an inspirational type of exercise program for cancer patients—both as they are going through treatment (post-surgery, radiation, or chemo) and once they are in remission—that would help ease the pain and heal their bodies and their souls."

KATHY

"I would love to have a little dress shop, very trendy, very upscale. Somewhere women would come to get 'outfitted' head to toe: the dress, the shoes, the earrings, the works."

JIM

[Author's note: getting Jim to start with "I would love" was a challenge. He firmly told me the only things you 'love' are your wife and your family. I think he finally did it just to get me to shut up. However, he did assure me that he really truly would be very happy with this Dream.]

   "I would love to spend my days driving around the countryside, fixing the things that people break, and telling yarns about all the historical places I came to along the way."


## How to Dream a Dream for Yourself that Will Pull You into a Successful Future

Dreaming your Dream can be a wondrous experience. It is an opportunity to truly let yourself explore the many facets of you, with a freedom we rarely allow ourselves. At this stage of creating a successful reality for yourself, don't limit yourself with "Oh that could never happen" or "I could never do that." Indulge your most creative, imaginative self, using the following steps as your guide.

## Personal Success Log 3: Your Dreams

### Step #1

Make a list of all the things you love to do, those things that through your life have excited you, inspired you, uplifted you. Look to the past, as well as your present. What have you loved to do? What always felt like play, gave you joy? Look to the past, not to re-create it, but to better understand yourself. People tend to be consistent with themselves. What you have loved to do has within it a deep and abiding truth about you. Don't worry about whether or not what you loved to do has anything to do with success. Just be willing to dream at this point.

"But I used to love to party! What's that going to inspire me to?" you cry out. "Sex, drugs, and rock and roll? I'm too old for that anyhow!" Well, what did you love about partying? The excitement of it? Being with lots of people? What was the *essence* of your love of partying? If what you enjoyed was the excitement and socializing, there are many dreams that include both. Being involved in art galleries, or the catering business, or being a sales representative for your local brewer, for example, can easily involve the excitement of parties and lots of socializing, all the while contributing to a healthy paycheck.

A client of mine had a 9 to 5 job in the advertising business. Although she made good money and was valued as a good employee, she hated the job. She loathed the constant stress and pressure, and found herself increasingly reluctant to go to work. She gained a considerable amount of weight, had constant health problems, and it became very clear she needed to create a different Future for herself. What this client loved above all was, of all things, rabbits. She was at her happiest and most fulfilled when she was interacting with her pet rabbit. Her dream was to somehow make a living that allowed her to be with lots of rabbits. At first that seemed like a completely impossible dream. Yet this client was able to turn her dream into reality by developing a successful business around the care and grooming of pet rabbits. The problem doesn't usually lie in our Dreams, but in our failure to be willing to dream them!

Don't concern yourself at this point with whether or not what you loved appears to lead readily to fame and fortune. Just be willing to look into past and present to what you love, to help you springboard into creating a wondrous Future.


## Step #2

Use meditation to help you Dream. Although there are many different ways to meditate, the basic principle of meditation is always the same. Meditation is a relaxed, focused state of attention. It is an excellent way to free up your imagination to Dream creatively. An easy approach to meditation is simply to sit comfortably and quietly, in a place where you will not be distracted by things (telephones, beepers) or people (children, co-workers), and close your eyes. Relax your body and allow your mind and emotions to become calm. Then ask yourself, "If I could have the life I wanted ideally, what would that look like?" Allow your imagination to roam freely. See as many pictures of your ideal life in your mind as you can. Don't put any constraints on yourself.

Then ask yourself, "If I could have the ideal job, or do the ideal activity, what would that be? What would be the most fun way I can think of to be productive? How would I best like to spend my time here on Earth?" Allow images of your ideal activity, job, and so forth to come into your mind. Play with the images, expand them, walk through them, make them more vivid. Have a good time! It may take some practice to do this, but with time, you will find that images come more and more easily.

"But I have a terrible imagination!" you say. "I can't see anything in my mind. I must be brain dead." I doubt it. You just may not have a facility for visualizing. Fortunately, there are other ways to get there. If you have too much trouble meditating or visualizing, go directly to Step #3.


## Step #3

Create a dream-collage. Get a pile of magazines and starting leafing through them. Whenever you see something that would be fun for you to do, or attracts as a wonderful way to spend your life, clip it out. Sometimes you'll be attracted by images and pictures, other times by articles. Allow yourself to be inspired by other people's lives. Knowing that someone else has created a successful and happy life around something as apparently "unusual" or "different" as that which attracts you can inspire you to follow your Dream.

If you have a marvelous imagination and don't need the help of anyone or anything to create a Dream, then go through some magazines in order to clip out images or articles that reflect or express your visualizations.

In either case, tape all your clippings to a large piece of butcher paper or tack them up on a corkboard, creating a collage. Put your collage somewhere where you see it every day. Spend some time at least three days a week sitting with your collage, just staring at it. Allow it to "speak" to you, to motivate you into finding your Dream, or into expanding your Dream if you already have one in mind.

## Step #4

Formulate your Dream. Without worrying at this point about whether or not your dream is feasible, gather the information you've learned about yourself and what you love from your list, meditation, and dream-collage, and come up with—a Dream. Make sure your Dream is indeed something exciting enough to you to pull you toward it. Remember, the whole idea of a Dream is to pull you toward a positive Future.

Make sure your Dream is *your* Dream. Don't choose a Dream because it would please your spouse, parents, in-laws, or step-children. Don't choose a Dream because it sounds good, would impress others, or fits the media's current version of "the good life." Choose the Dream that fits *you*, that sounds good to *you*, that excites *you*. You are, after all, the one who has to live your life. Choose the Dream that will pull you to a life *you* aspire to, that will fulfill you in ways that make sense to *you*.

Write your Dream out, starting with the words "I would love." Don't allow yourself to write anything down that you can't in all honesty start with the words "I would love." The only person you hurt in starting with anything less is yourself. That would truly be a shame, for you do deserve your Dream.

If you are one of the fortunate few who always have lots and lots of Dreams, then review your Dreams and ask yourself "Which of my Dreams pull the most strongly? Which really have the power to attract me into a vibrant Future?" If you have several, then prioritize them, so you can start with the first one.

Now that you've dreamt your Dream, it's time to begin the wondrous process of making that Dream come true. For it is only as you follow through to make your Dream manifest that you create that successful Future you so desire.

## NOTES

1. Richard Jerome, Susan Christian Goulding, "The Victim's Voice," *People Magazine*, May 26, 1997, pp. 67–70.
2. "There's The Beef," *People Magazine*, October 20, 1997, p. 157.
3. "Hotfooting It," *People Magazine*, June 15, 1998, p. 71.
4. Thomas Fields-Meyer, Meg Grant, "Keep On Pushing," *People Magazine*, February 17, 1997, pp. 111–115.

# CHAPTER FOUR

## HARNESS THE POWER OF YOUR DREAM

*How Do I Make My Dream Real?*
*How Do I Make It Come Alive?*

A Dream has the power to pull you through the Unknown into a success-ful Future—but only as long as you move toward it. Unless you actually take the steps to translate your Dream into reality, your Dream is but a vac-uous fantasy, something pretty that shimmers but will remain forever elu-sive. Winners dream purposeful Dreams, in order to help them create the life they desire. Winners' Dreams tend to be very detailed, concrete, and underscored by tremendous personal commitment, which gives those Dreams the substance required to become reality. If your Dream is to help you construct your life, it must have similar real substance. But how do you do that? How do you make your Dream real enough to be your guid-ing force into the Future? By using the power of choice.

    Choice is a focusing mechanism. Choice is how we determine whether we'll do A or B, spend time or money on X or Y; choice is how we focus our attention, energy, and resources. "But I already chose my Dream," you say, having followed the exercises in Chapter 3 and come up with your very own, very personal and wonderful Dream. "I dreamt it, didn't I?" you ask. And indeed, you did. But you haven't yet, in all likeli-hood, truly *chosen* it, meaning examined your Dream through a number of key perspectives to see if it is a Dream you are ready, willing, and able to act on. Acting on a Dream is how you bring it to life. Acting on a Dream is what makes that Dream come true.

These perspectives can be thought of as a number of steps, each leading you closer to a Dream with real substance, what I call a "chosen Dream." There are four steps to choosing your Dream:

- Making a *workable* choice
- Making a *wise* choice
- Making an *empowered* choice
- Making a *committed* choice

This chapter focuses on the first of these, making a *workable* choice.

## MAKE A WORKABLE CHOICE

The first step is to specify your Dream, meaning to define it in terms that are clear and workable for you, and releasing whatever fears and doubts you may have that get in the way of your seeing your Dream as genuinely doable.

The best way to illustrate how to choose your Dream is to show you how Paul, May, Kathy, and Jim each worked their way through the four steps to finding their "chosen Dream." Each of them started by giving a clear initial statement of their Dream, as I had asked them to at the end of the previous chapter.

PAUL

Paul's Dream was already well defined, so he had little trouble describing it in specific terms he could work with. Paul's challenge, in making his Dream a workable one, was in clearing his Dream of the fears he had attached to it.

*Paul's initial statement:* I want to be a consultant to young and growing companies—small companies, partnerships, professional businesses, and stores. I'll offer individually designed management programs that fit their needs and their budgets, which will include a maintenance program.

## *Dealing with Fear: The "Yeah-Buts"*

"Sounds great, Paul. How did you decide on the consultant status?" I asked. "I never want to be in the position again of being fired unexpectedly, for reasons entirely outside my control," Paul replied. "This way, if I get fired, it would only be because I did poor work, and if I'm working with a number of companies, even if I was fired from one company, I wouldn't lose everything all at once." "So working for yourself seems like a good solution," I said. "Yeah. Besides, no one wants to hire me, so what the heck—I'll hire me," Paul said wryly. "OK," I said. "Makes sense to me. Now let's take a look at whether this is a workable choice. In other words, have you made a choice that works for you, that you consider doable?"

"I don't know," Paul sighed. "When I actually look at it, the first thing that comes to mind is, OK fine, so I print up my cards and I'm a consultant but what if nobody hires me? If I can't find a job as a middle manager, what's to say I could find contracts to consult as one? And even if I do, what if I only get one or two clients? I won't be able to make a living at it, and then where will I be?" "Sounds like you have a case of the yeah-buts" I said. "Yeah-buts?" Paul asked, not understanding. "You don't question your ability to be a consultant; you say 'Yeah, that's doable' and then you have objections, '*But* it won't happen.' That's what I call the 'yeah-buts,'" I explained. "Oh, OK," said Paul, grinning, "I get it. And you're right, I have a bad case of the 'yeah-buts.'"

The "yeah-buts" come from Paul's fear of failure. He is confident on one level that he can do the job (work skills competency), but his fear undercuts his confidence. Fear operates as a security device; it is meant to keep us safe. Unfortunately, sometimes the very response meant to keep us safe will also imprison us. Paul's fear will paralyze him into inaction unless he deals with it. A fear is dealt with by examining it in order to determine whether or not the fear is performing a safety function. If it is, then the fear is keeping us from future harm, and we know that we must proceed with caution. If the fear proves to be simply a knee-jerk reaction to past hurt or having little basis in reality, it must be worked through and released if we are to successfully achieve our Dreams.

Paul's fear is of the "past hurt" variety. It comes out of his having experienced what he considers to be failure in his middle management job ("Couldn't keep my job through the merger, couldn't make the cut"). It is a past-oriented response. There is nothing in how Paul has specified his Dream—the Future—that suggests he will be axed out of work because of a merger. He has, on the contrary, carefully specified his Dream to avoid such a possibility. His fear provided a useful warning function: "Hey, you were hurt here. Let's set things up so you don't get hurt in the same way in the Future." Beyond that, his fear has no usefulness. What has hap-

pened is that Paul's fear of failing at his middle management job has gen-
eralized to a fear of failing in any occupational capacity. And he expresses
that fear, as do many people, as "yeah-but."

## Working through Fear

Fears are worked through by looking at them directly and determining which portions are helpful warning devices, and which parts can be
released. So I asked Paul, "Let's look at your fears, Paul, one by one. The
first is that nobody will hire you as a consultant." "Right," Paul said,
looking very depressed. "Yet you seem to have no worries about being
able to do the job," I continued. "No, I was good at it—at least that's what
all my evaluations said," Paul replied. "Have you ever tried to be hired as
a consultant?" I asked. "No," said Paul, slowly. "What are you getting
at?" "Well, if you feel capable of doing the job, yet you've never even
tried to get work as a consultant, then your fear is unfounded. You've
never even tested the waters," I said. "I never thought of it that way," said
Paul, thoughtfully.

"This particular fear, Paul, is a knee-jerk response to a hurtful past experience," I explained. "Your fear is responding to a situation from your
past that resembles your Dream only in the vaguest sense—being laid off
because of the merger and becoming a consultant both have to do with
work. That's it. The resemblance stops there." "So I really don't have to
pay attention to it," Paul said. "No, you don't," I replied, "because your
fear has no basis in your current reality. However, if you listen to it anyway, your fear will paralyze you and become a self-fulfilling prophecy.
You'll be too scared to really go for your chosen Dream, and thus end up
failing at it."

"All right," said Paul, "I can see the logic in that—and I can let it go. I
have a sneaking suspicion my fear of getting only one or two clients is the
same kind of fear." "It is," I replied. "Once again, you're projecting a fear
onto the Future that comes strictly out of your past, and that has no basis
in reality. You've never tried to get consulting clients before, so you have
no reason to fear that you can't do it. If you look at the world around you,
clearly it's a doable thing; lots of people are consultants and have plenty of
clients. Fearing that you can't do it is making yourself awfully special
('Everybody else can do it, but I can't'), in a very unhelpful way!" Paul
laughed, "All right, I get it."

"Looking at it now, without those fears in the way, is your choice workable for you?" I asked. "Is it something you can act on?" Paul thought about it for a moment. Then he looked up at me and said firmly, "Yes, I can do this. I can go forward with this choice."

Once you've described your Dreams in concrete terms, and then cleared it of whatever fears stand in the way, you've taken an important step in making your Dream workable.

MAY

May translated her Dream from the previous chapter into a clear and well-defined initial statement, thus giving her Dream enough concreteness to be workable. However, May's problem in making her Dream doable was in determining whether or not the choice she had made was the "right choice" for her.

*May's initial statement:* I want to have a studio where I teach an inspirational exercise program for cancer patients, both in treatment and in remission.

## Torn between "Right Choice" and "Wrong Choice"

"You're very clear with how you defined and made specific your Dream, May—that's great!" I commented. May nodded, "I feel very good about doing something that matters to me. It's just that . . ." May petered out, sighed, and seemed unable to continue. "It's just that—what?" I asked gently. "Well," May said, in an anguished voice, "what if I made the wrong choice? What if I do all this and it's not for me? What if I should have made another choice and now I'm going to waste years on this choice? How do I know if this is the right choice for me to make?" May was almost distraught as she spoke.

"May," I said, "hang on. Let's take a look at what's happening here. You're all caught up in 'what-ifs'—all of which are possible and legitimate, but none of which need to be a catastrophe." "What do you mean, Dr. Noelle? I'm confused," May replied.

"You're afraid of making a wrong choice, correct?" I asked. "That's normal and natural; many people are afraid of making the wrong choice. And there are ways of evaluating your choice to make sure it is the best possible choice you can make at this point in time, given what you know about yourself and your choice. We'll get to those in a minute. But for right now, May, what's important is to know that if you made a wrong choice, meaning a choice you can't act on, then all you have to do is make another choice!" "That's it?!" May said, astounded, "That's all there is to it?" "Yes," I replied. "Outside of suicide or homicide, there are virtually no irremediable choices. There are only choices that lead to new choices."

The willingness and ability to continually make new choices is critical to success in the Future. Since the very nature of the Unknown is that it is Unknown, we will—all of us—make what seem to be "wrong choices" at many points in time. The only way in which making "wrong choices" can become a deterrent to our success in the Future is if we *hold* ourselves to what turn out to be less-than-helpful choices. Winners are very willing to let go of choices that aren't working for them. Be willing to choose, experience, re-choose, experience, and re-choose over and over and over again. Sometimes you will choose a different path; sometimes you will recommit to the path you're already on. It doesn't make any difference which. Just get comfortable with, practice, exercise, and hone the ability to *choose*. Many "wrong" choices are in fact ways of finding out what the "right" choice is for you. Don't be afraid of wrong choices.

That being said, don't choose willy-nilly because you say to yourself, "After all, choice doesn't matter, I can always re-choose." Choose carefully, think through your choices so that you maximize the choices that in fact do lead to your Dream. Learn to imagine and visualize your choices to better enable you to evaluate them.

"Let's take a look at your choice, May," I said. "Let's see if it is indeed one you would feel comfortable and enthusiastic about acting on. Get comfortable in your chair and close your eyes." May did so. "All right, now see yourself in a studio, your studio where you will teach cancer patients and survivors your exercise program. Can you see it?" May nodded. "Good. Now can you see yourself actually doing the teaching?" May nodded and smiled. "Now can you see yourself in the office part of your studio, doing the administrative work?" May nodded, but this time she frowned. Seeing her frown, I asked her to stay with that image and continue visualizing administrative type functions. Then I suggested she visualize marketing and accounting type functions. May's frown deepened and she squirmed in her seat. She no longer seemed relaxed. I let the visualization continue for a little while, then asked May to open her eyes, and refocus herself in the room.

"What was going on for you there?" I asked. "You were frowning and didn't seem as comfortable." "I wasn't," May replied. "Something about all the administrative and marketing and accounting stuff—I really wasn't enjoying that." "OK," I said. "So what if you imagine hiring someone to do those functions for you?" I asked. May closed her eyes and was still for a moment. Opening them, she said, "Nope. I still don't like it. It makes me nervous to be responsible for the money coming in. It doesn't matter if it's me or someone I've hired, I'm just too worried about the money part. I can't see myself handling it without becoming a nervous wreck." "All right," I said, "then maybe your choice isn't one you'll be able to act on. There's nothing wrong with that. It just means you need to find a different expression of your Dream which you can act upon."

## Healing the "What-Ifs?"

"Think about the parts of your choice that made you nervous as you imagined them—the marketing and so forth—and the parts that made you happy," I suggested. "You mean the teaching, working directly with the patients," May said, smiling. "Yes, exactly," I replied. "Now, close your eyes, and see if you can come up with a choice that emphasizes the parts you like, and frees you from the parts you don't like in a way that is comfortable for you." "OK, Dr. Noelle," said May. "I don't know if I can do it, but I'll try." "Use your imagination," I said to May. "Play out different versions in your mind, just like we did earlier. That's how you'll find a choice that works for you."

Your imagination is a precious and valuable tool. Olympic athletes regularly use visualization techniques to help themselves perform at their peak, as do many other successful people.

Visualization can be thought of as "mental rehearsal," where you run through in your mind whatever it is you want to do, either in order to do

---

WINNER'S CIRCLE

Ilia Kulki, the Russian skater, winner of the 1998 Winter Olympics men's figure skating gold medal, talked about how on the day of the final competition, he was very stressed. There was so much riding on this final skating event! To help him perform at his very best, Kulki therefore proceeded to skate his program *in his mind* all day long, reviewing the parts that were difficult, going through what he needed to do to accomplish his jumps and turns, even as he rested his body. And win he did.

it really well, as did Kulki, or in May's case, to see where the problems may lie. Visualization enabled May to sense what areas she'd be uncomfortable with, and therefore helped her make an informed decision about her choice without having to implement that choice in reality. It also allowed her to run new possibilities through her mind. Here's the choice May came up with as a result of working through a number of choices in her imagination:

*May's new Dream statement:* I want to develop an inspirational exercise program for cancer patients, both in treatment and in remission, which I teach at various hospitals and other facilities, on a contract basis.

"Why does this work for you, May?" I asked. "How is this new choice something you can act on?" "Well," May replied, "I get to concentrate on the parts I really like, developing the program and teaching it, and I don't have to deal with the parts I don't like—the administration. In other words, I don't have to worry about getting each individual patient in as a client. I can work on getting a hospital as a client, and let them worry about the number of people who attend. Same thing with the administration. I only have to deal with the facilities as clients, which will be a limited number, so the administrative duties won't be nearly as much as keeping track of and billing lots of individual clients. Plus I can contract with hospitals for certain periods of time, without having to worry about individual patients dropping out." "And that feels good enough to you to be workable?" I asked. "Absolutely," May said. "I feel so much more relaxed about it. I'm still nervous and worried about whether I can do this, but at least I'm not nervous and worried about is this the wrong choice. It does feel like something I'd be happy and comfortable doing, even though I'm still concerned about how I'm gonna do it." "How you can go about actualizing your Dream is something we'll look at later, May," I said. "For now, congratulations on choosing a Dream you truly can act on. That's terrific."

Be willing to look at your "what-ifs" and handle them appropriately. Don't make the mistake of either brushing them aside, which isn't the same as handling them, or of taking them at face value, as if they were "truth." "What-ifs" pose questions to be asked and answered, thus assisting you in making good choices.

KATHY

Kathy's initial choice was clear and certainly to the point. She knew exactly what she wanted her Dream to be. The problem was in its workability. Kathy's dream was not one she could act upon, therefore although it was a valid Dream, it had no power to pull her into the successful Future she longed for. Kathy's challenge was to translate her lovely but impotent Dream into a compelling and forceful one.

*Kathy's initial statement:* I want to own and run a trendy little dress shop, where I help women choose outfits, including accessories, especially put together for them.

## Creating a Practical Dream

"A very clear choice, Kathy," I said. "The next question is, can you act upon it?" "Well, I can certainly help women choose outfits," Kathy replied, "so now all I have to do is find the money for the shop." "And learn how to own and operate a business," I said. "Oh, that," said Kathy dismissively. "There's nothing to that, you just take in the money and pay the bills." "Uh-huh," I said. "All right, then let's start with finding the money for the shop. "Oh, Heavens, I don't know," Kathy said, "I'm just choosing a Dream here, something lovely to pull me into the Future, right?" "Wrong," I said. "You're choosing a Dream you can act on—otherwise you're just indulging in fantasy. Can you see yourself acting on choosing outfits for women?" "Of course," Kathy responded airily, "That's easy. I love doing that." "Great," I said.

"Now, can you see yourself acting on finding the money for the shop?" I asked. "No," Kathy said, immediately deflated. "Other than finding some rich man to marry me, no." "Is that how you'd like to find the money?" I asked, "finding a rich man to marry you and finance it?" "Well, I wouldn't mind," Kathy answered truthfully, "but I seriously doubt that's going to happen. I'm no longer 22. Besides, if we're talking about a real Dream, I would vastly prefer not to be beholden to anyone, except maybe a bank." "Can you see yourself getting a loan from a bank?" I asked. "With what for collateral?" Kathy replied. "I don't own anything but a rather aging car and my clothes." We considered a number of other possible ways to raise money, none of which worked for Kathy.

"All right," I said, "so maybe the choice you've made isn't something you can act on." "But you asked me to come up with a Dream, and owning a shop is my Dream," Kathy cried out. "You're right, I did, and I think your Dream is a wonderful dream, Kathy, but you may have to define your Dream differently in order to be able to actually act on it. Because as it is right now, your Dream is just not workable. You cannot see yourself coming up with the money you need. That stops your Dream cold." "I know," Kathy sighed. "Well, it was a nice idea. Maybe someday it'll happen. Maybe I'll get an inheritance someday, or win the lottery, or meet an investor looking for a good thing; someday something's bound to happen."

Maybe, maybe not. "Someday," however, is what litters the junkyard of unfulfilled Dreams. Winners, people who have successfully realized their Dreams, use "someday" as in "someday it will happen," an intense motivator to make current workable choices toward those dreams. Kathy, unfortunately, is using "someday" as in "someday maybe it will somehow magically happen," which is highly unlikely. Kathy's "someday" doesn't motivate her to anything. It keeps her Dream in fantasyland, where without her active intervention, her Dream will remain forever.

## *Turning "Someday Somehow" into "Here and Now"*

In its present form, Kathy's Dream is unreachable. She can't envision getting the money for her shop in any believable way. If you don't believe at some level that you are capable of realizing your Dream, then it isn't workable, it won't pull you into the Future. When a Dream is too far away to be real, break it down into a series of more reachable choices, smaller Dreams, which will in turn lead stepwise to the Dream itself. That's how you reach an unreachable Dream, and how it can provide you with a powerful guiding force through the Unknown.

Wanting to encourage Kathy to break her Dream down into a series of reachable dreams, I asked her, "Kathy, keeping your Dream intact, but knowing that you will most effectively make it real by breaking it down into a series of choices, what might be a first choice you could see yourself acting upon?" A long silence ensued. "I haven't the foggiest idea," replied Kathy, depressed. "I don't even know where to start." "A good place to start, when you find yourself completely clueless, is to brainstorm with friends," I suggested to Kathy. "Is this something you could do?"

"I'd be so embarrassed!" Kathy exclaimed. "I don't understand," I said. "Well, here I am, with this ridiculously impossible Dream," Kathy said, "and I'm supposed to go ask my friends how to go about getting it? They'll just laugh at me." "Not necessarily," I said. "Not if you approach your friends by saying you need their help in brainstorming something. That you're unsure of how to break your Dream down into a series of

---

## WINNER'S CIRCLE

Janet Podleski and her sister Greta knew what they wanted to do. Their Dream was to create a cookbook based on their low-fat, wonderfully tasty recipes. And the sisters wanted to write their own special brand of cookbook—one that incorporated humor along with health-conscious recipes. The two women didn't know how to go about getting the book published—they just knew they had to write it. So Janet, now 33, and Greta, 32, took their Dream one dream step at a time. First, they surveyed the competition, answering the question, "Is it possible? Do we have something different and valuable to offer?" The answer was yes (Dream step 1). They then devised new recipes, thinking up jokes and funny titles to go with them. The book was now complete (Dream step 2). The women approached publishers but with no luck. The book was rejected time and time again. But having already accomplished Dream steps 1 and 2, the Podleski sisters were that much more determined to get to Dream step 3 (having the book published). This time they approached an investor, who liked their book so much, he provided the funds for the sisters to publish the book themselves! *Looneyspoons: Low-Fat Food Made Fun!* has been a wonderful financial success as well as the realization of the sisters' Dream.[1]

---

steps and you want to ask their opinion on what would be good steps. People like being asked their opinion. And if they are truly your friends, they will want to help you, not laugh at you." "Hmm," said Kathy. "Well, I'll try, but I'm not guaranteeing anything." "Good enough," I said. "And what you may find is that your imagination will be sparked by what they say. You may never use a single one of your friends' suggestions, but they may inspire you to a workable choice."

"You might also find it valuable," I continued, "to go around to successful small dress shops and ask the owners how they got started. Successful people are often pleased when someone is interested in how they got there. And again, you might either pick up some valuable information, or be inspired to new ideas of your own." "It's worth a try, I guess," said Kathy unenthusiastically, "but it still seems like I'm just spinning my wheels." "Well, give it your best shot, and see what you come up with," I replied.

Which she did. And much to her own amazement, as a result of brainstorming with friends, interviewing owners of shops, and the using her own inspiration and imagination, Kathy came up with a series of workable choices that could indeed lead to her Dream.

*Kathy's new Dream statement:*

- I'll get work as a salesclerk in a medium-sized trendy shop.
- I'll work out a deal with the owner that I can use a section of the shop to promote "Design by Kathy" outfits with accessories.
- Somehow I'll leverage that into a bank loan for my own shop.

"Can you see yourself acting on choices #1 and #2?" I asked Kathy. "Yes, I can," she replied. "You realize that you'll have to be successful at each step in order to move on to the next step?" I continued. "Oh, yes," Kathy smiled. "Is that workable for you?" I asked. "I'm not afraid of doing the work, nor of working hard," Kathy replied, "I just couldn't see how to get there from here before. Now that I have some idea of how it can work, yes it is workable. Because you're right, Dr. Noelle, my Dream does pull me." "Good," I said, "that's the idea. Now, looking at choice #3, that one seems less well defined." "It is, for now," said Kathy, "but somehow I think if I can succeed at both my first and second choices, I can find a way to make my third choice workable, even if I don't know at the moment what exactly that will be."

Kathy found a way to turn a "someday" lost in fantasyland into a "someday" that has excellent chances of becoming real. Too often, people never even attempt to fulfill their Dreams, because the task seems so daunting. Breaking your Dream down into a series of workable choices is one way of achieving "the impossible Dream."

### JIM

A Dream must have substance if it is to be workable. Jim's description of his Dream, although clear, had little reality because his choice had no substance. Meaning is what gives substance to things. Money, for example, has a great deal of meaning, and therefore, of substance in our culture. Money means the abundance or lack of material things. It too often means the difference between starving and surviving, and between surviving and thriving. Until you give meaning to your choices, your Dream is functioning as a lightweight, and it has little power to pull you toward it. Jim's challenge was to give his Dream substance by giving its various parts meaning. Then his Dream would indeed be workable.

*Jim's initial statement:* I'll drive around the countryside, fixing the things that people break, and tell yarns about all the historical places I come to along the way.

## *Giving Your Dream Solidity*

"Sounds good, Jim," I said. "Now how are you going to make this choice workable?" I asked. "What do you mean?" Jim asked in return. "Well, how is this going to happen? For example, where are you going to drive to?" I asked, looking for the substance of Jim's Dream. "I dunno," said Jim, "wherever the work is, I guess." "How are you going to find out where the work is?" I asked. "I dunno, guess someone'll ask for me or tell me," he said. "Well how is somebody going to find out about you so they can tell you?" I asked. "I dunno, guess they just will," Jim said, running his finger inside his collar. "And who are you going to tell historical yarns to?" I continued. "I dunno, whoever wants to listen, I guess," Jim said. "Do you want to earn any money telling your tales?" I asked. "I dunno, never thought about it one way or the other," Jim said, growing increasingly uncomfortable. "Would you like to?" I asked. "Yeah, sure," Jim replied. "Who wouldn't?" "So how are you going to go about telling your tales so you earn money at it?" I asked. "I dunno, maybe folks'll just give me money, like a tip, maybe," said Jim. "The same folks that you fix things for?" I asked. "Yeah, maybe," said Jim, grinning at the thought. "But you don't know how you're going to find these folk, right?" I asked. "No, I don't," Jim said, his grin fading.

Jim's choice, at this point, has too little substance to be of any value to him. Jim is afflicted with a very common problem: the "I dunno" syndrome. "I dunno," which we all fall prey to at one time or another, most often means: "I don't know because I haven't thought about it, and I'm not coming up with any swift ideas just off the top of my head." "I dunno" rarely means: "I truly do not know and could not come up with a single solitary thought if my life depended on it." When it comes to using a Dream to create a positive and successful Future for yourself, the "I dunno" syndrome is a sure road to failure. The antidote however is simple: think.

Too often people fear that thinking is for smart people and that if they weren't blessed with the brains of a genius or a Ph.D., they can't think productively. That is baloney. Most of us have average intelligence and some education, and that's all you need to think through the answers to your "I dunnos." You also, as Kathy did, have access to friends and acquaintances with whom to brainstorm, and others in the world to use as role models and providers of useful guidance. None of this requires more than average intelligence. For that matter, many delightful Winners who are challenged

---

### WINNER'S CIRCLE

Peter Leonard, a 54-year-old learning disabled handyman, won a seat in the New Hampshire House of Representatives on his seventh try. He has, despite his disability, submitted several bills to the state legislature, of which at least one has been passed as of the writing of this book. Had Peter Leonard stopped himself at the "I dunno" stage in his Dream to win a seat in the legislature, he would never have made it.

---

either in terms of intelligence or of education have still done remarkably well in thinking productively for themselves.

"I dunno" is frequently just intellectual inertia, born of lack of practice. As a culture, we have become far more practiced at consuming ready-made thought than at thinking for ourselves. For example, our media bombards us with ready-made opinion, which encourages us just to accept it rather than to think facts through on our own. Advertising gives us all the reasons why a product is beneficial, which we rarely check out for ourselves. Professionals give us advice, which we swallow whole, without necessarily thinking through the logic in what the professional suggests, and too infrequently do we tune in to our discomfort when we intuitively react against something we are told to do. Much of our willingness to accept ready-made thought is due to lack of time and sometimes to lack of interest, both highly understandable (although when it applies to things that are important to us, accepting ready-made thought is foolish and potentially damaging). Whatever the source and whatever the reason, accepting ready-made thought leads to an underdeveloped facility of thinking. This can get seriously in the way when you do need to think through choices.

## Curing the "I Dunnos"

The easiest way to cure the "I dunnos" is not to accept them. "Let's take my first question, Jim," I said. "When I asked where you are going to drive to, you answered 'where the work is,' which is great, but when I asked 'How are you going to find out where the work is?' you replied that you didn't know. So how about if we think on that one. And no fair saying 'I dunno.'" "OK." said Jim. "Gotcha." Long silence. I listened to the muffled sounds of traffic outside. Finally Jim said, "I think I'd better start with the other one." "What other one?" I asked, unsure of what he was referring to. "The other question before that—where the work is," Jim answered. "Oh, fine," I said, "what's your thought on that?" "Well," Jim said slowly, carefully, "I could go over to the local hospital, and the police station near me, and the school, and see if maybe they need some help fixing things that are broke." "That's a great idea, Jim," I said, surprised and delighted with how easily and quickly he'd solved his own "I dunno."

"And I saw a fellow, once, had a sign on his car doors—both sides—saying 'Hi, I'm Al the Plumber, you call, I'll plumb.' It was kind of funny, you know—got my attention. I could do something like that," Jim said, warming to his subject. "I could make a sign that says 'Hi, I'm Fix-It Jim. You Break It, I'll Fix It'—something like that. So's people just out and about would see it and maybe call on me." "I'm impressed, Jim, you do know what will work for you. These are very workable ideas that you can weave into a choice you will be able to act on. All you needed to do was think on them for a bit," I said. Jim nodded. He seemed pleased with himself, as well he should have been. It feels great to think things through for yourself, and what more marvelous thing to think through than how to make your own Dream come true.

"What about the historical tales part, Jim?" I asked. "Can you find a choice you can act on to fulfill that part of your Dream?" Jim chewed thoughtfully on his lower lip. "I don't—no, no I'm not going to say that," he said. Silence again. "I don't think people are going to pay me for talking while I'm fixing their toaster or furnace. I don't see how I'm gonna get a chance to do all of it."

"Maybe you can split your Dream into two choices, each of which would be a part-time activity. Then you can act upon both, pretty much at the same time," I suggested. Nowhere is it written that a Dream has to be fulfilled in one all-encompassing activity. Sometimes the most effective way to your Dream is to choose two or three different ways to express it, which together give you the fulfillment you desire.

"Hmm," said Jim, "Now there's a dandy thought. OK. If I look at telling tales by itself, well, let's see . . . I know kids go on field trips, and maybe I could get involved in that somehow, talk to them. Course, I don't think there's any money in that, and I would like to make money at this." Jim shook his head. "I'm stalled. I really don't know more on this one right now, Doc." "Ok," I said, "If you really don't know, then you don't. That's fine." I talked to Jim about brainstorming, and doing some research on the choices others have made in similar circumstances. I encouraged him to visualize and daydream on what different choices might look like and feel like to him. Some weeks later Jim came in with the following new Dream statements:

"I want to fix up my car so I'm the "Fix-It Man" and I want to be the regular fix-it man for the local institutions and facilities, as well as take on whatever customers see my car sign or otherwise come my way.

When I'm not busy with "fix-it" business, I want to sign on with the local historical society to be a tour guide on their charter buses. When tourists come to town, I want to be the tour guide that talks about the sites and tells the tales."

"Are these workable choices for you, Jim?" I asked. "Can you see yourself acting upon them comfortably and happily?" "Yes Ma'am—Doc, I mean," said Jim. "I can see myself making a living at them, too. That was what had me real worried when you started this whole Dream thing. That I wouldn't be able to make a living at it. But I can see making a living at these two things. The tourist trade is pretty good in the summer out here, and if I can hook up with enough places like the school and such, I should be able to do enough fixing to keep me in food and rent and a little something extra for savings. I can see it."

If you can see it, you can achieve it. Jim's Dream now has substance and meaning, which give it the power to pull him into a successful Future. A Dream can take many forms, what is important is that your Dream take the form that is workable for you.

## How to Develop a Workable Choice for Your Dream

Translating your Dream from your original imaginative no-limits concept to a Dream that can come true is key to your ability to succeed. Too many Dreams never see the light of day because we don't know how to get from the ideal to the real. Use the following steps to bring your Dream from an impossible "Out there, somewhere," to a possible "Here and now."

## Personal Success Log 4: Your Workable Choice

### Step #1: Specify Your Dream in Concrete Terms

Specify your Dream in terms that are clear and workable for you. State your Dream in terms that are concrete enough for you to act on. Use visualization to help you figure out the validity of your choice. See yourself in your mind's eye actually living your Dream, not the rewards the Dream might bring, but what the day-to-day living of your Dream would be. Then ask yourself: Have I made a choice that works for me, that I consider doable?

If you find that you can't see yourself living your Dream as you've currently described it, then reconfigure your Dream so you can. Just because you can't immediately see how you'd live your Dream doesn't mean you have to give it up! Don't let yourself get away with the "I dunnos." Use the examples of Paul, May, Kathy, and Jim to help you figure out how to make your Dream work for you. You may find that you alter one part of your Dream, or redefine your Dream into a series of choices, or split it into several Dreams that you may or may not seek to fulfill at the same time. What is important at this point is to have a clear statement of your Dream, which you can see yourself living day to day. Don't worry about how you are going to actualize your Dream. We'll discuss that in later chapters.

## Step #2: Release Fears and Doubts

Your Dream will only be workable if you release whatever fears and doubts you may have that get in the way of your seeing your Dream as genuinely doable. Fears are often hidden behind "Yeah-buts," and "What-ifs?" so look for those or variations thereof. Work through your fears by examining them to see if they are of the knee-jerk variety, an automatic response to past experience. Fears of making a wrong choice are defused by visualizing the day-to-day living of your Dream and thinking it through carefully. Once you've done that, realize that you'll really only know if you've made a "right choice" as you live it, and that choices can be made anew all along the way.

Having made a workable choice, it's now time to figure out how your choice works with who you are and what you want in your life. In other words, it's time to make a wise, empowered, and committed choice so your Dream can effectively pull you into the successful Future you seek.

## NOTES

1. Peter Ames Carlin, Joanne Fowler, "Flour Power," *People Magazine,* July 20, 1998, pp. 101–102.

# CHAPTER FIVE

## ENGAGE THE POWER OF YOURSELF

### *How Does My Dream Fit with Who I Am?*
### *How Do I Commit to It?*

A Dream must first be workable in order to be effective, thus "making a workable choice" is the first step in developing a chosen Dream. However, a Dream must also fit who you are and what you want for yourself in the larger context of your life. It must be a Dream you can and do act upon. This is what distinguishes compelling Dreams from those that stay in the land of "Ho-hum, wouldn't it be nice," never to be realized. Steps 2, 3, and 4 in developing a chosen Dream are:

- Make a *wise* choice
- Make an *empowered* choice
- Make a *committed* choice.

#### MAKE A WISE CHOICE

Determine whether or not your choice is a wise one, meaning a choice that works for who you are in the larger context of the life you wish to lead. A wise choice is one that is not only workable for you, as described in Chapter 4, but also one that takes into account what this choice will ask of you, what you expect of it, and whether or not this choice fits with how you see your life. If your Dream asks more of you than you are willing or able to give to it, then it is not the right choice for you. You will only become discouraged and unhappy. If you expect far too much of your Dream, you will be disappointed at the outcome. If your Dream is at odds with how you live your life, then you will either fail at your choice, or make yourself miserable trying to succeed at it. A wise choice is one where what you give to your Dream seems fair and just and what you expect from it is pretty much what you receive, one which allows you to integrate your Dream into your life patterns without too much adjustment or discomfort.

To help them determine whether or not their choices were wise, I asked Paul, May, Kathy, and Jim the following:

- "What will your dream ask of you?"
- "What do you expect of it?"
- "How does your dream fit with your current lifestyle?"

PAUL

Paul had some concerns with what his Dream would ask of him, and how it would impact his current lifestyle, especially his family. His expectations of what his Dream would give to him were realistic and felt satisfying to him. He wasn't thrilled, however, when we first started working on this aspect of choosing his Dream.

## Giving to Your Dream

"Oh, great, so now my choice not only has to be workable, something I can act upon, but wise!" Paul exclaimed. "Now how am I going to get to that?" "The same way you got to the workable status, by thinking it through," I replied. "OK, fine, whatever," said Paul. "So what am I supposed to think about this time?" he asked. "How about, what do you think becoming a consultant as you've described is going to require of you?" I asked. "Gosh, uh, let's see—time, probably some money, beating the pavement. Making contacts, talking to people." "All right," I said, "are those things you are willing to give to accomplishing your Dream?" "Put that way—yes, of course," Paul said. "How much time, then?" I asked. "Boy you sure like to dot all the i's and cross all your t's," Paul commented. "You'll be much more successful if you make as much of the Unknown known to yourself as possible," I replied. "Answering these sorts of questions is how to get there." "OK," said Paul. "How about if I give myself six months to get started, to actually see money coming in?" "Is that something you can live with, comfortably?" I asked. "Well I'd like to see money before that, but yes, I can live with it," Paul replied. Paul then thought through the monetary commitment his choice would take until he was comfortable with the amount.

## Being Clear about What Your Dream Will Ask of You

Then we discussed making contacts and "beating the pavement," as Paul called it. Here, Paul had some reticence. "I haven't been out there in the field—ever, really," Paul said, concerned. "I don't mind putting in the hours, but I don't know if I can make contacts and be effective selling my stuff." "If you felt you would benefit," I asked, "would you be willing to take a class, or read a book on the subject, or brainstorm with someone who's already a successful consultant to enhance your skills?" "Yeah," said Paul, "sure, that would be OK." "Then that's what your choice might require of you," I said. "That's not so bad," Paul commented. "No, why should it be? Making a wise choice isn't about making things painful or difficult for yourself, it's about making a choice which will work for you, a choice which will pull you into a successful and positive Future, a Future free of suffering and struggle." I said, "So it's wise to look ahead and make sure that the choice you are selecting isn't loaded with unpleasantness."

## Knowing What You Expect from Your Dream

"Let's move on to what you might expect from your choice of being a consultant," I said. "I expect money, of course," said Paul, "enough to live on, eventually." "You know some months are likely to be better than others," I said. "Is that OK with you?" Paul thought about it for a moment. "Yes, I think that's OK. I'd have to learn how to anticipate the short months, but I can handle that." "Anything else you'd like from your choice?" I asked. "Satisfaction. I expect this choice, this way of achieving my Dream to bring me good feelings, you know, the satisfaction you get from helping people, and doing something well. That kind of satisfaction," Paul answered. "Anything else?" I asked again. "Not really," Paul said, "that would be enough. Heck, that would be great."

### *Looking at How Your Dream Will Impact Your Lifestyle*

Paul's expectations of his choice were realistic and consistent with what he was willing to put out. I asked him now to think about how acting on his choice would impact his current life. After a while, Paul said, "I wouldn't have as regular a life as I did before. I'd probably work odd hours, maybe some nights and weekends. That's different." "How does that fit for you?" I asked. "It fits OK for me," Paul said, troubled, "but I don't know how my wife would like it. She's used to me always being home by a certain time, being there on the weekends. I don't know. I'll have to ask her, talk with her about it." "Good, I said, "that's important." A wise choice takes into account the other people in your life. It's not fair to them for you to make changes that will significantly impact their lives without discussing those changes with them ahead of time.

Taking the time and making the effort to determine if your choice is wise will avoid many problems down the road. As I told Paul, the more of the Unknown you can make Known, the more clearly you can see your way into your Future.

MAY

May had not given much thought to what she expected to give to her Dream and discovered she needed to set boundaries for herself. She didn't have a good grasp of what her Dream would give to her, other than in the most general terms.

### *When Giving to Your Dream Is Giving Too Much*

I started this session by asking May to think about what she would be willing to give to her choice. May replied, "Oh, that's easy—everything!" "Everything?" I asked. "You'd be willing to give up your child, your friends, your hobbies, everything?" "Well, no," May answered, "I didn't mean that." "What did you mean?" I asked. "I'm a very 100 percent person. I'm willing to do what it takes," May said. She furrowed her brow, continuing, "Except I don't know what it takes. I've never done this before." "Good point," I said. "So maybe in your case, May, it would be wise to look at what you're *not* willing to give to your choice. In other words, set some boundaries for yourself. A Dream is meant to fulfill you in a positive way, not overwhelm you and take over all of your life—unless that's what you want." "No, that's not what I want," May said. "Set boundaries, OK, let's see."

## Learning to Set Boundaries

May thought for a while, then said, "I want to be able to see Thomas off to school in the mornings, and I want to be home for him at night. So I guess I'm willing to give from about eight thirty in the morning to six o'clock at night during the week, and maybe some time occasionally in the afternoon on a Saturday, at least in the beginning." "What else?" I asked. May said determinedly, "I won't give up my health." "Good for you," I said. "I don't ever want to get as stressed as I did making patterns and dealing with people in the garment industry." May continued, "I'll walk away from my Dream before I let that happen." "Excellent, May," I said. "That's a great boundary to set." "Does anything else come to mind?" I asked. "Not right now. I mean, I'm willing to learn and study and get myself trained or certified, whatever is necessary. That part is exciting, actually." I suggested to May that she give some more thought later to any other boundaries she might wish to set for herself. May realized that an additional bonus to setting good boundaries was that she would be able to handle whatever adjustments in lifestyle her Dream might require of her. She felt good about that.

## Asking for What You Want of Your Dream

Then I asked May to take a look at her expectations of her exercise program choice. "My expectations?" May asked, surprised by my question. "Well, to get a paycheck—or more than one, I guess, if I get contracts with more than one hospital. To get the pleasure of helping people feel better." "Uh-huh," I said. "And what size paycheck are you expecting? How much?" I asked. May stared at me, a blank look in her eyes. "How much? I haven't a clue," she said. "That's a bit of a problem, wouldn't you say?" I asked. "How so?" asked May, "I'll just take what they offer me." "How will you know if what the hospital offers you is a fair price? And what will you do if the hospital doesn't know what to offer you and asks you for the value of your services?" I asked. May continued to stare at me.

"I hate this money part," she said finally. "I never know how to deal with it. When I was a pattern maker I just took what they gave me." "But

---

WINNER'S CIRCLE

Mother Theresa, a phenomenal woman, knew what she wanted to receive to
fulfill her Dream of caring for the sick and homeless, and didn't hesitate to
ask for it even in the most unexpected circumstances. When awarded the
Nobel Peace Prize, for example, she asked that her prize money be used to
feed the hungry. Mother Theresa knew exactly what she wanted and wasn't
afraid to ask for it.

---

you're trying to do it differently, this time, May. You are trying to fulfill a
Dream, not just take what someone hands you. If you don't have an
expectation of what you want to receive, you have no way of knowing if
indeed your choice is helping you fulfill your Dream or not."

May was quiet for a long time. Then she said, "I've always thought it
was bad to expect something for doing good things. That you should just
accept whatever people are willing to give you." "There's nothing bad
with accomplishing both: doing good deeds and having a comfortable life,
May," I replied.

Doing good and making money can go together. Even Jesus did not,
according to the Bible, say "Eat less" when faced with the dilemma of the
hungry crowd; instead, Jesus immediately sought a way to provide *more*
loaves and fishes.

A Dream scarcely qualifies as a Dream if you become a martyr in
order to fulfill it. Too many people believe that a Dream of helping others
must be done by sacrificing themselves. Not so!

---

WINNER'S CIRCLE

Michael Richards, 48 years old, and his wife Lynette, 47, fell into hard times
a little over 10 years ago, and virtually had to start over from scratch. They
began making candles in their apartment, enlisting homeless people to help
out. Their business, Candleworks, was an immediate success, and as the
business grew out of their apartment and into a company setting, the
Richardses continued to hire the homeless (who weren't homeless for long,
now they were employed!) as well as those suffering from physical or mental disabilities. Although the Richardses still live simply in order to keep expanding the business, they are immensely fulfilled and talk of the joy their
work brings them. Their business continues to grow and generate greater

*(continued)*

---

Just as there's nothing wrong with doing good and making money at the same time, there's nothing wrong with having expectations about earning money, as long as those expectations are realistic given the choice you are acting upon. So I suggest that you do a little research to find out what realistic expectations might be of the monies the type of program you want to develop could bring you—not in order to gouge the public, but in order to later on have something by which to gage, "How am I doing? Is my choice fulfilling me financially as well as emotionally?"

"Gosh," May said, "it feels really weird to talk so specifically about something in the Future." "No doubt," I replied, "but that's what Dreams are for. Only in vividly seeing, talking about, specifying, and imagining your Dream will you give it the power to pull you forward."

The more Unknown your Future, the more important it is to project "What am I willing to give to this choice and what do I expect to receive?" Then you will have a Dream of meaning, of substance, something strong to pull you forward.

KATHY

Since Kathy's Dream was formulated as a series of steps, we started by looking at the wisdom of the first step, working as a salesclerk in a small trendy shop. Kathy was quite clear and realistic about both what she expected to give (lots of long hours), and what she expected to receive (low pay with small raises or bonuses over time). She was willing to accept both as part of accomplishing her overall Dream. However, when I asked her to look at what impact working as a salesclerk would have on her current life, Kathy wasn't sure of how to do that.

## Visualizing the Impact of Your Dream on Your Lifestyle

"All right, then, close your eyes, and imagine what your day looks like as a salesclerk. I'll help by asking you questions," I suggested. Whenever you don't know how something will play out, or what an experience

---

(continued)

revenues each year, helping them as they help others. The Richardses were rewarded for their efforts in 1998 by Vice President Al Gore, who presented them with the National Small Business Owner of the Year Award for Welfare-to-Work.[1]

might be like, simply close your eyes, relax, focus, and imagine it. You will be surprised how accurate your imaginings will be.

Kathy closed her eyes, took a deep breath, and said "I'm ready." "OK," I said, "see yourself arriving at the shop; do you open up or is it open?" "I open up," Kathy said. "OK, then what I happens?" I asked. "I put my things away and start straightening up the shop from the night before," Kathy replied. "Good," I said, "keep going." "I wait for a customer. They come, I help them—that feels great," she commented, smiling, then continued: "I wait. My, this job has a lot of waiting in it," Kathy said, "I'm not crazy about that." "The delivery person arrives, I unpack a couple of boxes, I wait." Kathy opened her eyes and sat upright. "Gosh, Dr. Noelle, I never thought of all the waiting involved. That would drive me bonkers! Does this mean I have to make a different choice for my Dream?" she asked, panicked.

## *Transforming "Negative" Impact into Positive Productivity*

"Not necessarily, Kathy, let's talk about it. Didn't you have a lot of waiting to do as a hair stylist on sets?" I asked. "Well, yes, but I was never just sitting around waiting, there was always something to do, like style a wig, or people to talk to," Kathy replied. "Well, being a salesclerk isn't your Dream, it's just a step along the way, so what might you be doing while you're 'waiting' that could advance your Dream?" I asked. "Hmm," Kathy said, "I'd have to think about that . . . maybe I could contact former customers and suggest outfits for them. Of course, to do that I'd already have to have customers," she said, worried. Silence. Then Kathy said, "Maybe I could start by creating a contact and preferences sheet for each customer that walks in." She started getting excited. "Sure, that could work," Kathy continued, "just like I used to do with the celebrities. I'd keep a card on each one of how he or she liked their hair done—you know, products they liked used on their hair, how they liked their coffee, stuff like that."

"That's great, Kathy," I said, "that's good thinking. So looking at the impact being a salesclerk might have on your life, on what is and isn't comfortable for you—in this case, waiting—actually gave you yet another way to move toward your Dream: create your customer preference cards." "Wow, this is exciting," Kathy said. "Bet you never thought waiting could be productive before," I teased. "No, I didn't. OK, I see how to do this," Kathy said, "I'm going to close my eyes and do some more imagining, see where that leads me." A process I heartily encouraged.

## Thinking Differently, Thinking Wisely

When you look at the impact your choice may have on your life, you're not just looking at "What are the positive impacts, what are the negative impacts?" you're also looking at "How can I transform this negative impact into a positive impact?" You see, much of Winners' success has to do with their willingness to think differently.

It isn't old thinking that is going to catapult us into a wonderful and successful Future, it's new thinking, thinking in different ways about old situations. Think in terms of "what I *could do*" (a future-oriented thought) in this circumstance, rather than "what I *have done*" in this circumstance, which relies on how you behaved in the past.

JIM

Visualizing wasn't Jim's strong suit, but he closed his eyes, nonetheless, when I asked him to, and gamely tried to see what his day would look like as a fix-it man and tour bus guide. I wanted to help Jim determine the impact of his Dream on his day-to-day life. As Jim sat back, quietly visualizing, I thought about his expectations of what he would get (variable income, satisfaction of doing something he liked, and a less painful back)

---

WINNER'S CIRCLE

Selling Tupperware isn't exactly a new business. People have been selling Tupperware for years, hosting parties at individuals' homes to generate sales and revenue. So there's nothing innovative about 33-year-old Jeff Sumner selling Tupperware. However, the way Sumner sells Tupperware is unique. Sumner was tired of working as just an ordinary salesperson in a department store. His work didn't seem to be bringing him the success he wanted, and certainly wasn't fulfilling—until Sumner came up with a new and different way of selling, and applied it to Tupperware. Sumner, who is one of the top-selling salespersons in Tupperware's Pacific Region, uses his background as a performance artist to put on a lively and entertaining show for the Tupperware parties he books. Dressed in drag, Sumner lip-syncs Tupperware product knowledge he's transformed into lyrics set to current popular music. He invents Tupperware trivia games, and generally packages Tupperware in a fun, entertaining manner, which delights the attendees into buying lots of Tupperware. Winners aren't afraid to think differently— often, as Sumner, very differently.[2]

and what he would give (skill, attention, working his "tales" so they were entertaining and well spoken). His thoughts on the subject were solid and down-to-earth. I was curious to see what Jim's visualization would yield. I didn't have long to wait. Jim sat up and rubbed his eyes.

"Here's what I come up with, Doc," he said. "The one thing that'll be really different is all those people." "All those people?" I asked, not understanding. "You see," Jim said, explaining, "A trucker's life is a pretty lonely one—well, not lonely really, just that you're on your own, alone by yourself, a lot of the time. The only person I saw much was my wife, and maybe the waitresses at the stops I stopped at a lot." "Now if I'm doing this fix-it and tour guide thing," Jim continued, "especially the tour guide thing, I'm going to be seeing a lot of people, and I don't know how much I'm gonna like that. Or even if I know how to deal with it." I nodded and smiled, "So you have some 'I dunnos' here." "Guess I do, at that," Jim said.

## *Using the Known to Help You Deal with the Unknown Aspects of Your Dream*

"OK, let's feel it out a little, see if we can make your Unknown of seeing a lot of people a more Known experience for you," I suggested. "You use a CB radio in your truck, don't you?" Jim nodded. "Did you only talk to people you knew over the CB?" I asked. "No," replied Jim, "I talk to all sorts of people. Mostly truckers, like myself, but there'd be other folk talking on the CB, and I'd talk to them too." "Did you find it difficult to talk to these people?" I asked. "No," said Jim, smiling, "I like talking to them, it's kinda fun. I think I see where you're going with this, Doc. If I can talk on the radio to anybody and everybody, then why can't I talk just as easy to people when they're in front of me?" "You're right, Jim. That's exactly what I was thinking," I said.

If you're venturing out into unfamiliar territory, seeing how the unfamiliar new situation resembles a familiar past situation can be a useful way of using the past to help you step into the Future. The familiar and unfamiliar situations can be thought of as overlapping circles, with a little piece of common Known in the overlap.

The Familiar / Common Known / The Unfamiliar

That common Known helps make the transition from past known to Future Unknown easier, more comfortable. Jim's willingness to look at talking to people in his new ventures as similar to talking to people over the CB when he was a trucker was his way of using a Known situation to help ease the way into the new, Unknown situation.

## Mental Rehearsal Eases the Way

"So, how does that work for you?" I asked. "I think it works pretty good," Jim said. "I'll think about it some, play with it in my mind, like you say." Mental rehearsal is a valuable way to test out and practice new skills. Over the next few weeks, Jim imagined himself talking to lots of different people in his "fix-it" capacity, and talking to groups of people as a tour guide. When he wasn't sure how to handle a certain type of person or interaction, Jim would ask himself how he would have handled the situation if he'd been on his CB. Using that as a starting point, Jim would then translate the CB interaction into a "live" interaction. The more he rehearsed and played out the situations in his mind, the more comfortable he became.

## MAKE AN EMPOWERED CHOICE

Once you've specified your Dream, and cleared out whatever fears and hesitations are in the way of its being workable, then looked at your expectations thus making a wise choice, it's time to empower your choice. Empowering your choice means to support your choice with the power of your inner qualities. It means making sure you have what it takes to act on your Dream. If you don't feel that you do, your Dream will remain a fantasy. As daunting as it may sound, making sure you have what it takes to act on your Dream is actually remarkably easy.

PAUL

"All right, Paul, here's the moment of truth," I said. "Given everything we've talked about, can you actually do it? Do you feel that you have what it takes to activate your choice, to go out and fulfill your Dream?" Paul sighed, "sort of," he said. "Not a very compelling feeling, that's for sure." "So what do you intend to power your choice with?" I asked. "Power my choice with?" Paul repeated, not understanding. "What's the fuel, what are you going to use to give you the positive energy to go forward with your choice?" I asked. "I haven't the vaguest idea," Paul said. "Willpower?" he asked, dubiously. "Willpower is nice," I replied, "but too often willpower means grit your teeth and force yourself ahead. Not exactly the sustaining fuel I had in mind." "Well, what then?" asked Paul.

## Putting Your Inner Qualities to Work

I picked up my notes from previous sessions and leafed through them. "Ah here it is," I said. "Paul, remember when I asked you to describe who you are, and we came up with a list of your inner qualities?" "Yeah, sure," Paul answered. "Here they are," I said, reading off the list, "Honest, trustworthy, hard-working, a pretty good problem-solver, negotiator, doer, reliable, good with follow-through, patient, good listener, good at representing others, persistence. That's your fuel, Paul," I said, putting the list down and looking up at him. "That's what you will rely on to give you the power necessary to act upon your choice." "In other words," said Paul, "I'm going to use my qualities to help me do the whatever it is I need to do." "Yes, and to remind yourself that you do have 'the goods' as it were," I said. "I suggest you write out your qualities as separate items, and read them to yourself every day as you prepare to go about creating your new Future, to keep them well in mind, supporting you as you go along." "Do them as affirmations?" asked Paul. "Exactly," I replied.

## The Power of Affirmations

Affirmations are positive statements you repeat to yourself silently or out loud in a variety of situations, basically, whenever you wish to "feed" yourself mentally or emotionally. Paul's list of affirmations looked like this:

- I am honest and trustworthy.
- I do a good job; I am hard-working.
- I am a good problem-solver and follow through well. I am persistent.
- I am patient, a good listener, and a good negotiator.
- I represent myself and others well.

Affirmations are especially useful when you are setting about a new task or a new way of thinking. They will support and reinforce your new skill or way of thinking. Too often our negative thoughts get in the way of establishing more forward ways of thinking. Affirmations can counter these negative thoughts very effectively. Affirmations are a highly valuable tool in helping you solidify the power that lies within your inner qualities.

MAY

When I broached the subject of empowering her choices with May, she grew anxious and started twisting her hands together. "I'm fine with the Dream part, Dr. Noelle," May said, "but I'm very nervous about how I'm supposed to make this happen. I mean, I've never developed a program of any kind before, much less an exercise program. I don't have a clue about where to begin." Applying her inner qualities to this new task was critical to giving May the power to see her choice through.

## Translate Your Inner Qualities into the Skills You Need to Actualize Your Dream

"Let's look at your list of qualities, May," I said, "and see how they tie in to developing a program: conscientiousness, caring about people, ability to tune into other people easily, a survivor, persistent, patient, persevering, courageous, hopeful. Now, it would seem to me that caring about people and being able to tune to others easily, for example, would be very helpful in your considering what elements would fit an exercise program for your specific population." "Yes," May said slowly, "I know what worked for me, so I could start with those exercises, and then observe how they work for other cancer patients." "Maybe part of this would be that you could start a free volunteer program at one of the cancer support centers and have a forum in which to do your observing," I suggested, expanding on her thought.

"Yes," said May, growing less anxious as she began to see how her inner qualities applied to realizing her Dream. "And then," I continued, "your patient, persevering nature and caring for people would give you the staying power it's going to take to make the necessary adjustments and changes to your program." "Sure," said May, getting excited, "I see how this works." "And since you are courageous and hopeful, you'll be willing to make changes, knowing you'll come up with something truly of value," I concluded. "I got it!" May exclaimed. "This is great. So whenever I bump up against something where I panic and think 'I don't know how to do this, I can't do this,' all I have to do is look at my list of inner qualities and see which one can power me out of my panic into a constructive situation!" I smiled. "And that's how Dreams come true," I said, "from within you, your qualities reaching out to the vision that is your Dream." "I can do this," repeated May happily to herself. "I have what it takes—me."

May understood quickly how affirmations could be useful in empowering her choice. "I had a lot of experience with affirmations when I was healing from the cancer," May explained. "I will use them, but for me, Dr. Noelle, the real key to empowering my choice isn't my inner qualities in and of themselves, but how to use them to dissolve my insecurities, like you showed me. That is really helpful."

We are all so much more powerful than we know. All it takes is the willingness to look within, and use the strengths and talents already there. May's understanding that her inner qualities were the force she could use to "dissolve" her insecurities gave her the power she needed to truly act on her Dream.

KATHY

Kathy's initial comment on empowering her choice was a blithe "Oh, no problem—please, I've been outfitting people for years! I certainly have the power for that!" "Yes, I understand, and your eye for fashion and design is already well developed," I said, "but you'll be in a whole different ballgame this time, Kathy. You'll be dealing with customers, not friends or celebrities. I think you might want to look at how those of your inner qualities that have come out of your age itself will contribute to the success of your choice." Silence.

"I really don't like talking about my age," Kathy groaned, "even if it is in a positive sense." "I realize that," I said, "but since your age will be with you regardless of what you do, and since it brings with it tremendous value, I think it would be wise to use its gifts rather than deny them just so you don't have to look at the fact of your years." "All right, fine," said Kathy, not particularly happy about it, but going along with my suggestion nonetheless.

## Age-Acquired Qualities Can Hold the Key

Kathy's list of the qualities she's developed over the years are the following: being more tolerant of others; having a preference for doing just one thing, taking her time, and really doing it in depth; being a better listener; having a better sense of perspective (seeing how things will fit or work in the long run, without losing sight of the short term). I asked Kathy to look at the list and see how she could apply some of these age-related qualities to her choice. Kathy pored over the list for a while, then said, "Well, I can see how being more tolerant and a better listener is certainly going to help me deal with customers whose taste is different from mine. I mean I can't expect to outfit everyone only according to what I like." "Good point," I said. "What else?" "I can see how doing one thing at a time but doing it in depth will help me focus on a customer and really understand their preferences and how they like to look." Kathy laughed, "And much as I hate to say it, I think my relatively new sense of perspective will help me not go off the deep end when I don't get instant results from everything. I'll be better able to sit and look at the overall picture, see how things are fitting together."

"All these qualities help sustain your other fine qualities of design, Kathy," I said. "Together you have a formidable package, lots of power with which to fuel your choice." "Now all I have to do is remember these qualities when I need them," said Kathy. "And you will—just write them down and keep them somewhere handy, like on your bathroom mirror, or in your datebook," I replied. "And do my affirmations," said Kathy. "That always helps," I concurred.

Qualities are qualities! It doesn't matter how you've come by them: endowed at birth, learned through specific experiences, acquired over time. What matters is that you use them, as many as you can, to help your Dream come true.

JIM

Much to my delight and surprise, Jim quickly caught on to the notion of inner qualities as power fuel for his choice. "Well, I don't have much else than what's inside me, Doc," grinned Jim, "So's I guess it only makes sense to me to use what I've got."

Jim saw right away how his ability to tolerate a fair number of hassles without getting upset would be very useful in dealing with people

unhappy over the time and money it might take to fix their broken perco-
lators, screen doors, and lawnmowers. He recognized that his patience
with the ongoing "stuff" of life would undoubtedly come in very handy,
both in dealing with customers and in dealing with the inevitable delays,
frustrated tourists, and unexpected situations being a tour guide might
bring. The fact that he liked to set his own guidelines and rules would
greatly facilitate Jim's creating his own set of business practices.

## Use What Works

He did have a little trouble with the concept of affirmations, however.
"I'm willing to put a list up of my qualities where I can see them every day
and make sure I'm using them, like a checklist. But I'll be darned if I'm
going to go around muttering to myself all day long. People will think I'm
nuts!" Jim said, "Sorry Doc, I'll do it if you say I have to, but I don't cotton
to it." I laughed, "These techniques are only helpful if people do cotton to
them, as you put it, so just put your checklist up, Jim, and forget the 'muttering.' I have a feeling you'll do just fine without."

Everyone is wonderfully unique. Jim, robust individualist that he is,
seems to be confident and assured enough of his power that he has no
need of the extra boost affirmations could give him. That's fine. The guidelines given are techniques that have worked for many people, but should
always be adjusted to take into account your particular nature.

## MAKE A COMMITTED CHOICE

Once you've chosen a Dream you are willing to act upon, worked it
through to make sure it is a fit for you, and empowered your choice with
the clear awareness of your inner qualities and how they uphold your
choice, all that is left to do is commit to that choice. This is the last step in
choosing your Dream, and it is absolutely critical. Without commitment,
all the rest is just a lot of empty words.

What commitment requires, simply, is to take the first step. In Paul's
case, the first step meant his actually figuring out a basic management
plan to have something in hand to talk about, ordering his business cards,
and making the first calls to potential clients. With May, commitment
meant sitting down and beginning to design her exercise program, and

---

## WINNER'S CIRCLE

Christopher Reeve, once he realized the extent of his paralysis, threw himself wholeheartedly into the Dream of bringing attention, resources, and medical help to the cause of spinal cord injuries. As Reeve has often said, this is not a job he would have chosen, but it is one he embraces fully. He is tremendously active, giving speeches, visiting rehab centers, lobbying in Washington for more funds, and working on behalf of the Christopher Reeve Foundation. Reeve's first step was when he accepted producer Quincy Jones's invitation to make a special appearance at the 1996 Academy Awards. Reeve talks about how hard it was to go through with that appearance, not knowing if his body would stay still during the appearance, or would twitch and spasm, not knowing how people would react to the sight of him in a wheelchair and on a ventilator. Yet the success of his Academy Awards appearance is what gave Reeve the courage to accept the numerous public engagements that have resulted in raising more than $2,000,000 for his Foundation. The first step is critical. The first step is what allows Winners to do it all.[3]

---

contacting hospitals to determine interest. Kathy's first step was to get the newspaper and walk through the malls looking for a salesclerk job in a suitable shop. Jim's was having his car doors painted with his "fix-it" slogan, and starting to drive around to the local institutions to drum up interest in his business.

That first step can be absolutely terrifying. Even for people accustomed to challenges, taking that first step, committing to their choice, can be fraught with anxiety.

You show your faith in a positive Future by taking the steps to getting there. That is your commitment. A choice is worthless if not acted upon, a Dream but a fantasy if you don't do the work of making it real. The willingness to take one step toward your Dream, then another, then another, is the commitment that will assure your success.

## How to Develop a Chosen Dream that Works for You

"How am I ever going to do this?" you ask. "It's so much work!" Well, it may seem like a fair amount of work, but if you take it step by step, you'll see that it's not that bad. After all, you won't have every single one of the concerns or situations Paul, May, Kathy, and Jim each had, you'll only have a couple of your own. A Dream has so much power to pull you into the Future you desire, that it is well worth the time and effort it takes to choose a Dream that truly can fulfill that function.

## Personal Success Log 5: Your Wise, Empowered, and Committed Choice

### Step #1: Make a Wise Choice

Determine whether or not your choice is a wise one. Examine it to see if your chosen Dream works for who you are in the larger context of the life you wish to lead.

Ask yourself: What does my Dream ask of me? Am I willing to give to it what it requires? Use visualization to help you sort this out. Don't allow yourself to get away with being too general. Get specific with what will be required of you so you can assess whether or not you are willing to do it. Set good boundaries for yourself. Know what you are willing to give and not willing to give to this Dream.

If your Dream asks of you something that is unfamiliar and possibly intimidating, then see if it in some way resembles something familiar and comfortable for you. Use the idea of "overlapping circles of experience" to help you see your way from the old to the new. Work it through in your imagination. If you can do it there, then you can do it in "real life."

Ask yourself: What do I expect from my Dream? Be sure you are clear about what you expect. Don't just say "fame and fortune" or "a nice house" or "a good paycheck"; delineate what those expectations mean specifically. You don't have to know exactly, but you do have to give your Dream enough definition to pull you where you truly want to go.

Ask yourself: What will be the impact of this Dream on my life? On my lifestyle? On those who depend on me or whose lives are directly impacted by mine?

Use visualization to help you see the effect your Dream will have on your life. Be specific. Take into account what already works for you and doesn't work for you. If, for example, you are a morning person and can't keep your eyes open past 10:00 P.M., your Dream of owning your own restaurant needs to be specified to take this into account. A late-night dinner and after-theatre café is probably not the thing for you! Better to think in terms of a fabulous breakfast and lunch place.

Don't, however, abandon your Dream just because you find it has areas of potentially negative impact. Some of the apparently "negative" ways in which your Dream might impact your life could be readily transformed into "positives." Be creative. Ask yourself: How could this so-called negative really be of benefit to me? Brainstorm with friends or others to help you figure this out. Usually all you need to do is to choose a different specific expression of your Dream, not drop your Dream entirely.

Think about how your Dream will affect your family, significant others, friends, and whatever commitments (church, synagogue, bowling team, Little League, volunteer work, etc.) you already have. Discuss with friends and family the possible impact of your Dream and work out arrangements or understandings that all of you can live with. Don't assume that your family and friends will "understand." They may or may not. Certainly, they will understand a lot better if you've discussed it with them ahead of time.

## Step #2: Make an Empowered Choice

Empower your choice with the fuel of your inner qualities. Willpower only gets you so far. Your inner qualities, which are many and varied, will get you much farther. Review your inner qualities, your "Who I am," and pull out those that support your Dream. These are your grounding, the foundation from which you will actualize your Dream.

Enhance and strengthen that foundation by using affirmations. Repeat your affirmations, preferably out loud, with lots of emotion and conviction. When it comes to your success in the Future, don't cheat yourself. One affirmation, said with passion and zeal 3 times, is worth 50 affirmations repeated in lukewarm fashion by rote 100 times.

## Step #3: Make a Committed Choice

The last step in choosing your Dream is committing to your choice. This is the easiest step conceptually, but for many people the hardest actually to do.

In theory, it's simple. You just do whatever the first step is to your Dream. This does presuppose that as you specified your Dream (making a workable choice), and then made a wise choice, you also became aware of what your first step would be. If not, then take the opportunity now to figure out, "What do I have to do first?" For many people, this means outlining as many of the steps to their Dream that they can currently see, in order to discover what that first step is. If that's what you need to do, great, do it.

But you're not done yet. You must actually *do* that first step, and when you've accomplished the first step, do the second step, and so on. In the next chapters you'll see how to gather the resources you will need to do those steps. For now what's important is to understand that only as you are taking the steps toward your Dream are you truly committed to it, and thus likely to get there.

A Dream has the power to pull you across time and space to the successful Future you desire, as long as you don't hang back, resisting its pull. Get your feet out of that mud and step up! It's the beginning of a wonderful adventure.

## NOTES

1. Michael Neill, Joanne Fowler, "Shining Lights," *People Magazine*, June 15, 1998, pp. 117–118.
2. Roberta Cruger, "Pam Teflon," *Los Angeles Times Magazine*, January 21, 1996, p. 3.
3. Elizabeth McNeil, "Man of Steel," *People Magazine*, May 11, 1998, pp. 214–222.

# CHAPTER SIX

## BE RESOURCEFUL

### *What Are the Resources Available?*
### *How Am I Going to Achieve My Dream?*

If choosing your Dream answers the question *"What* am I going to do?" using resources answer the question *"How* am I going to do this?" Resources are the means you have available to achieve a desired end. One of the defining characteristics of Winners is their ability, even in the most destitute of circumstances, to see what resources are available beyond their immediate circumstances. Winners see resources as not only available but plentiful, a view grounded in their belief in a positive Future.

As long as you see the Future as narrow and dark, you won't conceive of any but the most limiting of resources. You'll tighten the proverbial belt, keep yourself at a survivalist level so as not to need any but the most restricted of resources. For example, survivalist organizations typically believe that the Future will be a dreadful one, and therefore have reduced their needs to the bare minimum. The *Salt Lake City Tribune* reported on June 21 of 1998 that many militia groups predict that in Y2K—cyber-speak for the year 2000—"the banking industry will collapse, food stocks will shrink and the government will have no choice but to federalize state law enforcement." When this happens, survivalists believe, the world will be divided into "those who succumb and those who survive." In preparation for this intensely negative Future, survivalists are stockpiling food and hoarding guns. John Trochmann of the Militia of Montana, a survivalist group, is quoted by the Beloit Daily News (July 14, 1997) as saying "Hedge your bets, put away food, put away water," as he sold such manuals as "The Sniper Handbook," and "Building an Underground Home." Other survivalist organizations have gone "back to the land" where they grow their own food, use little if any technology, and have closed themselves off from the rest of the world. One such organization, Pastor Pete Peters's Christian Identity group, believes that race war is imminent and only those who join his group will survive. Identity members assure their survival by training in camps, and stockpiling food and weapons. Guided by their fatalistic beliefs, these groups don't see any way of using resources other than restricting themselves.

Once you open up to the idea that the Future is full of positive possibilities, however, see yourself as having the inner qualities that enable you to be successful whatever success requires as our world changes, and have chosen a Dream to pull yourself forward and up, you can also begin to see the virtually limitless resources available to you to help you accomplish your goals.

If technology has brought with it a radical and often chaotic change in how we work, play, and interact, it has also made resources available on a scale never before enjoyed by the average person. The Internet alone has made people aware of the vast array of resources available to everyone on the planet who has access to (not necessarily ownership of) a computer. Your local library has tremendous resources, many of them also accessible "on-line." The problem for most of us isn't that resources and information aren't available, but that we don't know what is available, don't recognize certain resources for the goldmines that they are, and frequently don't know how to use these resources when we become aware of their availability.

Winners are uncommonly good at recognizing and using resources. Their ability to do so is predicated on their belief that whatever it is they need, it is "out there" in one form or another, and on their willingness to search for resources creatively.

## RECOGNIZING RESOURCES

Most of us think of resources in a very limited fashion. For many of us, the idea of "resources" is contained in one word, "money." But money is but one resource, and not necessarily the most useful. If, for example, you have a pile of money but little awareness of how to manage that money, you may find—as have many overnight "I-won-the-lottery" millionaires—that the money just seems to "vanish."

Information is often a more powerful resource than money in and of itself, because with information you can obtain access to a never-ending wealth of solutions to a multitude of problems and challenges. For example, with information on how to manage finances successfully, the above lottery winner would be in a much better position to keep and grow his or her fortune.

The primary resources to help you move into a successful Future are the following:

- information
- your imagination
- your use of your time
- your past experience
- other people
- your spirituality

These resources are not separate and discrete categories. On the contrary, as you will see, each one feeds into and enhances the others.

## Information

Information is a precious commodity. It is frequently noted that those who control information in the 21st century will be those with the power. One of the reasons for the incredible explosion of the Internet and the World Wide Web is the almost instantaneous access it provides to more information than anyone had ever dreamed possible. When I entered "job" and "search" as the criteria for a search on the Internet, the search provider promptly offered me 88,040 matches! That's 88,040 different resources from which to *begin* a job search, resources such as "The Business Job Finder," "Career Resource Homepage," and "Resources for Job Seekers and Employers."

But the Internet is not the only source of information. Books, libraries, newspapers, magazines, television, radio, and films are some of the other excellent sources. One of my personal favorites is the library, and that wonderful seemingly endless source of valuable information, the reference librarian. In my experience, the information a reference librarian has to offer is only limited by the number of well-targeted questions I can come up with. In addition to these resources, Winners are uncannily good at using a little recognized yet tremendously powerful source of information—their imagination.

## Imagination

"My imagination!" you exclaim. "Hogwash. I need a steady job, plain and simple, that has a good retirement attached to it, that I can do without ruining my health." "And how do you think you're going to get that steady job?" I ask. "Look in the classifieds," you reply, down-to-earth person that you are, "and ask around." "So you have two sources of information," I say, "the classifieds and your friends." "Yeah, so what's so bad about that?" you ask, challenging me. "Nothing. It's just very limited," I respond. "You are providing yourself access to only two resources from which to secure something as important to you as your livelihood." "Well I don't see how my imagination is going to kick in and help," you counter. "OK," I reply, "let's try this: you say you read the classifieds to help you get a job. Where else in the paper do you look for jobs?" You answer my question slowly, doing your best to be patient with my obvious lack of common sense, "I don't. The classifieds is where they announce job openings."

"Right," I say. "And what about the information in the rest of the paper?" You frown, confused. "What about it?" "Well," I reply, "if you read the whole of the paper, not just the classifieds, with the idea in mind that 'I'm going to see how many different ideas I can find in this paper to help me either find or create a job that will work for me' you'll be surprised at what you find. That's where *your imagination* kicks in. You stop thinking of job-hunting in the paper as looking in the classifieds, and start treating the paper like a giant source of ideas and information. You're not looking for '*the* job' to pop out at you, you're looking for ideas on how to get there. So you start noticing low cost training classes in this or that, free seminars that introduce you to different ideas, community college classes and open houses for adults, support groups for people in transition, stories about how so-and-so turned a love of trinkets into a thriving mail-order business." "Hmph," you say thoughtfully, "I never thought about it that way."

---

## WINNER'S CIRCLE

Garton, now 52 years old, had a simple Dream some 20 years ago, a dad's dream—to be close with his kids. Being divorced, Garton worried about how he was going to accomplish that. That's where his imagination kicked in. On the days his daughters were at his home, he would write poems to them on their lunch-box napkins. Some of the poems were silly, some serious, but all showed how much Garton cared about his kids. He did this year after year, and Garton's daughters always knew how much their dad cared. That caring created the bond between daughters and father. This Dream had yet another ending—an unexpected one. One of Garton's daughters had kept all of his napkin notes, and once she was grown, she suggested to her dad that he publish them. He did. After 99 rejections from publishers, Garton's book *Napkins: Lunch Bag Notes from Dad* was so well received, it landed him a spot on the Oprah Winfrey Show. Sometimes Dreams come true—and even grander than you ever expected. Imagine one Dream, and another may pop out, a marvelous two-for-one.[1]

---

Most people don't. But Winners do. Winners are particularly adept at using their imaginations. Take Courtney Garton, for example.

Imagination can be used in as many ways as you can imagine. As described above, once you look at them imaginatively, both your local and bigger city newspapers are among the most valuable, easily accessible, and underrecognized sources of terrific information. "Of course that would take a lot of time," you say, "to go through the paper like that." "That's another underused resource," I reply, smiling, "time."

## *Time*

If imagination is the most commonly underrecognized and undervalued resource, time runs a close second. Yet time is what gives you the possibility of exploring other resources such as information, time is what frees you to sit with your imagination, time is what you use to connect with other people, who in turn are valuable resources. Time, well used, makes the difference between another step toward your Dream and standing still. Often, when you're in a period of transition between your current life and the one you are seeking to create, the resource you have most in abundance right at your fingertips is your time.

Winners don't waste time. That doesn't mean Winners run around frenetically cramming activity into their every minute. On the contrary, Winners often use their time to think, daydream, slowly sift through piles of information for that one useful item, and nap or sleep to rejuvenate themselves, all apparently passive activities, but during which Winners are actively engaged in purposefully pursuing their dreams. Winners use time in a myriad of ways, but one thing they don't do is waste it.

Unfortunately, most of us waste tremendous amounts of time. Worry is perhaps the biggest arena in which we waste time (and energy). Winners consistently surprise me with how little time they spend in worry. Worry is to be differentiated from the thinking process that leads to decision making. Worry is when you go over and over and over the same concern *without* coming to some sort of plan (decision) about how to resolve your concern. Worrying about past events ("Did I do that right? Did I make the right decision? What did they think of me?") only keeps you focused on the past, wasting time that could be applied toward resolving things in the Future.

Worry is the projection of your fears into the Future. Worry does nothing for you. Worrying about the what-ifs ("What if this doesn't work? What if I can't make a go of it? What if things get worse?") keeps you focused on what *won't* happen rather than on what *can*, wasting time that once again could be used in seeking positive alternatives. Worry has never produced a single constructive deed. Constructive thinking, as opposed to worry, is thinking about your concern with a commitment to resolving your concern in as positive a fashion as you can at the time. Constructive thinking leads to decision making. Worry leads to an endless loop of fear–worry–more fear, while you waste precious time.

People often confuse wasting time with the time they spend in recreation. Recreation is not wasted time—it is essential to a balanced life. Doing things in which you find no satisfaction is wasted time. Doing things out of habit, without stopping to explore whether the thing still has value to you, is wasted time.

"I get it," you say. "Sitting around watching the ball game between two teams I could care less about is wasted time. Sitting around watching my beloved home team run all over the field is a good use of time." "Yes," I reply, "it's recreation." "Except for the times I'm doing it 'cause I can't think of anything else to do," you continue. "Right," I reply. If you learn to think of time as a resource, you'll use it wisely.

## Past Experience

Your past is not in and of itself a negative attribute. Much in your past can be used in positive fashion to help you accomplish future success. When you look to your past with an eye to "What can I find in my past that can contribute to achieving my Dream?" you are using your past in a future-oriented way, and then your past can be of great benefit. The danger lies not in looking to the past for pat answers or ready-made solutions. Looking to it as a resource is highly valuable.

---

### WINNER'S CIRCLE

Willye White, 58 years old, has a glorious past. She was the first American woman to win an Olympic medal in the long jump and the only American woman to compete in track and field events at five consecutive Olympics. Her current Dream has nothing and everything to do with her past. White dreams of helping children in disadvantaged situations know they don't have to live in those situations forever. She tells them that there is a world beyond poverty and crime, and that they can get there. White doesn't try to help those children by turning them into Olympic athletes, or by sharing her story of how she lifted herself out of the cotton fields of Mississippi onto the Olympic team. Instead, White dips into the resource of her wonderful athletic training and knowledge to teach these children how to make something good and fulfilling of their lives. Through the Robert Taylor Girls Athletic Program that she developed, White uses athletics to teach children living in the Robert Taylor Homes (the largest public-housing project in the United States) valuable life lessons. She uses bowling to teach the kids math skills, swimming to teach the children trust, and basketball to teach teamwork. She shows the kids how to share and have a winning attitude. White talks about deprogramming the children from violence and reprogramming them for peace. White's use of her past as an imaginative and fruitful resource is typical of Winners.[2]

A different, yet equally resourceful, use of the past is exemplified by Richard Batt.

---

### WINNER'S CIRCLE

Batt is president of the Franklin Memorial Hospital in Farmington, Maine. A man walked into Batt's office one day, utterly miserable over the fact that he could not pay for his son's hospital bills. After reviewing the bills and adjusting them as best he could, Batt, knowing the man was a writer, asked offhandedly if the man could help revamp the hospital's brochures. The man was overjoyed at the opportunity to do something to help out, and that started Batt thinking. Barter is a time-honored American way of paying for services. What if the hospital offered low-income patients the possibility of trading their skills for services rendered? Out of Batt's imaginative thinking (using imagination as a resource) and his willingness to dip into the past as a valuable resource came "Contract for Care," an innovative fee-for-service program that allows individuals just above the federal poverty level to pay their hospital bills. The result? Patients feel good about paying off their bills, and the hospital gets much needed services. Is the program working? Yes. Would this work everywhere? Probably not. But *something* will work everywhere. Recognizing and creatively using whatever resources are available is truly a Winner's trait.

---

## Other People

People, and whatever connects you to the people in your world, are a wonderful resource of one kind or another. Think of your friends, the bulletin board at your local supermarket, co-workers, the local throwaway paper, adult education classes, support groups, the Little League team, your local coffee shop, Internet chat rooms, and all the other myriad connections to others in our world as resources—not to use, as in "take advantage of," but to learn from, as in listen to, observe, read, ask questions of, brainstorm with.

Take support groups, for example. They are a wonderful source of information, brainstorming, enthusiasm, ideas, and helping hands. On the Internet, when I entered "support" and "groups," the search provider came up with 56,110 matches, each of which could lead to yet more support groups. These groups covered a wide range of interests, from support

---

### WINNER'S CIRCLE

Kathleen Potter, now 52 years old, was diagnosed with Usher's syndrome when she was nine. Usher's syndrome usually causes deafness, and eventually can lead to blindness. By the time she was 39, Potter was blind, deaf, and mute. Did that stop her from leading a happy and productive life? Not at all. Potter began by attending an Usher's syndrome workshop where she found out that blind people in Asia often become massage therapists. Armed with this information, Potter enrolled in the Culver City Institute of Psycho-Structural Balancing. Her classmates and instructors helped her improvise in the classroom to get the training she needed. Later, she applied to the well-known Massage Therapy Center in Los Angeles, California. The director, Ahmos Netanel, was impressed with her technique, but not impressed enough to hire her. Potter reapplied a year later, having considerably improved her skills. This time, she was hired. Netanel helps with Potter's introduction to new clients who aren't used to communicating with someone who can only communicate through touch. All along the way, Potter has reached out to and accepted others' support in the realization of her Dream, to earn her living as a certified massage therapist. Potter's is a powerful example of how Winners view other people as resources, not as "marks" to be taken advantage of and used, but as willing participants and helpers on the road to success.[3]

---

groups for healthy aging, to an international network of environmental support groups, to groups dedicated to helping those who are victims of violent crime.

Knowing that you are not alone, that there are literally hundreds of thousands of people you have access to, who can be of assistance to you in one way or another, is very empowering. You don't have to "go it alone," you can enroll other people's support, imagination, resources, and ideas in the pursuit of your own Dream. Winners rarely hesitate to call upon those around them (near and far!) to help them achieve their chosen Dream.

## *Spirituality*

Spirituality is our connection with something greater than ourselves, however you conceive of that. For some people, it's the universe, the force of love, a greater intelligence, nature; for others it's a more defined pres-

---

### WINNER'S CIRCLE

Kaile Warren's life was hitting rock bottom a couple of years ago, both his home remodeling business and his marriage were failing. In despair one night, he prayed for a break. Much to his surprise, he woke up in the middle of the night to a vision—a vision of three simple words, "Rent-a-Husband." From that vision, the 38-year-old Warren has built a service that provides "husbands" who, for an hourly rate, handle all sorts of ordinary household chores, from building a back porch to screwing in a light bulb. As a home remodeler, Warren had always noticed the need for such a service, but how to tap into that need and how to create a business out of it never came to him until he had his vision. In the two years "Rent-a-Husband" has been in existence, Warren has already franchised his company both in the United States and abroad. Warren's success and profits just keep growing.[4]

---

ence such as God or Goddess; and for still others, it's a specific presence such as Jesus, Buddha, angels, and other spirits. Spirituality is a private matter, between the individual and that something greater than him or herself, to be differentiated from religion, which is an organized expression of spirituality.

Spirituality, your connection to what, for purposes of this book, I will call Spirit, is often a powerful resource for Winners.

You can commune with Spirit through meditation, individual prayer, communal prayer, visioning, journaling, any number of ways, all of which open up avenues to yet more resources. As Warren's example shows, a little spirituality can go a surprisingly long way.

PAUL

Which of the resources you use and when depends on what you need to actualize your Dream. Paul's primary need at this stage of creating his Future was for clients. At first, Paul's idea of the resources available to him to find clients was quite limited.

"So, Paul," I asked, "how are you going to go about fulfilling your chosen Dream of being a management consultant to small companies or businesses in transition?" somewhat paraphrasing his choice. Paul looked at me, depressed. "I don't know, Dr. Noelle," he said, "other than beating the pavement handing out my cards, I don't know." I thought for a moment. "Maybe a better way to go about this would be to ask you what you need, Paul. Then we can figure out what might be good resources for you." "OK," Paul replied. "What do I need? Clients. I pretty much have the rest, the management skills and tools, and I think I have a good fix on how to package and present those to people. What I don't have is the people to present my programs to. Clients!" Paul repeated.

"This is where your imagination needs to kick in," I said. "Try thinking creatively about using the newspaper, for example, Paul. Where in the paper might you find clues to small companies in a growth mode?" I asked. Paul thought for a moment. "Stories in my local paper about up-and-coming businesses," he said. "Maybe looking in the classifieds to see in the smaller ads who's hiring. That's usually a good indicator of growth or transition." "Yes," I replied, "those are good ideas." "I wonder if newspapers list when various medical or dental practices change hands," Paul continued, thinking out loud, "or become incorporated—that could be an indicator." "And if the paper itself doesn't carry such information, you might be able to find out who does through a city administrative office—such changes must be registered somewhere," I suggested. "Yeah," Paul said, no longer depressed, and beginning to sound excited, "yeah, someone's got to have that information. And then I tailor my presentation to the type of company I'm approaching, and—" Paul broke off and looked at me, smiling, "yeah, I see how I can do this. Just look out and ahead." "Out and ahead?" I asked. "Yeah, out to the world around me and ahead to possibilities rather than inward into myself, and backward into the only way I would have done it in the past," Paul replied. "Well put," I said, impressed, "well put."

Newspapers, of course, are but one avenue of the written media Paul could use. I wanted to help him think in terms of other avenues, so I suggested that he then look at what his past experience might yield in terms of client sources. "Gosh," Paul said, "no one at work that I can think of." "Well," I asked, "how about suppliers, vendors, service agencies your company used? Might any of those qualify as small growing companies?" "Sure," Paul said, "of course they could, and I'd have an in with them because of my former employment—why didn't I think of that?" he asked, annoyed with himself. "Because you're new at this, Paul, that's all. You have a fine imagination, you're just not used to using it in this way," I replied.

"Where else might you look?" I asked, continuing. Paul concentrated, then said, "I could talk to my own accountant, dentist, the auto repair shop I use, people like that. They might either be in a growth phase themselves, or know of others who are." "Connecting with people from your past and present as resources is very helpful," I said. "You're definitely getting the hang of this. Recognizing the resources available to you, right there, close to home, is very important to your ability to succeed in the Future. Let's shift gears now, and see how you do with brainstorming resources less near and familiar to you." "What's that?" Paul asked, intrigued. "The Internet," I replied.

Paul groaned. "I can handle a computer just fine, Dr. Noelle, but the Internet—I have no patience with sitting there waiting painfully for a page to appear, going one link to the next just to come up with useless information! I'll do much better scanning the papers," he said. "I wasn't thinking of your using the Internet to find clients directly," I replied. "Actually, I was thinking of it more as a way for you to get the word out on both who you are and what you have to offer, at the same time as you find out what your client base's current needs are, so as to be able to present more individually tailored programs." "Oh," said Paul slowly. "OK . . . and how am I going to do that?" "Well," I replied, "I'm not an expert, so I can't tell you exactly how to do it, but I know there are such things as "chat rooms" on the Internet, where individuals chat about subjects of common interest. What if you created or joined a chat room where you could give information about your services, receive information about what people want and need, and get people interested in possibly hiring you by giving away some of your thoughts on how to resolve their problems?" "In other words, get the word out," said Paul. "Yes, and I'm sure there are any number of other ways you can use the Internet to do so," I said. "All you have to do is—" "Use my imagination," Paul interrupted, grinning. I nodded, "Yes, and right now you have the time available to investigate the wealth of leads (information and people) your imagination will come up with."

Once you let your imagination roam freely through the variety of resources available in the world, you'll be amazed at what you can come up with.

MAY

May's resource need was quite different from Paul's. She was interested in a more intangible resource. May needed creative ideas to support the development and presentation of her exercise program.

"My most immediate need," said May, "is to get help in actually developing my exercise program and then creating a pitch or brochure to promote it. That's where I feel stumped. I mean, I certainly can describe the exercises and stretches I learned, but I feel like that's just not enough. I need to develop my own approach, my own style, something that defines

---

### WINNER'S CIRCLE

Anthony Robbins, now an extraordinarily successful entrepreneur, seminar leader, author (*Unlimited Power*, *Awaken the Giant Within*), and founder of many companies, turned his life around when he was in an almost destitute situation as a young man, by observing and modeling his behavior on that of successful people.

---

my work, but I don't know where to begin." "A good place to start figuring out your approach is to look at how other people have approached similar programs," I replied. Winners often use other people's successes as inspiration and fuel for their own.

I encouraged May to think in these terms. "What resource might provide you with information about how other people have successfully created their exercise programs?" I asked. May was silent for a moment. "I could go to the library and check out videotapes from other exercise programs. Even if they aren't related to my special area of interest, they might give me ideas."

"So you might figure out your approach by noticing what you like and dislike about someone else's approach," I said. "Uh-huh, plus," May continued, warming to the subject, "I could look up health-oriented magazines and newsletters, and see what's being done in the area. You know, physical therapy developments, new modalities, that kind of thing." "So you're using both your time and imagination to help you get the information you need to develop your program, May," I said. "Is there any other way you can think of to get the information to help you develop your approach?"

May looked down for a moment, and when she looked back up at me, spoke almost shyly, "I know this is going to sound funny, Dr. Noelle, but sometimes when I need help with something, I go hiking, and I'll find some really pretty spot to be in, somewhere where people won't be coming by much. And I just sit and let the beauty all around me inspire me. It's kind of like praying, only I don't say a prayer. I just soak it all up, and then, out of nowhere, usually when I'm on my way back down into civilization, I'll get ideas on how to help with my situation. So I think I'll do that. I think once I've looked at other people's exercise programs and the health literature and all that, I think I'll go be by myself with some big old tree, the earth and the sky, and just sit. Let it come. 'Cause it always does." "Yes, it does," I agreed softly.

Being with nature is how May connects to her spirituality. Knowing what your way of connecting is, and using it to help you achieve your goals, is a very personal and very powerful resource.

"What else is on your list of 'what I need to make my Dream come true'?" I asked May. "It would be really great," May said, "if I could test out my idea of a program by having cancer patients actually do the program and give me feedback on how well it does or doesn't work for them. But where am I going to find people willing to do that? And for free?" "In other words, you need to connect to people as a resource," I said. "Yes," May replied. "Well, you spoke to me of the support groups that helped you through your healing, May," I replied. "Might those same support groups be a source of people to help you with feedback?" I asked. "Gosh," May said, "I don't know, but it sure is worth a try. Cancer support groups would certainly be really motivated and interested in this sort of thing. Besides, if I couldn't get people from the support groups to help me directly—you know, work the exercise program themselves—they might be willing to help me locate people who would be willing to do so."

One thing leads to another. That's the beauty of resources. You don't have to have them all yourself, you don't even have to know what they will actually end up being, all you have to do is pick one and start working with it. Inevitably, one resource will lead you to another, if not directly, then indirectly by the new thoughts that the resource will inspire.

"You mentioned needing help creating your pitch or brochure," I said, moving on to the next of the means May had said she needed to fulfill her chosen Dream. "Yes," May said, "I'm hopeless when it comes to promoting stuff. And I don't have the money to hire a publicist or advertising person." "What do you have that is worth money to someone?" I asked. "Do you mean my car? my clothes?" May asked, surprised. "No," I said, "I'm sorry, I didn't explain myself well. I mean, what service can you perform or product can you make that would have value to someone? That you could trade in return for their skills in writing brochures, for example." Trading is a time-honored way of getting what you need when you're low on funds. "Oh," said May, "I get it. Great idea! . . . Only I don't have anything to trade," she continued, suddenly deflated.

"Yes you do," I said. "You have one valuable skill to trade right now, your ability to design and make clothes, and another skill you'll have very soon, an exercise program that can benefit cancer patients and survivors." "So I could trade a certain number of sessions of my exercise program to someone in return for their help in writing and designing my brochure?"

May asked. "Of course," I replied, "why not?" "But where would I find such a person?" asked May. "Probably the same place you might find volunteers willing to help you test out your program," I replied, "support groups, and the people support groups then lead you to." "I could also go to some of my old employers in the garment industry, and work out a trade to do some work for them in exchange for some hours with their advertising people," May said, excited. "For that matter, there are some firms in the garment industry that are known to support pro-health causes. I could maybe go to them with this idea even if I haven't worked for them before . . . Wow—I never thought there would be so many possibilities of how to get this done. This is great!"

Imagination is the key. May's willingness to look at her skills and support groups in a new light is what opened up new avenues of possibility for her.

"What about finding the facilities to actually sell your exercise program to?" I asked. Do you feel like you need a resource for that?" "I think I'm pretty comfortable with that part, at least for now," May replied. "I plan to go on-line to locate hospitals with large cancer departments, foundations that work with hospitals and support groups, and other cancer-related facilities." "So the computer skills you developed as a pattern maker will come in handy," I said. "Very," May replied, "as will my 8-year-old's facility with whizzing around the Net," she continued, smiling. "He will probably be able to do that part of the research quicker than I ever could!"

KATHY

Kathy's initial view of resources was very restricted. She could see no way to meet either of her needs—not her need for customers to buy from her nor her need to eventually get money for her own shop. Kathy feared that the only avenue open to her was the mysterious land of the World Wide Web, which she wanted nothing to do with.

"Don't even talk to me about computers!" Kathy cried out. "I don't know the first thing about them and I really don't want to have to learn." "All right," I said, "so don't. There are an infinite variety of ways to access resources, and computers are only one." Kathy breathed a sigh of relief. "Good. I've been dreading this session," she continued. "I was sure you were going to tell me the first thing I had to do was learn how to work one of those blasted things." "No," I replied, "the first thing you have to do is figure out what you need in order to make your Dream of eventually having your own dress shop come true."

"Customers and money," said Kathy, promptly, "and I haven't a clue how to get either of them. All I can see at present is that without happy satisfied customers I can't parlay being a salesclerk into having a corner of a shop to myself, and without money, I'll never be able to get from a corner of someone else's shop to my own shop." "So let's take those needs one at a time," I said. "Let's start with investigating resources to give you customers." "OK," said Kathy," because I figure that's the only way I'm going to get a corner of the shop to operate as my 'outfit heaven,' if I'm bringing in enough customers on a regular basis to convince the boss that it's a good idea."

I nodded, then sat there and thought for a while. Finally I said, "You have a very rich past. How about using that past to springboard you into your Future?" "I do?" Kathy asked, "what do you mean?" "You've been a hair stylist to television and film personalities, right?" I asked. Kathy nodded. "And you have contact numbers for most of them, right?" I continued. "Yeah," replied Kathy, "but I can't just call them up and say "Come buy at this shop! Especially when I'm just a salesclerk!" "No, but you can call them up and say "I've found the most wonderful outfit for you I think you'll just love, it'll work perfectly with your—, and then fill in the blank from whatever you remember about that personality. Either they'll be interested or they won't, but I'll bet you some will be interested." "Of course they will," Kathy said, enthusiastically. "Oh, and I know just what to put together for each of them. There's Linda, she'd love—" "Kathy," I said, interrupting her as she was about to launch into a full description of what would work for each personality, "before you do that, why don't we keep looking at other resources you may find helpful." "Oh, sure" Kathy laughed, "it's just I get so excited!" "I know," I said, smiling, "and your excitement in and of itself is a powerful resource with which to generate excitement in other people. But for now, let's look at other sources of customers."

Kathy thought hard, a determined look on her face. "There's always other cast members and, of course, there's all the crew that I've met over the years. You know, showbiz is very image conscious in front of and *behind* the camera. So I could use the same approach with crew as I would with personalities." Kathy's willingness to look to her past not in order to repeat it, but to mine it for the gold of what it can bring now, is a typical Winner's trait.

"That's great, Kathy," I said, "so now let your imagination step outside of show business, and see what other sources of customers you might find." Kathy furrowed her brow and was quiet for a few minutes. Then she said slowly, "I remember that thing you said the other day about time, about using time as a resource. Well, I have a lot of that now, I might as well use it productively! What do you think, Dr. Noelle, if I created a sort of Tupperware party that I might call an 'accessory party.' I could bring a whole bunch of accessories—you know, scarves, earrings, clips, bows, all sorts of things—and accessorize the ladies' outfits." Now Kathy was using not just her time and imagination as resources, but also the tremendous resource of other people. "I think that's a great idea, Kathy," I said, delighted and surprised at her wonderful capacity of imagination. "And," said Kathy continuing, "I could probably start these off by giving free talks to local ladies' groups on 'how to be in fashion and trendy for under $50'—or something like that. Hopefully from the talks and the 'accessory parties' I could get more customers to actually come in the shop and be outfitted." "I have no doubt that would be the result," I said, agreeing, "and you've greatly broadened your customer base, so you're not relying on just one segment of the population."

"There's another advantage to creating a broad personal customer base, Kathy," I said. "What's that?" she asked. "Well, some of your customers may be wealthy, and down the line, you might consider them as potential investors," I suggested. Kathy's eyes lit up, "Yes! So maybe instead of having to get a bank to loan me money, I could have a 'ladies' club' of investors! That would be so much fun," she exclaimed delightedly. "And," I said, "the bank might be more willing to kick in whatever else you needed if you did have investors." "This is great, Dr. Noelle," Kathy said. "I can actually see how I'm going to do this. And I am going to do this!"

In discussing further the resources Kathy might use both to generate and to manage the money she would need to make the leap from having a corner of someone else's shop to having her very own shop, we talked about her reading self-help books about creating a small business, financing options, and so forth. We discussed the various classes that exist for adults seeking this kind of information, including the seminars sponsored or recommended by the small business associations. The more we talked about different resources, the more Kathy engaged her imagination, and she slowly realized "There's no limit to this stuff, Dr. Noelle. The more I'm willing to spin off ideas, the more ideas come to me."

That's the beauty of imagination. It literally is limitless. You may get stumped from time to time, but when your imagination starts flowing again, it knows no bounds. And if you do find yourself stumped, the best thing to do is find someone to brainstorm with, someone to bounce your ideas off of. Somewhere in that process, your imagination will get kick-started again, and you're off and running. In your imagination, you hold the key to all the other resources. With your imagination you scout the present for possibilities. With your imagination, you then project the impact of those possibilities on creating success in your Future. Imagination is truly the Winner's secret to a successful Future.

JIM

Jim used his imagination wonderfully to find resources for "fix-it" clients and tour agencies. Jim's next concern was finding the resources to help him communicate his uniqueness as a tour guide to the agencies in a way that would encourage them to use his services.

"So what is it that you need to accomplish your chosen Dreams?" I asked Jim. "And how are you going to go about getting what you need? Let's start with your 'fix-it' business." Jim nodded, looked me square in the eye and said, "I've been thinking about it, Doc, and I figure I need a fair number of people who'll want me to fix things, pretty much on a regular basis. That's the first thing." "OK," I said, "any thoughts on how you're going to find these people?" "Yes I have," Jim said. "You know all that time I've been driving the truck, up and down the state, I've delivered to retirement homes, hospitals, restaurants, public works buildings, all sorts of places. They know me! If I come in and tell them what I'm up to, some of them will give me work. And I can take it from there—you know, either drive a regular route to these people, or come out every couple of weeks, or something like that."

I was amazed. Jim's previous approach to problem solving had been a litany of "I dunnos." I asked Jim where did all his innovative ideas come from? "Well," Jim said, "I've been thinking a lot about how I've done things in the past, just letting things come to me, and I guess I was ready for a change. A way of doing things differently, you know. And I did do some of that muttering," Jim confided, referring to the affirmations I'd recommended, "but only around the house, mind you—and it does seem to help me think differently."

Jim was richly using his past experience as a resource. It is easier to start off with people who know you, at least a little, than to launch into cold calls or their equivalent. "What other information could you use to help you find more fix-it clients?" I asked. "It's important to give yourself more than one resource." "The telephone book," Jim stated. "I figured I could let my fingers do the driving," he said smiling. Telephone books, like newspapers, are underused and yet very valuable sources of information. "I could get lists of institutions, hotels, motels, schools, churches, and the like, from the telephone book, and go around and introduce myself," said Jim. "You could indeed," I said. "Sounds like the resources for your fix-it client base are pretty well thought out. How about your other Dream of being a tour guide for the local historical society or other tour agencies?"

"Well, the telephone book is pretty good for digging up who does that sort of thing. I don't figure my 'client base' as you call it is much of a problem. No, the problem as I see it, is how do I get the tour agencies to hire me?" Jim said. "Hmm," I replied. "Good question. . . What's different about you? What do you have to offer that is something the tour agencies would want?" I asked, encouraging Jim to engage his imagination. He thought about it for a minute. "My tales," he said, "the stories I know and can tell about the different places." "All right," I said, "so if that's what's different about you, how do you go about letting the tour places know about your uniqueness?" In other words, I was asking Jim to think about what are the resources that he could use to promote his uniqueness.

"I saw a thing this insurance guy put together," Jim said, thoughtfully, "a newsletter, I guess you'd call it. It had some tips on how to save money for retirement, a couple of jokes, maybe a little story on what the government was doing with social security, that kind of thing. It was interesting. Caught my attention." He stopped, thinking for a moment, "Maybe I could put together something like that, with maybe just a "teaser" kind of tale in it, you know, part of the story, not the whole story, that kind of thing—along with maybe a tip on something local the tourists might enjoy, like a new restaurant, or an out-of-the-way antique shop, or something like that. And send it out every month to the tour agencies, get their attention. Maybe I could call it "Jim's Gazette," something like that."

Jim was using the wonderful resource of other people, how other people have achieved their Dreams, to inspire him to his own success. "That's a great idea," I said. "You're not only using a tool that's been successful for someone else—the newsletter—but you're also using your knowledge of the local area as a resource." "Yeah, and whatever interesting tidbits I pick up as I'm driving around for fix-it jobs. I pick up a lot of stuff like that, looking around," Jim said. "And you're deliberately connecting with people through your newsletter, which of course is one of the most powerful resources," I continued. "And of course I'll introduce myself around, but that's not a problem, I'm comfortable with that part," Jim said. "I did some of that 'mental rehearsal' stuff you call it, and I could see myself calling on the tour agencies just fine." Jim never ceased to surprise me. Considering his previous complete unfamiliarity with such techniques as affirmations and visualizations, he took to them like a duck to water.

"Good," I said, "so the next 'need' becomes—what are you going to use as the resource for actually getting your newsletter written and printed?" "I wasn't thinking printed," Jim said. "I was thinking more just running off copies. See, I have this niece who's a genuine computer person, she knows everything there is to know about them. But she knows next to nothing about cars. I'll bet if I'm willing to fix up her car and take care of it for her, she'd be real willing to read my scrawl and make it look nice on her computer." "A trade, in other words," I said. Once again, Jim was using his past experience—in this case his knowledge as a car mechanic—to assist him in creating his future success.

## How to Find the Resources that Will Work for You

We have so many resources available to us to create wonderful Futures. It's just that when we're in the midst of a major life change, we too often forget about the multitude of resources that are out there, readily available and frequently, at little or no cost. Whether you're in a crisis situation or proactively seeking to create a better Future for yourself, *assume* that somewhere out there are the resources you need to be successful. It is a safe assumption! The world has become both so vast and so accessible that, given creativity and persistence, you will find your resources. Use the following steps to show you how.

## Personal Success Log 6: Your Resources

### Step #1: Stay Awake and Alert to the World around You

You can't go forward successfully into the Future if you don't have some idea of what is going on in the world around you. It's impossible to take advantage of opportunities you don't know exist. Therefore, be awake and alert to the world around you on a regular basis. Watch the news not with an eye to "Ain't it awful!" or "What's the world coming to?" but with an eye open to "What's out there? What new options, new ideas, new possibilities, new hope?"

Changes happen so quickly that it becomes important to find some regular source of new information that works well for you. Your local newspaper is a wonderful source, and a major newspaper an even better one. Your local library will carry it if you don't want to subscribe. The Internet, for those who either have computers or have access to a computer (Did you know many public libraries have computers you can use for free?), is a wonderful source as well. Effective use of the Internet is more complex than reading a newspaper, but there are many courses offered in how to do so, and of course manuals such as the ever-popular "for Dummies" series. Weekly magazines such as *Time, U.S. News & World Report,* and *Newsweek* all are good sources of information and, again, available for free at your local library.

Then, depending on your interests, there are a multitude of specialized magazines, both on and off the Internet, which will keep you apprised of "what's going on in the world." Television magazine-format shows and talk shows are useful, especially as starting points, since television rarely has the luxury of time to go into subjects in the depth that provides the greatest wealth of information. Radio has many interesting and informative shows, which if they don't cover a subject as thoroughly as you might need, at least give you a good place to begin, and will spur ideas. Again, use your imagination. Read books, and go to movies as a way of gathering information, in addition to being entertained.

## Step #2: Open Yourself to the World around You

The more you are willing to reach out to others, the more you will cultivate sources for all kinds of resources. "But I'm shy," you protest. "I don't like walking around telling everyone my problems!" Opening yourself to others isn't about weeping and gnashing your teeth in public. Opening yourself up to others is a willingness to ask about what interests you, to observe and ask how others go about things so as to get ideas on how you might do so.

Support groups are a powerful way to find people who have had similar problems or are in similar situations to your own, and then sharing with one another what's working and what isn't. Be wary, however, of support groups that only "moan and groan." There's nothing wrong with investigating which support group might be good for you, and only joining one after you've done enough research to determine that.

If there is no support group that addresses your particular situation, then find a church, synagogue, book club, bowling team, or community group of some kind where there are people you can relate to. When you get involved with a group of individuals, it's as if you multiplied yourself by however many people are in the group. Since everybody is different, everybody has a different view on things and different sources they rely on; you exponentially increase your personal access to resources by involving yourself with a group.

### Step #3: Create Your Personal Resource File

Make lists of everything and everyone in your world you can think of as a resource. Describe what resources that individual or source might provide for you, and keep these lists handy for future reference. Add the names of people and resource possibilities to your list as they occur to you.

### Step #4: Use Your Imagination

Always remember: your greatest resource is your imagination, your creativity, not "How it's always been done," or "How I've always done things," but "Here's how I *could* do it," "Here's a *different* way I could try." Continually exercise your mind, and practice using your imagination to look into the Future. Your Dream is the light guiding you through the Unknown to your success. Your resources are the steps you take to get you there.

Your attitude, however, is what determines whether you will take those steps successfully or not. There are attitudes that will solidly support the realization of your Dream, and others that will only drag you down. Winners (no surprise!) have winning attitudes.

### NOTES

1. "Love, Dad," *People Magazine,* July 27, 1998, p. 72.
2. Tom Brokaw, "American Close Up," NBC Nightly News, February 23, 1996.
3. Mark Miller, "That Physical Touch," *Los Angeles Times Magazine,* September 14, 1997, p. 5.
4. "Man around the House," *People Magazine,* April 27, 1998, p. 89.

# CHAPTER SEVEN

## DEVELOP A WINNER'S ATTITUDE

### What Will Get You There, What Will Hold You Back?

There are certain attitudes, certain ways of approaching your life and the people in it, that will engage the Future and help you go successfully into it. These are in sharp contrast to those attitudes that are detrimental to your creating a successful Future, attitudes you can't "take with you." A winning attitude is one that looks to the Future and actively seeks to explore the Unknown. A winning attitude is courageous, curious, proactive, enthusiastic, hopeful, open-minded, joy-driven, giving, responsibility oriented, and protects by setting boundaries. These are the approaches to their lives and situations that Winners use. What you can't take with you if you are to create success are attitudes that focus on the past and that resist all that which is Unknown. These attitudes include wanting to know all the answers ahead of time, apathy or passivity, self-righteousness, blaming self or others, self-pity and martyring, anger that turns into bitterness, resentment, or rage, and defensiveness. You just can't be successful in the Future if you're dragging behind you all that negative baggage.

Does this mean that Winners don't get depressed, discouraged, apathetic, resentful, have a pity party, mope, or get angry or defensive? Of course not! Winners are people, and people go through the entire range of responses to life when they find themselves in tough situations. The difference is, Winners don't dwell on these. They don't stay there for long. Winners are good at catching themselves in less-than-productive modes and lifting themselves up and out. How do they do that? Well, before we look at how Winners get out of what doesn't work, let's look first at what does.

## What a Winner's Attitude Is Made Of

### *Courage*

Courage is the willingness to step off into the Unknown of the Future, with the possibility of danger lurking at every step, or into a fearful Known—with the possibility of danger lurking at every step. Heroes don't become heroes by simply strolling down an obviously peaceful and blessed path. Courage comes from the French word for heart (*coeur*), and as the song says, "You gotta have heart" if you are to go into possibly fearful places and be a Winner.

A heart functions best when working in tandem with your head. You will have the courage you need, the willingness to face the dangers that may lie ahead, if you learn to take *considered risks*.

---

### WINNER'S CIRCLE

Twenty-eight-year-old Susan Silberman was a fitness trainer and avid cyclist when a reckless driver crashed into her and her bike, causing her injuries that led to the amputation of her lower left leg. Silberman's dream, despite her doctor's pessimistic evaluation that she would neither run nor ride a bike for two years, was to ride successfully in the long-distance fund-raising bicycle treks she loved so much. Winner that she is, Silberman thought out her recuperation and training extensively. Once she learned to walk with her prosthetic leg, Silberman moved from her home in Illinois to San Diego, where the warmer weather would make her training easier. She failed one attempt to ride in a trek, so she went back and trained more, often pedaling 200 miles a week. Silberman completed the six-day Minneapolis to Chicago trek, raising money for AIDS services, in July of 1998, just two years after the crash. Had Silberman not thought through the dangers and problems inherent to fulfilling her Dream, and trained to meet those challenges, she would not have been successful. Her recognition of the risks involved and willingness to deal with those risks is the mark of a Winner.[1]

A considered risk is the opposite of a blind risk. A considered risk is a risk you take with your eyes wide open, well aware of what might go wrong, and which you have therefore thought through extensively before committing yourself to the endeavor. Paul, for example, is taking a considered risk in attempting to establish himself as a consultant. He has come up with a number of different ways (resources) to find clients, to assure that he won't fail from lack of clientele before he even begins. May is building her exercise program with the help of feedback from cancer patients so that she does not create a program that only works for her.

These are some of the ways Paul and May thought through their Dreams *before* venturing out into the world, to increase their opportunities for success. Your courage depends on your willingness to look ahead to scout possible pitfalls. The more you think through your Dream, assessing the risks involved and figuring out ways to deal with them, the more willing you will be to go forward into the Unknown, seeking your success with all your heart.

## Curiosity

Curiosity asks "What's out there?" Curiosity is what led you as a child to explore every nook and cranny, to drive your mom nuts as you got into places she never dreamed you'd get into (having forgotten that she did the same as a child). Curiosity is what we too often lose on the road to becoming an adult.

A Winner's curiosity can be thought of as a positive "what if?" that is to say a "what if?" followed by the expectation of a positive outcome rather than a negative one. For example, curiosity asks "What if I approach this individual in this way with my idea? What might happen then? What if I try this other approach? Then what?" or "What if I go there? Where might that lead?" always anticipating a positive outcome, if not a direct solution to your problem, then an indirect one by teaching you something valuable. This is a very different "what-if" from the anxiety ridden "what-if" most of us are subject to: "What if I fail? What if this is stupid? What if I never make it?"

You will need to be well armed with positive curiosity to succeed in the Future. Your Future, being unexplored, uncharted territory, needs to be explored as it unfolds, just as a child explores the different rooms of a home as they are made available to him or her. Curiosity allows you to

## WINNER'S CIRCLE

Struck with Parkinson's disease at age 33, Tom Reiss refused to let Parkinson's define his life. In particular, Reiss sought to find a way to correct how he walked, which was impaired due to his disease. Reiss found that when he walked in certain places, such as climbing regularly spaced stairs or shopping at his local supermarket where the floors were covered with evenly spaced black-and-white tiles, his walking became almost normal. Armed with curiosity, Reiss investigated. He came up with all sorts of innovative ways to re-create the even spacing of stairs and tiles that enabled him to walk correctly. At one point, he even attached playing cards to the tips of his tennis shoes with coat hangers to help give him evenly spaced visual cues! His curiosity kept him searching. When Reiss heard of a virtual reality device that superimposed a virtual TV screen image onto whatever lay a few feet ahead, he investigated. His curiosity paid off. The virtual reality goggles enabled Reiss to walk almost normally, and since then, Reiss, now 45 years old, has dedicated himself to developing and refining glasses specifically designed for helping others like himself who suffer from Parkinson's. Curiosity is more than just an amusing twist of thought. Curiosity is often the very basis of a Winner's success.[2]

take full advantage of your new situation. When Jim, for example, starts his tour guiding, he may start by telling his tales at the actual site. If he's curious, however, he may explore other possibilities such as telling his tales while on the bus, before arriving on site. He may find that the tourists prefer an initial story, with perhaps some intriguing details given later at the site. His curiosity, and willingness to follow it through, are what will lead him to yet greater success.

## *Enthusiasm*

Enthusiasm is a self-generated excitement about life, about what you are doing, about your day, about all sorts of things. Enthusiasm is contagious. When you are enthusiastic about something, you attract people, you draw people in just by virtue of your enthusiasm. When Kathy talks to me about her Dream, her shop, she is so inspiring I can practically see the shop and the clothes. She makes her Dream almost as real to me as it is to her. Enthusiasm communicates to others that your idea, your project, your service is a valuable one, an interesting one, one that merits attention.

WINNER'S CIRCLE

Ralf Hotchkiss's enthusiasm is contagious. In a wheelchair since he was 18 years old due to a motorcycle accident that paralyzed him from the waist down, Hotchkiss, now 50, considers himself liberated by his wheelchair, and refuses such terms as "wheelchair-bound" or "confined to a wheelchair." He has devoted his life since the accident to designing and building wheelchairs—as have many others. What is unique is how Hotchkiss has shared his knowledge and enthusiasm for what wheelchairs can do for people. His company, the "Whirlwind Network," works in collaboration with 33 wheelchair makers in 25 countries. The companies share ideas, brainstorm together, and have their ideas tested at Hotchkiss's facility in San Francisco. It is Hotchkiss's extraordinary Winner's attitude and positive approach to wheelchairs that uplifts those around him and makes his "Whirlwind Network" an exhilarating success.[3]

You cannot afford to be lackluster about your Dream. If you aren't passionate about your Dream, why on Earth would anybody else be? "Well, that's all very good to say, Dr. Noelle," you say, "but I'm scared! There's an awful lot of ways I could fail, people might hate my idea, who knows? They might even laugh at it. How can I be enthusiastic in the face of all that?" By remembering that everybody gets scared. Everybody fears failure. Winners aren't Winners because they're invulnerable (despite what popular movies would have you believe). Winners win because they are enthusiastic in spite of their fears, because they let their commitment to their Dream override the paralysis fear might cause. So it's not about not being scared, it's about being enthusiastic *anyway*, about going forward with passion and zeal *anyway*.

## Proactiveness

Being proactive means to willfully engage your Future, to reach out to it so that it can pull you forward, just as you reach out a hand to someone so they can pull you up. Winners don't sit on their behinds, waiting for success to drop in their laps. Even Winners who are physically challenged and sometimes are physically immobile are proactive where it matters—in their approach to their situation and their attitude toward life.

To be proactive is to be constantly looking for ways to be actively involved in the fulfillment of your Dream. Being proactive means reaching

## WINNER'S CIRCLE

R. David Smith wanted to be a firefighter when he grew up. That was never going to happen, for Smith was born without a left forearm. However, when it came time for Smith to go out in the world and earn a living, he dealt with his situation proactively, by figuring out how he could come as close as possible to his Dream. Smith decided to become a stunt performer and actor. For the past 18 years, he has been using his missing forearm as an asset. It allows movie producers to add greater reality to scenes showing limbs being blown off, yanked off, or whatever other gruesome fate the writer has in mind. Smith has shared his success with other disabled individuals, especially amputees, teaching them specialized stunts as well as practical show-biz information. He and his group of "Stunts-Ability" students are shining examples of Winners at work, proactive one and all.[4]

out and seeking answers, solutions, better ways of doing things *before* you have a problem. Paul, for example, is proactive as he actively searches for different sources of potential clients. He doesn't expect clients just to drop out of the sky, he proactively seeks them out. May doesn't just assume her program is valid for cancer patients because it is valid for her, nor does she wait until someone comes up and says "Gee, this doesn't work for me" before factoring in what others think. She proactively seeks to test out her program by offering it to cancer patients for free and asking for feedback.

"But I'm coming to you, Dr. Noelle," you say, "because I already have a problem, because my life sucks! How can I possibly be proactive? I have to go back and fix this mess before I can get 'proactive.'" No you don't. You don't have to go backward to fix your problem, you have to go *forward* to create a life that works for you. It's not the same thing. If you have been downsized, it won't do you any good to try to go backward and get your old job back; your chances of success are very poor. If you are truly in love with your old job, if it is your Dream, then you have to find a way to choose your Dream so it can flourish in a different economy, a new company, perhaps an entirely new way. All of these require proactive approaches.

Being proactive puts you in charge of your life. Being proactive means you are captain of your ship, eager to set your course, and looking ahead to which way looks best, not waiting until there's a storm to suddenly wake up and take notice. Being proactive will help you get your life on a success track and keep it there.

## Hopefulness

Winners are hopeful. Winners see among all the possibilities an array of positive probabilities, and they set their sights on those positives. "Great, just what we all need," you say, "a little denial. Come on, Dr. Noelle, that's the sure road to disaster. I mean, that's how I got into this mess in the first place, thinking they'd never fire me, that I wouldn't get laid off, that I was indispensable. Hah! I got cured of that one fast. So excuse me if I don't buy into this 'setting your sights on the positive probabilities' routine."

Setting your sights on the positive does not mean denying the negative. Setting your sights on the positive means that *being fully aware of what the negative possibilities are,* you choose to focus on the positive ones.

You cannot go forward into a positive Future if you don't see at least some possibility of it happening. That's what hope does for you. Hope keeps the light of the Future burning bright enough for you to see, so you can pull yourself to the success out there, to your Dream. Without hope, life is hardly worth living. It's hardly surprising that one of the classic indicators of depression is hopelessness.

Everyone loses hope from time to time—that is part of being human. Winners maintain a basically hopeful attitude throughout their lives, and don't let those times when they lose hope overwhelm them.

---

### WINNER'S CIRCLE

For Kirby Puckett, 36 years old, the negative isn't just a possibility, it's a reality. The 10-time All Star Minnesota Twins player lost the vision in his right eye to glaucoma in 1996, and with it, lost a phenomenal baseball career. Had he so chosen, Puckett could simply have retired from public life and nursed his sightless eye in joyless silence. Puckett, however, is not that kind of man. Puckett talks of loving every minute he played baseball with all his heart, and fortunately, of never taking it for granted. Just as he doesn't take his life now for granted. He refuses to let his sightless right eye get him down. As Puckett says, the only thing he can't do is play professional baseball. As a Twins executive vice president, Puckett is using his popularity to help promote awareness of glaucoma and its prevention. In addition, he and his wife have founded a scholarship program at the University of Minnesota. Puckett believes he has much to live for, and looks forward to the future where he believes anything is possible. Such tremendous optimism and hopefulness are the hallmark of a Winner.[5]

*Open-Mindedness*

To be open-minded is to be willing to explore new ways of doing and being. To be open-minded is to be receptive to technological innovations, to new ideas, but also to be receptive to other people's ideas, to doing things differently from how you've always done them. Winners are remarkably unafraid of what's new and different from themselves, surprisingly eager to embrace the unfamiliar. "How faddish!" you say. "So it's just toss the old out and grab whatever new gimmick, or psycho-babble, or person comes along? Sounds mighty superficial to me."

Being open-minded doesn't mean throwing away what's valuable from the past. Being open-minded means not resisting the new or different just *because* it is new or different. It means being willing to consider what's unfamiliar to you with the same regard and seriousness as you would consider the tried-and-true. Jim, for example, was open to someone else's idea—painting a "Mr. Fix-It" sign on his car doors. Paul was open to using the chat room idea on the Internet to generate interest in his consulting as well as get valuable feedback from people.

"But I hate technology," you exclaim. "The last thing I want to do is spend my life figuring out the latest software or the newest electronic organizing gizmo." Fine, then don't. But be open to the possibility that the "latest software" or "newest electronic organizing gizmo" may be very helpful to the Dream you seek to realize. If indeed you find that it is, then given your preference not to work with it yourself, find a way to get someone else to work it for you, so you don't deny yourself the advantage of the new technology.

Being open-minded also means being willing to listen to other people's comments and suggestions about your Dream without necessarily implementing those comments and suggestions or defending against them. Just because someone suggests something doesn't mean you have to use it *or* reject it. Winners listen! They listen a lot more than most people because they know that they will then think their options through with the added bonus of someone else's opinion. They recognize the potential value of another mind.

Most of us upon hearing a negative comment, for example, immediately become either defensive or crestfallen. You launch into either: "What do you mean, you think this is a stupid idea! You don't know what you're talking about, I've spent hours looking into this," or "Oh, you're probably right. It was a dumb idea to start with. Forget I said any-

WINNER'S CIRCLE

Had George Dawson been close-minded, he would never have learned to read. At 98 years old, Dawson had been working since he was 8 years old, a day laborer since he was 12. There was no time or place for school. Ashamed of his illiteracy, he'd tried to keep it hidden as best he could. Dawson had survived several wives, one child, four siblings, and a lifetime of hard work. In his retirement Dawson spent his time fishing and growing and cooking much of his own food. One day, a teacher from the local adult education program came by and told him he could learn to read. Dawson kept an open mind as he listened to the man and figured if everybody else could learn to read, so could he. And read he did. Now Dawson, at 100 years old, reads the Bible at Sunday services until the pastor tells him to stop. The teachers at the literacy center say that Dawson is like a magnet for new students—people enroll in the class just because Dawson is there.[6]

thing." Neither response serves you. A Winner's approach would be to welcome the new, to say something like, "What about it is stupid? What about it makes you think it won't work?" You would be amazed at what you learn if you're willing to ask such a question in a neutral, nondefensive tone of voice.

Be open-minded. Be willing to listen. Be willing to think about what people tell you and evaluate their suggestions for their benefit to you. Keep an open mind to what you read in books, papers, and magazines and to what you see and hear on the radio, on TV. Be open to receiving ideas from all sorts of sources to help you fulfill your chosen Dream. Most people by George Dawson's age have long ago traded in an open mind for a set way of seeing and doing in the world. Not Winners—they stay open-minded forever.

## Being Joy-Driven

"Now if that doesn't sound like a lot of New Age drivel, I don't know what does!" you say, thoroughly disgusted. "Be joy-driven. In a pig's eye! What is that supposed to mean? Bounce through life with a smile plastered on my face? I prefer some reality to my life, thank you very much. Joy-driven indeed. I'd like to see you joy-drive your way through a construction job, or hustling clients, or trying to close a sale."

## WINNER'S CIRCLE

Anthony Robbins, the extraordinarily successful entrepreneur, author, and leader in the science of peak performance, is perhaps one of the most joy-driven individuals on the face of the Earth. In a few short years, Robbins turned his life around from being a miserable, depressed, lonely man barely keeping body and soul together with low-paying jobs, into a dynamic, successful man whose enthusiasm and appreciation for life is boundless. His Dream is to help people awaken their special gift, the uniqueness Robbins believes lies within us all. Robbins feels privileged to be able to share his ideas and feelings with the millions who tune into his television show, read his books, and attend his seminars. His attitude is typical of Winners, who express enormous gratitude for their lives, for what they can do in life, and for the Dreams they unfold. People gravitate to Robbins because of his passion for life and living. Being joy-driven is central to Winners' success.

The operative word here is joy-*driven*, not "joyous." Although being joyous throughout one's life is certainly a Dream in and of itself, what I'm referring to here is what motivates Winners in the pursuit of their Dream, and that motivator is primarily joy.

Joy changes the way you look at life. When you're joy-driven, you seek the deep satisfaction working with your hands can bring to, for example, your construction job; you know the pleasure of doing a fine job so the persons who will occupy the space you build will be happy there. You don't hustle clients, because when you're joy-driven you don't need to. When you're joy-driven you're enthusiastic about your product and your service, and you are eager to let everybody know about it, to offer it to one and all. Such eager enthusiasm attracts far more clients than a soulless "hustle." "Closing the sale" becomes an opportunity to offer something valuable, and to rise to the challenge of demonstrating its value in a way that is meaningful to the buyer.

Winners tend to seek that which will give them joy, sometimes also called satisfaction.

This being said, Winners do tend to be literally joy-driven, to seek out and choose Dreams that give them joy. Indeed, if your Dream doesn't give you joy, how are you going to muster up the enthusiasm or courage you need to see it through? Why would you bother being curious unless you thought there was something wonderful in it for you?

---

### WINNER'S CIRCLE

Candace Lightner founded "Mothers Against Drunk Driving," a tremendously successful grassroots movement, out of her personal loss. MADD's mission is to stop drunk driving and to support victims of this violent crime. I doubt that Lightner was joyous as she pursued her Dream of removing drunk drivers from the road so that other mothers wouldn't lose their children as she had. However, Lightner could easily be motivated by the intense satisfaction she would receive as deaths caused by drunk drivers became fewer and fewer.

---

Being joy-driven doesn't mean smiling all the time; being joy-driven means pursuing that which gives you joy. Joy can come from the satisfaction of a job well-done, from helping others, from knowing that you are contributing to the overall success of a larger organization, from any number of things. Everybody is different and has a unique sense of what "joy" is. For some, for example, joy is living simply themselves in order to be able to give scholarships or other contributions to those in need. For others, joy is putting their kids through school. For others, joy is building their Dream house. And for still others, joy is getting off the welfare rolls. But regardless of what your personal definition of what "joy" is, being joy-driven means two things:

1. You only undertake those projects that give you joy.
2. You find the joy or satisfaction in everything you do, everything you involve yourself with.

You laugh, "Right, and driving in five o'clock traffic is a kick! A hoot! I can really approach that one with joy!" Actually, you can. If driving in five o'clock traffic is part of what you need to do to fulfill your Dream, then you can have the joy of knowing, traffic or no, that you are on your road to success. You will still not like sitting in traffic, but you will know it has purpose, and because it has a place in the larger scheme of your Dream, you can accept it. You can also learn to use that time productively to further your Dream (think things over, listen to audio-books, get ideas from the radio)— and then you will get satisfaction from what you can accomplish during your "gridlock" time, even if you never enjoy the actual gridlock itself.

## *Giving*

Giving is half of the equation "giving and receiving." One of the secrets to receiving much in life is to give generously. Unfortunately, most people hearing the word "give" equate it with "give money" or "get taken advantage of," as in "give too much." But giving, as Winners do it, has little to do with money and even less with being taken advantage of. Giving is a natural and necessary contribution to the flow of abundance. Winners give of their time, energy, ideas, kindness, smiles, encouragement, inspiration, hope, positivity, and other such qualities far more than they do of their money. Winners give of what they have to give, to the degree that feels right for them. Oh, certainly, Winners who have, for whatever reason, received great sums of money often do give that money to those in need, but that isn't the first and most important way in which they give. Winners give *of themselves* because that's what Winners do. And in so doing, Winners plant the seeds of their receiving in the Unknown of their Future.

"How can that possibly work?" you ask. "Sounds like so much goody-goody mentality to me." Perhaps. But how it works is relatively simple. When you give of your time, energy, kindness, supportiveness—whatever it is that you have to give—the people who have received from you will want to give back to you. Not perhaps right then, nor perhaps in

---

### WINNER'S CIRCLE

Myrtle Faye Rumph is a case in point. In 1989, her only son, Al Wooten Jr., 35 years old, was killed in a drive-by shooting. All that her relatives could talk about at the funeral was revenge. Rumph had a different idea. She wanted to honor her son's memory, not avenge it. With what she had in her savings, she opened the Al Wooten Jr. Heritage Center, a storefront office in South-Central Los Angeles. Her dream was to make it become a youth center, somewhere young people could come, rather than spend their time on the streets—a place to learn, a place to play, a place where they could be safe. When Rumph ran out of money a year later, she sold her house to get enough funds to keep the Center going. She truly believed that by giving to the community, she could make a difference. And her giving paid off. Five short years after the Center opened, it was already an unqualified success. The Center boasts a library, a computer learning center, a recreation room, and well-appointed offices. It has become what Rumph wanted it to be—a haven for young people, a good place for them to come.[7]

the same way you gave to them, but at some time, in some way. If not the people you directly give to, then those who have observed your generosity of spirit will want to give to you when you need something. Essentially, by giving generously, you set up a dynamic that makes giving and receiving easy. It starts to flow. Now this, of course, assumes that you are not giving with strings attached, not "giving to get" but just giving, trusting that in so doing, you will receive. Giving as a Winner does also assumes that you give without draining or martyring yourself. You give what you have to give, in ways and to the degree that is comfortable for you. That way you don't feel "taken advantage of." Giving in the present assures that you will receive in the Future, and that's where you'll need it, because that is where you are creating your success.

Giving comes naturally to Winners. When many others would turn inward and despair, Winners give.

Giving in the present is what allowed Myrtle Rumph to receive in the Future. Giving—hers and others'—is what made her Dream come true.

## Taking Responsibility

The idea of taking responsibility truly has a bad rap in our culture. Taking responsibility has become unfortunately associated with blame. "Take responsibility" usually means "Something went wrong and it's your fault! Take responsibility for it!" Who would want to? Getting tagged as the idiot, the wrongdoer is no fun. No wonder we tend to shirk responsibility.

And yet . . . taking responsibility is a powerful Winner's tool. Taking responsibility is your willingness and ability to respond to situations. It's not about taking blame. It's about being in charge. When you are willing to respond, you're taking charge of the situation. If you've made a mistake, welcome to the human race. You didn't think Winners made mistakes? On the contrary, they do, but they are willing to take responsibility for their mistakes and learn from them. They are also willing to take responsibility for their successes and learn from them—something too few of us do.

Winners take responsibility for their lives, for their Dreams. They don't expect anyone else to realize their Dreams for them.

None of this would have happened had James Hunt not taken responsibility for his life and taken action to realize his Dream. Winners succeed,

---

WINNER'S CIRCLE

Bobby James Hunt, 53 years old, lost his full-time job as a steelworker in Pittsburgh in the 1970s. He would get called back for various lengths of time when the mill needed extra crew, but then get laid off again. This pattern went on for eight years. Hunt didn't like the way his life was going and decided to take charge. He was inspired by one of the gifts being offered at a fundraising auction—a scholarship to a beauty school. Although he didn't win the auction prize, he was interested enough to go ahead and enroll in the school anyway. For six months, Hunt worked at the mill by day, and went to school by night. The mill eventually closed and Hunt opened his beauty salon. For the next five years, Hunt and his wife lived off her salary. Every dime he made went back into his business. Fifteen years later, Hunt owns two hair salons, a beauty school, and a video production company that makes educational videotapes about hair care. He has authored three books and has donated $220,000 in cash and scholarships to cosmetology schools in Pennsylvania.[8]

---

not because they are inherently smarter, more talented, or born with wealth and privilege; Winners succeed because they take responsibility.

Winners ask for help, for support, for members to play on their team, but they do not ask others to take responsibility for either their success or their lack thereof. If your employees steal from you, for example, the stealing is their responsibility, but yours is to learn how to select more honest employees or to install security systems that make stealing more difficult so that your Dream of a business survives. If you've had a rough childhood or a drinking problem, it's your responsibility to deal with it and heal yourself, not to let it impact others hurtfully, or get in the way of your Dream.

If you are unwilling to take responsibility, then you are leaving the fulfilling of your Dream up to other people at best, and abandoning your Dream at worst. For example, if you have to wait for all employees to be honest in order to prevent theft from your store, you are in deep trouble. You are no longer in charge of your Dream. If you have to wait for the aftereffects of your rough childhood to disappear, you may be dead before that happens, and your Dream along with you. If you believe your drinking problem is what's in the way of your Dream, then take charge, take responsibility, or else you will ruin your Dream along with your liver.

There's a great deal of joy in taking responsibility for our Dreams, and Winners know that joy well. Take the blame out of responsibility and let it be what it is—the ability and willingness to *respond*.

## Protecting Yourself by Setting Boundaries

There is danger in the Unknown of the Future, much of which you can address by considering your risks, as we discussed in the section on "Courage." But you can also, as Winners do, learn to set boundaries to protect yourself. May, for example, knows that her health will be endangered if she works too many hours, so she consciously and deliberately sets boundaries delimiting how many hours she will work. Similarly, May wants to make sure her relationship with her son is not endangered by her Dream, so she sets boundaries on the time she is away from him.

Boundary-setting can be thought of as answering the question "What am I willing and not willing to do in the name of this Dream?" Boundaries are both a way of protecting your physical, emotional, and mental well-being, and a way of protecting your principles, or character. Boundaries are proactive. You set boundaries *before* you're in trouble, which is what differentiates boundary-setting from protecting yourself by being defensive. People become defensive *after* they are in trouble. Boundary-setting is a proactive way of taking care of yourself. Good-boundary setting makes the need for defensiveness infrequent.

### WHAT YOU CAN'T TAKE WITH YOU (NEGATIVITY)

Negativity can be defined as whatever prevents you from moving forward. Negative *beliefs* about the Future, as we saw in the first chapter, prevent you from moving forward into the Future at all. Negative *attitudes* prevent you from moving forward into the Future successfully. They hold you back either by turning your focus toward the past, or by stalemating you in the present. Unfortunately, given the accelerated rates of change, if you're not going forward in life, you'll probably be going backward.

## Wanting to Know All the Answers ahead of Time

Wanting to know all the answers before you venture forth is a little-recognized negative attitude, a stumbling block to success. It is certainly an understandable desire; you feel a lot safer about going out there into the Unknown of your Future if you know ahead of time every problem you're going to face, every situation you'll encounter, and preferably have the wherewithal to deal with each ahead of time. Given the increasingly unpredictable nature of our world, however, this is virtually impossible, so demanding that you know all the answers before making a move amounts to stopping yourself dead in your tracks. It's not going to happen. Be willing to let go of your need to know all the answers and accept knowing *enough* of the answers to proceed.

So, for example, May doesn't know all there is to know about exercise programs for cancer patients, but she knows enough to start developing one, and trusts that along the way she will receive sufficient feedback from her "volunteer exercise program testers" to develop a worthy and useful program. If May waited until she was an expert in exercise programs for cancer patients, she'd be 10 years down the pike and starving before she ever got anything underway. And since science is constantly evolving, by the time May was an expert, that information would probably already be outdated! Instead, May has the courage to go forward, knowing *enough* to begin.

So too, Kathy doesn't know all there is to know about how she is actually going to transform having a corner of someone else's shop into her own shop. As a matter of fact, Kathy knows very little about the details of that conversion, but she does know that she has access to enough resources to support her vision. If Kathy waited until she knew exactly how the transformation was going to take place, it would never happen, because there is no way she can know that until it is actually taking place. What she can do is talk to others who have performed similar conversions in their own businesses, such as caterers who started by working on their own out of their homes, and then leveraged their initial success into a company financed in a variety of ways. She can learn from them what are some of the possible ways such a conversion might occur. What she will never be able to do is plot ahead of time the "how, where, when" of her conversion, and if she waited to do so before actually beginning the process, she'd never start.

"But I want to know what is going to happen," you say, frustrated. "It's too frightening just to go forging into the Future without a game plan!" Who said you had to go out there without a game plan? On the contrary, all the steps in this book *are* your game plan. Because new technologies and ways of doing things change so fast, your game plan must now be based on *how* you go about achieving your dream, that is to say, which attitudes, resources, and beliefs you use, because those are under your control and are therefore stable. You can no longer rely on the old game plan, which was based on *"What* I do it with,*"* that is to say which specific job, policy, or technology was available, because these elements are now out of your control and are therefore unpredictable.

As much as we resist the thought, the Future is Unknown! Demanding to know what the unknown is, is impossible. That is why an approach allowing us to go safely and successfully into the Unknown that does not rely on that which we already know is so important and valuable. Saying to yourself, "This is what I know about the situation, this is what I don't know, and this is where I can get answers and help for the parts I don't know" is a far better guarantee of your success in the Future than attaching yourself to "I have to know it all before I move an inch."

## Apathy or Passivity

Apathy is most often expressed as "I don't care" and succinctly summed up in the popular term, "Whatever." Few attitudes are as deadly to your success in the Future as this one. If you don't care, who will? If you say "whatever," whatever is precisely what you will get. You cannot create a Dream unless you care deeply about it. There isn't a Winner in the world who has been merely lukewarm about his or her Dreams. Winners share a passionate conviction that is inspiring to all those they meet.

Second cousin to apathy is passivity. Apathy is a lack of interest, an indifference to life. Passivity is a lack of activity, allowing yourself to be acted upon rather than being active. Passivity means that you stop thinking and feeling for yourself, stop making decisions you have thought through for yourself, and instead accept the decisions others make for you, and accept other people's opinions, thoughts, and feelings about your life rather than coming up with your own. Passivity has nothing to do with whether or not you are sitting down. Passivity has to do with your active involvement in the workings of your life. You will not create a Dream for yourself unless you are willing to take charge and be active on your own behalf. Sitting back just doesn't cut it. For example, Winners who have been paralyzed and rendered quadriplegic, and thus are incapable of being physically active, are unbelievably active when it comes to their involvement with life. Stephan Hawking and Christopher Reeve are outstanding examples of Winners who are superbly active, while outwardly hardly moving a single muscle.

Apathy and passivity keep you stalemated in the present at first, whereupon you'll usually slide rapidly into an undesirable Future you chose by doing nothing to prevent its occurrence. Apathy and passivity are like a nightmare, leading you places you never wanted to go, yet feeling yourself pulled there by forces beyond your control. Apathy and passivity may sound neutral, but they are not. They are in fact powerful forces pulling you down, away from your Dream and its fulfillment.

The antidote to not caring, to apathy, is to imagine, think about, and especially *feel* "What would be a wonderful Dream for me?" until something clicks for you. Allow yourself to be vulnerable to yourself, to acknowledge what secretly delights and inspires you, regardless of what anybody else may think about it.

Let yourself care about something—an achievement, an accomplishment, a very private step up for yourself, or let your heart yearn for goodness, beauty, or truth, a cause of some kind, whatever shape it comes in. Often, we just haven't thought we had a right to a Dream, and therefore forgot to Dream one. Or it seemed like "just so much nonsense" when, in truth, Dreams are critical to your success in the Future.

Passivity often comes from fear, as in "It won't work anyhow, so why try?" or "I can't do it, so why try?" Winners try again and again and again, picking themselves up after every attempt that doesn't turn out the way they want. "I can't do it, so why try" is often a cover for "I don't know how to do it, so why try," or "I don't think I have what it takes to do it, so why try." Kathy, for example, was convinced she could never own her own shop, so she had abandoned her Dream years ago. It's only as she worked her way through the process of making her Dream real by figuring out the

---

WINNER'S CIRCLE

Chicago police officer Jim Mullen could easily have let apathy take over his life. Wounded in a shootout with wrongdoers, the 33-year-old Mullen was paralyzed from the neck down. He could have simply accepted the medical disability payments that were permanently assured him and left it at that. But Mullen had a Dream—to remain on the job and to remain in uniform. He could not conceive of just letting things be, he had to go forward, into his vision of a positive Future. And he succeeded. Mullen is an outreach coordinator for Chicago's community policing program, bringing much needed attention to this valuable program. He uses his own experience in talking to high school students and others about how "crime doesn't pay."[9]

steps to getting there that she realized she could indeed have her Dream. Kathy's passivity in regards to her Dream stemmed from lack of know-how. Once she saw how her Dream could become real, she became wonderfully active. May was very fearful that she didn't have "what it takes" to create her Dream, and thus had hardly even allowed herself to think about possibly helping other cancer patients and survivors. Her passivity was quickly transformed into activity once she built her confidence in who she is, and recognized what resources were available to her.

Jim's original litany of "I dunno," a typical apathetic response, when asked what Dream he might have was actually a cover for "I've never given it any thought." Once he did give some thought to a Dream, he found something he could indeed care about, and his apathy vanished.

"But it's so much work!" you say, comfortable in your passivity and dreading all the activity that success in the Future seems to require. "I'm not sure what I want is worth all that effort." Perhaps you are confusing effort with struggle. Many people do. Struggle is when you are exerting tremendous effort against resistance or opposition. Struggle is usually painful, lonely, hard, and you're right—who would want it?! Effort is simply the use of energy. Lifting your fork to your mouth is, in truth, an effort, although for most of us, it doesn't feel that way. Anything you do in life other than the usually automatic bodily functions of breathing, digesting, blood circulating, and so forth requires effort. And yes, being successful in the Future requires effort. But it does not necessarily imply struggle, i.e., effort in the face of great resistance! Remember, the Future is wide open, full of as many positive possibilities as negative ones. If you steer yourself toward the positive possibilities, you will encounter much less resistance, therefore much less "struggle" will be involved.

What most people mean when they say "I don't know if what I want is worth all that effort" is that they don't know what it takes to be successful and *assume* it means tremendous and painful effort. Success in the Future requires a great deal of imagination, creativity, and willingness to look to new and different ways of doing things, and in that regard requires effort. The more skilled you become at working with your beliefs, developing who you are, cultivating the active use of your imagination, and turning to resources for help and support, however, the less effort you will need to put out for a given result.

"But I really could fail!" you cry out. Of course you could. But if you create a solid foundation with your beliefs, know who you truly are, dream a Dream and choose that Dream, know your resources and have a positive approach, it's going to be a lot harder for you to fail! You may not have 100 percent success, but you will succeed.

## *Self-Righteousness*

Self-righteousness can be thought of as a "my way or the highway" attitude. Self-righteousness says "I'm right and I'm going to do it my way no matter what." Self-righteousness is yet another way to stay stalemated in the present, which if maintained rapidly devolves into an unfortunate Future. Self-righteousness is detrimental to your success in the Future because you have no way of knowing which way is "the right way" when you're venturing into the Unknown—all you can know is that there is *a* way. To stubbornly proceed along your way, regardless of the feedback or results you're getting, may give your ego enormous satisfaction, but it's not likely to put you in the winner's seat.

The middle managers who have suffered most in the downsizing of companies and corporations across America were those who, once ousted from their jobs, insisted on applying only for middle management jobs. "I'm a middle manager," they would say, self-righteously, "I've always been a middle manager and that's what I'm going to be." The problem was that the functions of middle managers had been to a large extent rendered unnecessary by new technology and methodology, or absorbed into other positions so that there was an overabundance of middle managers in a market in which the number of job openings for middle managers was extremely limited. The middle managers who have been most successful at assuring a comfortable Future for themselves are those who did not insist on remaining middle managers, but either learned new skills entirely or found a way to convert their management skills into other occupations that were valid in the current job market.

Donald Snyder, author of *The Cliff Walk; A Job Lost and a Life Found* (Little, Brown, New York, 1997), talks about how after he was laid off from his job as assistant professor at a university, he stubbornly refused to consider anything other than a position in the academic life he was used to, and put himself and his family through absolute agony for years, until he finally stepped aside from his self-righteous position, and was willing to take very different steps to rebuild his life.

Self-righteousness can only hurt you in your search for a successful Future. It is the opposite of open-mindedness. When you're being self-righteous, you close yourself off to all other possibilities, and thus greatly limit your probability of success. You cut yourself off from the array of re-sources so critical to success in the Future. Being willing to see things from other people's point of view, for example, immediately doubles, triples, and eventually geometrically increases the number of ideas and resources available to you. Why would you deny yourself access to all that out of a need to "be right"!?

A winner's approach is to proceed along the way he or she has thought through and determined to be the best way for now, relying on feedback to help him or her steer and guide a sure course to the Dream. A winner values his or her success more than the ego satisfaction of saying "I'm right."

Self-righteousness, as in "my way or the highway," is not to be con-fused with taking a moral stand. Having moral principles and high values that set a standard for your behavior are part of boundary-setting; "This is what I will do; this is what I'm not willing to do." Principles and values have to do with such things as honesty, treating others fairly, having com-passion, and so forth. They in no way cut you off from listening to and using what others may have to offer you in your journey toward success.

## Blaming Self or Others

Blaming, as opposed to taking responsibility, is probably the surest way to keep yourself mired in the past and guarantee the failure of your Dream. When you blame yourself or another, you are looking backward, focusing on who did or caused whatever it was, and then tying up your energy in reprimanding yourself or the other for the situation, which is long gone. "It's your fault," you say, "if you hadn't been such an idiot and done such and such, we wouldn't be in the mess we're in," and then dwell on the subject as if by doing so, somehow everything would get better again. It never does. Blaming only makes people feel bad and wastes time. Eventually you have to deal with the situation anyway.

"But it was the company's fault," Paul said to me vigorously when we started talking about blame. "They did to it to me. I certainly didn't merge myself out of a livelihood." "I'm not arguing that fact for an instant," I replied. "I'm just pointing out how blaming them doesn't get you any-where." "What do you mean?" asked Paul. "Well, does blaming the com-pany get you your job back?" I asked. "No, of course not," replied Paul. "Does it help you create a new position for yourself?" I asked. "No," Paul said. "What does it do for you?" I asked. "Makes me feel better," said Paul. "Why?" I asked. "Because at least then I don't have to feel guilty about not working," Paul answered. "OK, so it assuages your guilt. Anything else?" I ask. "No, not that I can think of," Paul said. "All right," I continued, "then how long would you like to spend relieving your guilt?" Paul laughed, "About a minute, I guess." "Well, then," I replied, "that's about all blaming is worth—a minute." "Got it," Paul said.

To say "It's the economy," or "It's my lack of education," is even more counterproductive than blaming a person or a company, because the econ-omy or your lack of education, being inanimate, is insensitive to your woes and isn't going to do anything about them. All you succeed in doing in blaming your past or an abstraction such as the economy is postpone that time when you have to actually deal with the economy, however it is, or your lack of education, whatever that is.

Winners are remarkable in their lack of blaming behavior. Even when a crisis is clearly someone else's doing, Winners tend to get on with re-solving the crisis to their Future benefit as quickly as possible. They just don't let blaming get in their way.

## Self-Pity and Martyring

When things go wrong or a crisis hits, and your plan isn't working as you expected, or your success isn't flying in at the speed of light, it's quite normal to feel sad, upset, hurt, or disappointed, even to spend a little time feeling sorry for yourself as you lick your wounds. The operative word is "spend a *little* time." Winners don't sit around and whine. They may get upset, feel disappointed and frustrated, and cry, but they don't indulge in pity parties.

Self-pity, with its "Oh poor me, ain't it awful" refrain, keeps you ru-minating about the past. It keeps your focus squarely on what happened to you and how awful it felt. It does nothing to heal your wounds or allow you to move once again into your Future. For Kathy, for example, to dwell on the fact of her aging, and bemoan that every hairstylist position in the entertainment business seemed to be given to younger, hipper, trendier

---

WINNER'S CIRCLE

Dr. Beck Weathers had quite a bit of healing of past wounds to do. Weathers, caught in a snowstorm while hiking up Mt. Everest with a group of fellow climbers, initially was thought to be dead. Miraculously, the 50-year-old Weathers survived, but lost his nose, his right arm from just beneath the elbow, and the fingers of his left hand due to frostbite. Weathers's healing, however, wasn't just physical. He realized, when he came home, that he had given up his family for his passion of scaling mountains, and yet that family, when he was near death, was the single most important thing to him. Rather than dwell on the misery of losing portions of his body, and his life that had been filled with mountain climbing and adventure, Weathers turned his focus to repairing his relationship with his wife and children. He then turned his focus to his Future. Weathers modified the equipment he used as a pathologist so that he could return to work, hiring an assistant to help out, and once again, looking to success in the new life he had created—where family comes first. A Winner, indeed, Weathers learned, healed, and moved on.[10]

---

stylists, did nothing for her success in the Future. To *notice* that her chosen field seemed increasingly closed to older individuals and thus was squeezing her out (fairly or unfairly, the purpose of this book is not to take on age discrimination!) was helpful to her success in the Future. She can't make herself younger (plastic surgery only does so much), so it wouldn't be wise to choose a Dream apparently more available to younger people.

There's a big difference, however, between *noticing* something, and having a *pity party* over it. You may indulge in a pity party when you've noticed something but refuse to take it into account in a way that moves you forward into success. Winners notice the inequities of life, all right, and they certainly notice all the dire things that can happen along the way—going bankrupt, losing a child, being stabbed, crippled, downsized, or fired, for example—but once they've had a brief spell of wound licking, that's it, it's over. Winners turn their focus as quickly as possible onto their Future—which may very well include some healing of past wounds—and get on with it.

Martyring adds a blaming chorus to the self-pity refrain: "Oh poor me, ain't it awful, nobody understand me, nobody appreciates me, after all I've done for them, poor me." When you're martyring yourself, you want others to know about it and appreciate how much you are suffering. Martyring keeps you not only stuck in the past, but also in an overt blaming posture as well. Neither is conducive to your forward progression into a successful Future.

"But I really am unappreciated, misunderstood, undervalued," you cry out. "I really do do everything for everybody else and never get a word of thanks or gratitude. It is awful." "I believe you," I say. "Now tell me how ruminating over people's failure to appreciate you helps you create your Future success." Silence. You're at a loss for words. Then you say, "See you don't understand me either. I told you nobody understands." I am sorry you feel so very misunderstood, I tell you, but martyring yourself is an exercise in futility. The people who currently fail to appreciate you and never utter a word of gratitude for all your good deeds are unlikely to sit up and take notice just because you're moaning about it. In all likelihood, they will just continue their usual failure to appreciate you. So if your Dream includes doing something where you are appreciated and understood, sticking around your present situation and moaning about it isn't going to do the trick. If you're feeling martyred, better to (once again) notice that, and proceed to choose a Dream that shifts you from an unappreciative present to an appreciative Future. You can't do that while your energy is all tied up obsessively reviewing how miserably ungrateful everyone is of your good deeds.

Self-pity and martyring are like a glue, affixing you rigidly to an unsatisfactory present. Pry yourself loose and use the energy that's been holding you in place to propel you into the Future of your Dreams.

## Anger that Turns into Bitterness, Resentment, or Rage

Anger can be a marvelous motivator. Anger over being mistreated or hurt has fueled many a Winner's Dream of justice and compassion. But anger must be released once it has performed its original motivating function. Why? Because, if you hang on to your anger, you continually focus on the event or situation that caused the anger in the first place, namely, something in your past. Anytime you are focusing on the past, you are not focusing on your Future.

Furthermore, anger, focused on, doesn't just sit there. Anger, like anything else you focus on, grows. And when anger grows, it becomes either bitterness and resentment, or full-blown rage. In The Cliff Walk, Donald Snyder talks about being so resentful of his still-employed and still-affluent neighbors after he had been laid off that he and his young son shot arrows into the neighbors' backyards. Frustrated desires for success easily lead to such petty acts of resentment, yet the resentment does nothing to advance your success.

When you are bitter and resentful or enraged, you don't create a Dream, you create a Future of revenge, a nightmare. You are not even being true to yourself, for your nightmare is one of reaction to what someone did to you. You are limiting your vision of success in the Future to one narrow event in your life, determined by your past.

Anger that degenerates into resentment, bitterness, or rage tends to narrow your focus. When you approach life with resentment, bitterness, or rage, it is very difficult to see the positive possibilities, difficult to hold positive beliefs about the Future, and difficult to be curious, open-minded, or hopeful. When you're filled with resentment, bitterness, or rage, it is difficult to interact with other people. People will tend to shy away from you, for bitterness, resentment, and rage are violent energies that frighten most people away. You thus lose the resources so critical to your success in the Future.

When anger comes, channel it wisely and safely, heal its source, and let it go quickly. Just because someone hurt you in the past or present doesn't mean you should give them the power to continue to hurt you in the future! Don't damage your opportunities for a genuine Dream by harboring old angers and grudges, or fanning the flames of resentment and hurt. You deserve far better than that.

## *Defensiveness*

Defensiveness is the tendency to defend what already is, whether that be your game plan, your belief about something, or your approach to a situation. When you defend something, you are maintaining the status quo (the present that quickly becomes the past), usually regardless of whatever new input may come your way. Success in the Future, however, requires an expanded awareness of what is around you, a willingness to *continually* explore new and different alternatives.

"Well, that's all very well and good," you say, "but I like my game plan! I did all of your steps 1 through 5 and you're saying now that I'm supposed to just dump my chosen Dream just because someone challenges it or disagrees with me? Fine kettle of fish that is! I'm not giving up my game plan," you continue, defensively, "no way, no how." Fine. Who asked you to? Being nondefensive doesn't mean roll over and play dead.

You stand up for yourself by the choices you make and how you follow through on those choices. Defensiveness doesn't enter into the picture at all. Being nondefensive means being willing to listen to what others have to say about your game plan, incorporating what makes sense to you, and leaving the rest alone. Winners are not doormats—far from it! Winners often have strong opinions about what they are doing and how. But Winners are rarely defensive because they know that defensiveness closes the doors to possible sources of valuable information.

Winners take suggestions. Winners listen to what else is possible, what other ways there are of doing things, what other means exist to do them. Winners keep their options open so success can develop in any number of ways, not just the one they anticipated. In creating your success, be willing to listen to all input from others without defending your stance—just listen. Just because someone makes critical comments about your ideas doesn't mean you have to hear the criticism as an attack. Winners don't tend to feel threatened by someone's comments on their Dream and thus are able to hear what the person has to say nondefensively. Listen to others' comments from a Winner's perspective. Thank them for their input and later, think over what was told you, weigh it, evaluate it for potential usefulness—"Is what this person said to me helpful in advancing my success?" If yes, use it. If not, discard it.

If, however, you find that upon occasion you are defensive when someone points out a weak point in your chosen Dream, for example, or argues that you'll never get there, then learn to catch yourself as quickly as possible and shift gears. Go into "inquisitive mode." "Enquiring Minds Want to Know," the slogan of the newspaper *National Enquirer,* is very apropos. Let your modus operandi be that of an enquirer: "Can you tell me more about how you see this weakness? How do you think it may get in the way of my success?" "What about my Dream makes you say I'll never get there? Can you tell me more?" and *listen.* Leave your ego (which is screaming by this time "How dare they! Who do they think they are!" and other such unhelpful phrases) out of the discussion, and be open to gleaning as much helpful information as possible. The person may tell you absolutely nothing worthwhile, but he or she may just tell you something surprisingly on target, which you may have missed entirely.

Do you then give up your Dream, since it has been deemed "faulty" by someone? No, of course not. You figure out how to readjust your course so you're firmly on the road to success, do whatever it takes, and keep moving. You'll be all the more successful because of it.

## A SPECIAL NOTE ON FEAR

You look at me pensively. "Dr. Noelle, aren't you leaving a real biggie out of your list of "what gets in the way?" you ask. "What's that?" I respond. "Fear," you say. "Isn't fear the negative approach most in the way of moving forward into a successful Future?" "No," I reply, "fear isn't what stops people; everybody fears something somewhere along the line, Winners as much as anybody else. What stops people is giving in to the fear." "So Winners aren't unafraid?" you ask, surprised. "No, Winners feel fear, probably a lot and often; they just deal with it differently." Christopher Reeve, in his book *Still Me*, is very candid about the fears he has had, all along the journey from his accident to the present day. He just doesn't let those fears stop him.

For many people, fear is paralyzing. Once they feel fear, they are literally stopped from any further activity. But fear is part and parcel of the human condition. We're not likely to know less of it in the Future; if anything, the Unknown being in and of itself fearful, we're probably going to know more. Just because we are not likely to rid ourselves of fear as a feeling, however, doesn't mean we have to use it as an approach to life and to our Dreams.

*Winners feel fear, but they don't adopt a fearful approach to life.* They acknowledge what frightens them and find a way to deal with the emotion that it is. They then are free to pursue their Dream.

Fear only gets in the way when you let it. Be willing to deal with your fears as they come up, however you do that, be it through journaling, talking

---

WINNER'S CIRCLE

Emily Lyons would have every reason to let fear stop her for good. Lyons, a 41-year-old nurse, was the victim of a recent terrorist attack on an abortion clinic in Birmingham, Alabama. She lost the sight in her left eye, her right eye and her legs are severely damaged, and her entire body is covered with hundreds of purple welts, the result of the nails and gravel packed in the bomb. In all likelihood, Lyons will not be physically able to return to nursing. However, determined not to let the bomber stop her lead the life she wishes to live, Lyons's Dream is to become a speaker on women's rights once her health permits, despite her innate shyness. Is she aware that such a choice could expose her to further danger? Yes. But she doesn't intend to let that intimidate her.[11]

---

### WINNER'S CIRCLE

Tom Whittaker, who strives to be the first amputee to make it up Mr. Everest, is open about having fears about surviving a climb up a mountain where so many have died. But he doesn't dwell on it. Instead, the 49-year-old Whittaker acknowledges the reality of his possible death, and deals with it by cherishing the special time he deliberately spends with his daughter.[12]

---

with friends or a counselor, through prayer, or any other of the numerous ways that exist. Then, although you may bump into fear on occasion as you move toward your Dream, it will not prevent you from achieving it.

## How Winners Deal with Negative Attitudes

"You said at the beginning of this chapter that Winners are good at catching themselves in less-than-productive modes and lifting themselves up and out," you tell me, looking studiously at your notes. "How do they do that?" "In a number of ways," I respond.

Winners are very good at reaching out to others. So when Winners find themselves sabotaging their own success by being self-righteous, self-pitying, or holding any of the other damaging attitudes, they will call a friend, go to a support group, meditate, pray or use other ways of reaching out to Spirit, or refer to a book of inspirational sayings, many of which can be done at 2:00 A.M. or whatever completely inconvenient time such attitudes often surface. Further outreach would consist of going to church/synagogue/temple, talking with a counselor, taking a self-development class, listening to self-help tapes, reading books devoted to self-improvement, going into nature for a spell, or taking a retreat, for example. Winners don't like anything coming between them and their success, so they are either unusually quick to sense that they are in a negative mode, or willing to let those around them alert them to their less-than-success-producing state. They are then eager to do what it takes to get out of it; in other words, Winners take responsibility for their negative attitudes quickly and decisively.

Awareness of your negative attitudes and your willingness to do what it takes, using the Winners' ways described above to shift negative attitudes when needed, is all that is required. Remembering your Dream and how much it means to you is often helpful in motivating you to get past any negativity rapidly.

## How to Develop Your Winning Attitude

Create a successful Future for yourself by adopting the attitudes of a Winner. Leave your negative and less-than-productive attitudes in the past, where they won't get in your way. Look forward eagerly and enthusiastically to the Future, sow the seeds of hope, open-mindedness, and proactiveness that will grow your successes full, rich, and abundant. Use the steps that follow to help you recognize and choose those attitudes that will serve you best.

## *Personal Success Log 7: Your Attitude*

### *Step #1: Evaluate Your Winning Attitude*

You can't change something if you don't know what it is. The first step to developing a winning attitude is to assess what your current attitudes toward life and your situation are. Go through each of the components of a Winning attitude—courage, curiosity, proactiveness, enthusiasm, hopefulness, open-mindedness, being joy-driven, giving, taking responsibility and boundary-setting—and see where you stand relative to a Winner's position on each.

Be honest with yourself. Don't make yourself out to be a saint or a devil—you're probably neither. Figure out which of the winning components you have and to what degree. Sometimes you'll find that you have a Winner's attitude in one area, but lack that same attitude in a different area. Be specific. Help yourself by evaluating yourself accurately.

### *Step #2: Identify Your Negative Attitudes*

It is never a pleasant task to see that what's in the way of your success—is you. The good news is, your negative attitudes are yours and yours alone, so you can change them. Go through those attitudes that won't work for you in creating your success in the Future—wanting to know all the answers ahead of time, apathy or passivity, self-righteousness, blaming self or others, self-pity and martyring, anger that turns into bitterness, resentment, or rage, and defensiveness—and identify those you hold and to what degree. As with the Winning attitudes, you may find you have negative attitudes about one area, but not about another. That's fine. Just be honest and neither assume you're flawless nor conclude you're a hopeless case. If you're like most of us, you have some baggage to release. That's all.

*Step #3: Make the Necessary Adjustments*

Take the areas in which you feel you are deficient, be they insufficient Winner's attitudes or an overdose of negative attitudes, and work with them. Follow the suggestions given in the pertinent passages, and refer to other sources—self-help books, counselors, journaling, prayer, classes, whatever works for you—as needed. Do what it takes to help yourself develop the attitudes that will assure your success in the Future, and to release those that will hold you back. Be sure to use the many resources you learned about in Chapter 6 to help you.

A Winner's attitude is what will guide you surely to success in the Future. Flexibility and your willingness to adapt and change course along the way are what will keep you there.

## NOTES

1. Beth Karlin, Lisa Newman, Lorna Grisby, Lorenzo Benet, "On the Road Again," *People Magazine*, August 31, 1998, pp. 129–133.
2. Galen R. Brandt, "Walking Again," *New Age Journal*, September/October, 1997, pp. 116–119.
3. Michael Ryan, "I've Been Liberated By a Wheelchair," *Parade Magazine*, August 3, 1997, p. 12.
4. "Part of a Lifetime," *Los Angeles Times Magazine*, March 26, 1995, p. 12.
5. Margaret Nelson, "With No Regrets," *People Magazine*, March 3, 1997, pp. 67–69.
6. "Man of Letters," *People Magazine*, April 6, 1998, p. 112.
7. Miles Corwin, "Grief, True Grit Leads to Memorial for Slain Son," *Los Angeles Times*, October 29, 1995, Part A.
8. Michael Ryan, "Success is Sweeter When It's Later," *Parade Magazine*, April 27, 1997, pp. 10–12.
9. "Force of One," *People Magazine*, January 19, 1998, p. 64.

10. Michael Neill, Carlton Stowers, "Days of Reckoning," *People Magazine,* September 29, 1997, pp. 91–94.
11. Bill Hewitt, Amy Laughinghouse, Gail Wescott, "Battling Back," *People Magazine,* June 1, 1998, pp. 119–121.
12. Christina Cheakalos, Johnny Dodd, "Higher Purpose," *People Magazine,* May 11, 1998, pp. 60–62.

# CHAPTER EIGHT

---

# BE FLEXIBLE, BE WILLING TO CHANGE

*Where Am I Relative to Where I Want to Be?*
*What Adjustments Do I Need to Make?*

A willow survives a storm by bending, and buildings survive earthquakes by moving with the Earth's movements, not against them. It seems to be a law of nature that surviving turbulence requires flexibility. That which is too rigid, breaks. So too for human beings. In the chaotic times ahead, flexibility will be essential to survival. We can predict neither the timing, direction, nor magnitude of the changes we will see in the years to come, we can only predict that they will come, and thus make ourselves ready for them. Readiness cannot come from knowing what the changes will require, the Future being Unknown, readiness can only come from how we approach those changes.

"How very poetic," you say, somewhat sarcastically, "but what does it mean to me? Flexibility is the opposite of rigidity, I got that, but what else?" Flexibility, in the sense used here, means sensing when changes are needed, and being able and willing to make those changes. "And what, pray tell, does that have to do with my success?" you ask, seeking more specificity. "Everything," I reply. "In order for your success to be solid and sustained, you must be able to adjust continually to the rapidly changing world we live in. Otherwise, your success, even if you attain it, will be short lived." "More work!" you exclaim, despairing. "Not really," I reply, "just a few guidelines to keep you steady on your success course."

Sense when change is needed and adjust your course accordingly, by attending to the following:

1. Periodically evaluate where you are relative to your Dream.
2. Actively seek and welcome feedback.
3. Be willing to change.
4. Run systems checks on your beliefs and attitudes.
5. Be willing to dream new Dreams.

## PERIODICALLY EVALUATE WHERE YOU ARE RELATIVE
## TO YOUR DREAM

As you go about realizing your Dream, periodically evaluate your current position by asking yourself the following:
*Where am I relative to where I want to be?*
When I asked this of Paul, six months after he'd begun working on building his success as a consultant, he said, "Well, let me think . . . I have a number of clients I'm working with, so in terms of being accepted as a management consultant, that's happening. I have a few clients I've contacted but aren't yet signed on. I'm making some money, but not enough to cover my bills; I'm still dipping into my savings, so that's not being where I want to be." "How will you know when you are successful?" I asked. "What will tell you your Dream has come true?" "When I have enough money?" Paul asked, unsure of how to answer me. "No doubt that's part of it," I replied, "but I expect part of your Dream is also to feel secure by having enough money coming in on a regular basis." "Absolutely," Paul said. "How will you know when that part of your Dream has happened?" I asked. Paul looked at me and smiled, "Guess I'll have to have some goals." "That would be very helpful," I said.

Since you know what your end goal is (your Dream), track your progress by creating a chart that states your Dream in the form of target goals. Charting where you are relative to those goals gives you the stepping stones on the way to your Dream. For Paul, this first meant figuring out how many clients he would need to work with, on contracts averaging a certain amount of money per quarter, to yield the financial security he wanted. Second, Paul needed to put "satisfaction" down as a target goal, as in the satisfaction derived from his "helping people, and doing something well," an important part of his dream.

"Can you give me an estimate, in percentage," I asked, "of where you are relative to 100 percent success in terms of financial security and satisfaction?" Paul sat and thought about it for a while. Then he replied, "I'd say I'm about 30 percent of where I want to be financially, and about the same, actually, in terms of satisfaction." "Great," I said. "That's a terrific result after just six months."

It's very important to create a concrete representation of your Future. Your Future can literally slip away from you without the benefit of concrete anchoring. Periodically evaluating and plotting graphic indicators of your current position relative to your Dream keeps you grounded. It also gives you support, showing you concretely that you are going in the direction you want to go in. If you're not, such an evaluation gives you a reality check, so that you can make appropriate changes.

"Why didn't you ask me to create target goals in terms of numbers of clients?" Paul asked. "That's how a lot of businesses do it." "I know," I replied, "but how many clients you have may or may not be a good gauge of your financial security. You may choose to have many small clients at lesser rates or a few clients at higher rates, or even a mix of both. A Dream isn't as easy to quantify as a company's financial targets." "How about creating my target goals in terms of money?" Paul asked. "You could certainly do that," I replied, "but you stated your dream in terms of being a consultant to young and growing companies, not in terms of making X dollars. Therefore it makes sense to create target goals that express your Dream as clearly as possible." "So it wouldn't be wrong to express target goals as dollar amounts," Paul said. "No, of course not," I replied, "as long as that was an accurate reflection of your Dream."

Other questions to ask yourself in evaluating where you are relative to your Dream are these:

*"Where is my attention? What am I focusing on? Where is this leading me? Is this where I want to be going?"*

"Boy, that's a funny one," Paul commented. "How so?" I asked. "Well, I just never thought of asking those questions," Paul said. "Can you answer them for me?" I asked. "To start with, can you tell me what you are paying attention to these days? What you are focusing on relative to your Dream?" "Sure," Paul said. "I'm probably paying most attention to getting new clients." "And where is that leading you?" I asked. "To getting closer to financial security," Paul said, looking at me strangely. Surely I couldn't be that slow. "Yes, but is it the way you want to get there? In other words, Paul, by focusing especially on getting new clients," I asked, "are you actually creating a situation for yourself where you constantly have to be on the lookout for new clients, rather than perhaps giving some attention to developing already existing clients as referral sources, to help provide you with new clients or as sources of continuing business?" "Huh," said Paul, "I hadn't thought of that." "That's why periodic evaluations are so important. You need to stop and take a look at what you're paying attention to, at where your focus is. Whatever you focus on grows. I can't emphasize that enough. You want to make sure that what you are growing is what you *want* to be growing," I said. "So it's not about whether my choice in scouting for new clients is 'right' or 'wrong,'" Paul said, "you just want me to stay aware of what I'm doing and consider the consequences." "Exactly," I said.

The Future is something we create one step at a time. Each action you take here in the present, has consequences for your success in the Future. Just as a gardener attaches the growing limbs of a rosebush to a trellis to

---

## WINNER'S CIRCLE

John Feight had a successful career in advertising for many years. He had dabbled in painting since his mid-20s, but he got serious about his art when he went to Paris in 1974 to try to sell some of his work. That's when it first hit him that he wasn't happy. Somehow, to be happy, his Dream—painting— had to be helping someone. So he took the first step in adjusting the direction of his Dream. Feight volunteered to paint murals in local hospitals in his spare time. He then came to another realization that caused the second major adjustment in the direction of his Dream: finding a way for hospital patients to create art might be more beneficial than his doing so. So Feight began drawing outlines on canvases for patients to fill in. Patients feel a healing sense of accomplishment from having painted something. They no longer feel so terribly disempowered and helpless. Feight gave up his advertising job, established a foundation, and at 58 years old, says he is passionate about what he does. And Feight's Dream has taken yet another turn as he sees, day in and day out, the wondrous effects art can have on people. His goal is now to make health professionals all over the world aware of the healing powers of art, and he is well on the way to doing that. To date, Feight's Foundation for Hospital Art has donated more than 15,000 artworks to about 500 hospitals in 165 countries. Because Feight stayed (and stays!) in touch with his Dream, he has consistently taken steps to make sure his Dream is on track, both benefiting people and making him happy. Therein lies the secret to this Winner's success.[1]

encourage it to grow in that direction, so must you attach the points of your attention to the direction of your desired growth. Only by stopping from time to time to reflect on where you are putting your attention will you become aware of the direction of your growth. As long as you take such a pause periodically, you will be able to make whatever changes and corrections to that direction are needed. This way you avoid the dreadful surprise of finding out you've been going for too long in a direction that isn't getting you to your Dream, and now have to scratch the whole thing and start over. You assure your success by checking your progress often.

## ACTIVELY SEEK AND WELCOME FEEDBACK

Use feedback to answer these questions:

*How am I doing? What are the results of my current activities? Are these activities advancing my Dream?*

When I asked May if she had sought feedback regarding her exercise program, she replied "Oh no, I'm afraid of asking the hospitals for feedback!" This was eight months down the road, and May had succeeded both in developing her program and in placing it at several local hospitals. "You weren't afraid of asking your volunteer cancer patients for feedback about your exercise program. That's how you developed it," I reminded her, "by creating your program, having your volunteers exercise accordingly, then tell you what worked for them and what didn't." "I know, Dr. Noelle," May replied, "but those were people like me—I knew they'd understand. I knew if what I was doing wasn't right, they wouldn't criticize or judge me, they'd just help me make it better." "How is that different from asking the hospitals?" I asked. May sighed. "What if they don't like the program now," May said. "What if they take a critical look at it and say 'This is really not worth it, let's not renew her contract.' I can't afford that, I only have three contracts, and I really need to keep them at this point." I nodded.

I understood May's fear well, having heard it many times before. Too often we equate feedback with criticism. We fear that asking for feedback will encourage others to suddenly look for "what's wrong" with our product, our services, our relationship, ourselves. We're afraid of the consequences of their seeing "what's wrong." You don't realize that if something's "wrong," people are already well aware of it! They're just not telling you. And whether you are aware of it or not, you are already suffering the consequences (or reaping the rewards!) of how people view you and what you have to offer.

Reluctance to seek feedback leads to the "don't rock the boat" or the "if it ain't broke don't fix it" school of thought. Unfortunately, many businesses, individual ventures, and projects are going out of existence after enjoying a brief period of success because success increasingly requires constant growth and renewal. The less you can see ahead into the Future, the more important it becomes to solicit feedback. You cannot rely on your service, product, equipment, or whatever it is you produce or contribute to fit the needs of a constantly changing world if you aren't aware of what those needs are. The "if it ain't broke don't fix it" adage no longer applies. "Even if it ain't broke, find ways to grow it and strengthen it" would be a more accurate 21st century slogan.

"There are many ways to ask for feedback, May," I said. "People generally respond very favorably to being asked their opinion, especially if you put your questions in the context of wanting to continually improve your service to them. Besides," I continued, reminding her, "a hospital is a collection of individuals, not some faceless entity." May thought for a moment. "So maybe I could start by talking to the administrator I work with," she said. "And maybe create evaluation forms for the patients to fill out occasionally, like every six weeks or so." "That would be great," I said, encouraging her. "Feedback is just getting information—that priceless commodity—to allow you to do even better."

When I broached the topic of actively seeking feedback with Jim, he had a different objection. "They'll tell me when they don't like something, Doc, people always do," he said nonchalantly. "I don't have to go looking for it." "No people don't," I said. "Often, they just go off to someone else providing the same or similar service without saying a thing." This was one of the valuable lessons I had learned from client satisfaction surveys taken at various law firms. Clients more often than not left the firm when dissatisfied without ever telling anyone the reasons why. Usually, the sources of their dissatisfactions could have been easily remedied, had the lawyers in question known what those were. "Remember, Jim," I said, "the more you can make the Unknown of your Future Known, the better the likelihood of your success. When you actively seek feedback, you are literally making the unknown—what people think of what you are offering—known. If it's all positive, wonderful! If it's not, equally wonderful, because now you can do something about it. If you don't know how people are receiving what you offer, you keep yourself in the dark. That only hurts you in the long run."

Actively seeking feedback will also help you evaluate whether or not the activities you are currently engaged in are indeed advancing your Dream. Paul, for example, received feedback that his clients really appreciated his management program, but felt they had difficulty in communicating with him, that he had poor "people skills." "I feel awful," Paul said, "I never should have asked for feedback! Look what it got me; they think I'm a lousy communicator." "Did you lose any of your clients through asking for feedback?" I asked. "No," Paul admitted, "But they must look at me differently now." "How, Paul?" I asked. "The only difference is before they privately thought you were a poor communicator, now they think it and you know it. Nothing has changed on their end, except possibly their increased respect for you, given your willingness to ask for their opinion." Paul sat silently for a moment, then asked, "What do I do now? I feel at a loss."

"The purpose of asking for feedback is to do something with it once you get it," I replied. "When you evaluate feedback, positive or negative, ask yourself, 'Given the feedback I'm getting, are my activities advancing my Dream?' Go back to your Dream, Paul, and assess your feedback from there." "OK," Paul said, "apparently the actual product I'm offering is in line with my Dream, but how I'm delivering that product isn't." "Sounds accurate to me," I said. "Looking at the feedback from that perspective, what does it tell you to do?" "I can either revamp my Dream—make a different choice—or I can take classes, whatever, learn how to become a better communicator," Paul replied. "Right!" I exclaimed. "Either way, you will be increasing the likelihood of your success in the Future. That's all we're talking about here, Paul, how to be successful in an Unknown Future. If you have feedback, you can adjust your course so you keep progressing in the direction of your desired success."

You can no longer rely on past performance to determine future performance. People's needs, desires, how they see their businesses, their goals, how technology affects us, all of these elements and so many more impact the effectiveness of your performance. Without feedback, you are literally steering in the dark. Why would you make it more difficult than you need to, to get where you're going? Actively seek and welcome feedback; it is one of the secrets to success in the coming century.

It's not enough, however, to solicit feedback. You must also be willing to use that feedback constructively.

## Be Willing to Change

Be willing to act on the answers to the following question:
*What adjustments do I need to make to assure my steady progress toward the fulfillment of my Dream?*

Feedback is only as useful as what you do with it. Change is hard for many of us, and often, once we've mustered the courage and strength to make a major change, such as that made by Paul, May, Kathy, and Jim, it's tempting to sit back, and rest a while before making another change. For good or for ill, however, the ever-changing nature of our Future makes the willingness for us to continually change a precursor to success. If you stand still in the 21st century, you will be going backward.

"Not again," you groan, "I can't just keep changing and changing! It's just too difficult. I'll settle for a smaller Dream, or less success." There is no need to settle for less, or give up your Dream, because change is part and parcel of success in the Future. Change is not synonymous with catastrophic upheaval. Once you've chosen your Dream and are actively in the process of realizing it, "change" comes in the form of small adjustments to your course, just as when you're driving, you continually, and virtually unconsciously, make small adjustments according to the weather conditions, road conditions, and behavior of other drivers. Once you've adopted an attitude of *willingness* to change, you will find that the adjustments in and of themselves aren't difficult to make.

Kathy was distressed as she discussed with me the feedback she'd received. She didn't yet have repeat customers (she'd only been with the shop a couple of months), so she requested feedback from her sales manager. "I'm just miserable," Kathy said, almost in tears. "My manager said I handle customers beautifully—I'm patient and good in working with them. But she said my way of dressing myself and my hairstyle and all is too extreme for many of the customers. My manager said she noticed that the more conservative customers tend to turn away and walk toward another salesperson rather than let me wait on them. No one's ever said anything about my way of dressing, Dr. Noelle, I'm so upset about this, I feel like such a fool!"

Kathy's concern was understandable. How one presents oneself through dress and grooming does matter, and more so in certain businesses than in others. "I'm sorry you feel so badly, Kathy," I said. "But I don't think the situation is as bleak as you feel it is. How did your sales manager respond to your request for feedback?" "Oh, she loved it," Kathy said, "she said she was very impressed I was interested enough in doing a good job to ask for feedback. She said she'd remember that when it came time to consider raises." Kathy wiped her eyes and blew her nose, then continued, "But that doesn't make me feel any better; I mean what she told me makes me feel just awful!" "I can understand that, Kathy," I said, "but let's talk about it for a minute, OK?" Kathy nodded.

"Your former life as a hairstylist was on TV and movie sets, right?" I asked. Kathy nodded again. "And there is a great deal of freedom on TV and movie sets as to how people dress, right?" I continued. Kathy laughed despite her upset, "Oh, yes! And you wouldn't believe what some people consider clothes!" "So in that context, you were probably appropriately dressed and groomed," I said. Kathy agreed, "People loved my clothes and the way I fixed myself—I was always getting compliments." "You've moved into a different environment now, a different world, which has different ideas of what is and isn't appropriate dress. The feedback you got is very valuable, Kathy. The world you're trying to succeed in simply requires a different mode of dress. That's a relatively small adjustment." "Yes," Kathy said, "I guess so, seen that way." "If you choose to adjust the way you dress somewhat in order to help customers feel more comfortable in approaching you, you will have more customers. You need customers in order to fulfill your Dream," I pointed out.

"But isn't that not being who I am?" Kathy asked. "Isn't that being phony?" "Well," I asked, "do you dress the same way for a quiet evening with friends as you do to go out for a night on the town?" "No," Kathy said, "Of course not." "Are you being phony in either case?" I continued. "No," Kathy said slowly, "I see. I dress according to what is appropriate for the situation. So I could rethink what is appropriate for this shop, looking at it as a situation, and dress appropriately." "Yes," I said. "It is that simple."

A common characteristic of Winners is their willingness to keep learning. Paul really wanted the satisfaction that working one-on-one with individuals in coaching them through their management challenges brought him. He recognized that he wasn't going to be able to fulfill that part of his Dream if he wasn't willing to change, and so he made the decision to take classes to become a better communicator. Learning is part of making what is Unknown Known to you, so as to increase your opportunities for success.

The more you see feedback as a valuable tool clearly guiding you to the changes that will speed you on your way to success, the more you will welcome it and the more easily you will make the necessary adjustments.

## WINNER'S CIRCLE

Caren Mahar, 37 years old, has made many adjustments since her daughter Katie was diagnosed with xeroderma pigmentosum (XP). XP is a rare genetic disorder that makes a child's skin hypersensitive to ultraviolet light. It is so severe that even the briefest exposure to sunlight often causes burns leading to skin or eye cancers. Many of those afflicted die before they reach their 30th birthday. When Katie was diagnosed with XP at the age of 2 after a series of terrible burns, Mahar went into high gear. She did everything she could to keep Katie out of sunlight, and a year later, with her husband Dan, Mahar started the XP society—the United States' first support group for families coping with XP. At the same time, Mahar was trying to raise money any way she could, to generate more research into XP. That's when she got a devastating piece of negative feedback that could have stopped her in her tracks. Mahar was told that unfortunately, the $10,000 she had painstakingly raised would have virtually no impact on the scientists' efforts. Winner that she is, Mahar recovered from the bad news, regrouped, and came up with a wonderfully creative adjustment to her Dream of a positive Future for her child: Camp Sundown. Camp Sundown, provided free to children suffering from XP and their families, offers all the fun of summer camp—at night! Children and their families spend the afternoon indoors doing arts and crafts, and the safe nighttime hours having hayrides, sing-alongs, walking trips, and playing baseball. The Camp is funded out of Dan Mahar's $39,000 salary and lots of help from volunteers and the community. Children come from as far away as the Ukraine and Nepal to enjoy the benefits of "normal" living with other children like them. Mahar's creativity and willingness to change allowed her to adjust to the negative feedback she received in a way that provided great positive benefit.[2]

Developing a willingness to change is like developing any other skill; the more you use it, the easier it gets. Change is something you can learn to get really good at. Be creative. For example, much of the time our tendency is to consider the extreme opposite of whatever negative feedback we've been given as the only possible adjustment we can make. Not so! Paul's consulting business, for example, wasn't doomed to failure because he lacked communication skills, nor did he need to drop his desire to personally coach clients through the management process, both of which are extreme responses to the negative feedback of "poor communicator." Improving his skills over time, as he's chosen to do, will allow him both to keep his dream and to be successful. When you're looking for solutions to the negative feedback you've received, write down the extreme solutions first, and then start brainstorming with yourself, friends, a colleague, anyone who is willing to help, and start coming up with as many solutions as you can that are somewhere in between those extremes.

Make adjustments also to accentuate the positive feedback you receive. Feedback isn't just about negativity! Jim, for example, found out that the two travel agencies he'd signed on with as a tour guide were very satisfied with his work for them. The only feedback they gave in addition to "very satisfied" was that the tourists just loved the "secret scandals" he sometimes included in his historical tales. Thus encouraged, Jim began actively to look for "secret scandals" for more of the sites on the tour itinerary, which made him even more popular with the tourists. Kathy, finding out that her sales manager really valued how she handled and worked with customers, took even more care in working with them, which impressed her sales manager further.

Don't take anything for granted. You need to make as much of the Unknown known to you as possible, positive as well as negative. This is your Dream you're on your way to, not "just some job" or "just something to do." Use feedback of whatever type—positive or negative—as guideposts to your success. Be willing to adjust your course in response to the feedback. Nurture and continue to grow the areas in which you receive positive feedback, and find more effective alternatives in the areas that are receiving negative feedback.

Feedback from others is very valuable, but so is the feedback you can give yourself, especially as it relates to your beliefs and attitudes.


## RUN SYSTEMS CHECKS ON YOUR BELIEFS AND ATTITUDES

*Is the way ahead clear? Am I open and available to my success? Are my beliefs conducive to my success? Are my attitudes engaging it?*

Your beliefs about the Future are what provide the foundation to your success. Your attitudes are what engage the Future in a way that brings in your success—or fails to. Beliefs and attitudes aren't stagnant. They shift and change over time. If your beliefs and attitudes aren't providing you with the foundation and approach necessary to fulfilling your Dream, then the way is difficult, if not entirely closed off. You are no longer open or available to your success.

Periodically, stop and take a look at what your beliefs are about the Future, and how you're approaching your Future with your attitudes. Just as technicians periodically run a "systems check" on their computers and other machinery to make sure all is running as it is supposed to, so too do you need to run a systems check on your beliefs and attitudes to make sure that both are functioning in a way that will maximally support the fulfillment of your Dream.

## *Beliefs*

Ask yourself, "How do I see the Future right now? When I imagine the Future, do I see it as bright and inviting, full of exciting possibilities, or is it dark and frightening, with disasters and crises lurking too near?" When I asked May to imagine her Future in this way, after about eight months into working her exercise program with hospitals, she said, "I see it as mostly bright, Dr. Noelle, but it's sort of like a tunnel, very narrow. I see my Future as bright, but only as long as I really tow the line."

I thought about what she had said for a moment. Then I asked, "May, if I understand you correctly, you see your Future as bright only as long as you work very very hard." May nodded, "That's it." "That's just a belief though, May," I said, "that's not a fact. Are you aware of that?" May frowned, "No, not really. It feels like a fact." "When you look around you, do you see people working less hard and still being successful at their chosen Dream?" I asked. "Oh, sure," May said, "but I don't know how they do it. They must be really smart or something." "Maybe, maybe not," I said. "All it really tells you is that the statement 'you have to work very very hard to fulfill your Dream' isn't a fact, in and of itself. If it were a fact, everybody would have to work very very hard to achieve their Dream, and that clearly isn't the case."

"What is certain though," I said, continuing, "is that if you have a belief that ties in your success in the Future to having to work very very hard, then that's precisely what will happen. You will only see, among all the alternatives out there in the universe, those that require you to work very hard. You will only act upon the possibilities that involve hard work. That's where your focus is. The upshot is you will have to work very very hard. So I suggest that you work on changing that belief, so that you can change your experience of how to achieve success. Otherwise you'll burn out before you've had a chance to enjoy your Dream!" May agreed rue-fully, "You're so right—I already feel that way sometimes."

You can't know what your current beliefs are unless you take a look every so often. Nothing is set in cement—including you! Sometimes your experience as you proceed along the road to your success will bring up a be-lief you didn't even know you had. At one point Kathy was horrified to dis-cover she had a belief that women could only attain a certain level of success. She discovered this belief when she was on the brink of beginning to look for investors for her own shop. Suddenly she couldn't imagine a Fu-ture beyond working for someone else. The idea of actually owning her own shop was quite literally unimaginable, although logically, Kathy knew that many women own businesses of all kinds. Kathy was horrified because she had always considered herself a liberated woman, yet she found herself held back by what she considered to be a very antiquated chauvinist belief.

Beliefs are not outgrowths of logical thought. Beliefs are convictions held on an emotional level, sourced in the unconscious programming we receive from infancy on, via parents, schools, the media, other people, au-thorities, and whatever we pay attention to in the world around us. Beliefs often don't come up until a situation arises that calls upon that belief. Once Kathy discovered her belief, however, she was able to change it and con-tinue toward her Dream.

## *Attitudes*

Running a systems check on your attitudes is a matter of reviewing the list of Winning attitudes, and the list of attitudes that will only hold you back.

Periodically ask yourself the following questions:

- Am I being courageous enough? Is there any area in which I lack sufficient courage? Am I considering my risks enough?

Succeeding in the Future does not require 100 percent courage—or 100 percent of any other attitude. As you evaluate yourself, always be looking to "Am I doing well *enough* on this dimension?" As long as you are honest with yourself, you'll assess your attitudes accurately enough (there's that word again!) to work successfully with them.

- Am I being curious enough? Proactive enough? Am I reaching out enough toward my Dream?
- Am I enthusiastic enough, hopeful enough? Am I keeping an open mind to what's around me?
- Am I seeking my joy? Am I joy-driven enough? Or am I settling for "Oh, well, I guess this is OK"?

Settling is very tempting, especially when you've been very active in pursuing your Dream and find yourself bumping up against lots of obstacles. The mind, body, and soul get tired, and suddenly settling seems like a dandy idea.

Kathy, for example, found herself in this position before she discovered the belief that was holding her back from finding investors for her own shop. It seemed no matter where she turned all she heard was "not interested." At the same time, her "Kathy's Korner" was doing very well in sales and she was the number one salesperson at the shop where she was employed. She had good security of employment, and knew she would earn consistent raises. Kathy was very tempted at that point to settle for "Kathy's Korner." Once she discovered her limiting belief, however, Kathy's energy and passion returned full force. Kathy realized she didn't want to stop at "Kathy's Korner," and the idea of settling disappeared.

"But how do I know that I haven't just chosen a different Dream?" you ask. "When is settling not settling but making a better choice?" When you feel deep inside that your choice is a joy-driven one, and not a disappointing "oh well, I guess this is all there is" choice. If Kathy had said to me something like, "Oh, I just love 'Kathy's Korner,' I've never been so happy and fulfilled, I could do this forever," I would not have called that settling. What Kathy said to me, however, was, "I'm just so tired, I don't think I can do this. What the heck, having my "Korner' isn't so bad, I guess I can live with it." That is not a joy-driven statement! It is settling.

When the body, mind, and soul get tired, sometimes a rest is in order. It can be very beneficial to take a break from pursuing your Dream, so that you can come back to it fresh and invigorated. Artists and other creative people have long understood the importance of taking a break. Pursuing a Dream is a creative endeavor. Your imagination and curiosity are just as engaged and focused as an artist's are. Taking some time away from the intense pursuit of an activity or project allows you to come back to it with a better perspective, a better sense of whether or not your Dream still inspires you.

A break can also provide you with the opportunity to take some time to run your systems checks. Often you'll find you're being stymied by a less-than-helpful belief or attitude, which once revised, frees up your positive energy.

*Do I take enough responsibility? Am I looking for the ways I can respond to situations and events, regardless of how those situations came about? Am I more interested in solving problems than in pointing the finger?*

If you find that you are turning to others to *fix* things for you, as opposed to turning to others to *support* you in your endeavors, then you are probably not taking enough responsibility. If you find yourself looking for "Who's at fault?" rather than delving into "How do we handle this?" you are falling short in the responsibility department. "But it doesn't feel fair!" you cry out, "other people get to find fault, and blame and get away with it just fine. Why does it always have to be me?" you wail. Because you're the one who wants to be a Winner. You're the one who wants a successful Future. Get yourself back on track. Gnash your teeth and let out a yowl if you need to, and then turn your attention to the task at hand, taking responsibility. The willingness to take responsibility puts you in charge of your life. Only when you are in charge of your life can you create success for yourself.

*How am I protecting myself? Am I setting good boundaries for myself?*

For many people, boundary-setting feels like such a "downer" in the midst of their enthusiastic reaching for their Dream. Yet good boundary-setting is essential to achieving your Dream and enjoying it. Jim, for example, eventually became so popular with tourists, that between his "Mr. Fix-It" jobs and being a tour guide, he was working seven days a week during the height of tourist season. His health became precarious, and when he ran a systems check, Jim realized he was not safeguarding his well-being. So although Jim was having a wonderful time with all the attention and income he was receiving, and truly fulfilling his chosen Dream, he decided to make a boundary adjustment. He reduced the number of "Fix-It" jobs he took on during the peak tourist season, so that regardless of the time of year, he always had at least one and a half days off every week. Once tourist season was over, he became more available for "Fix-It" jobs.

A Dream ceases to be a Dream when it endangers your well-being, be that mental, physical, emotional, or financial. Kathy, for example, had the opportunity to take out a loan that could have provided her with the seed money for her shop. Kathy, however, had nothing to put up as collateral, but she did have a friend who was willing to cosign on the loan. When Kathy looked at her paycheck, however, which was still her only source of revenue, she realized that in order to pay off the loan, she would be stretched so thin financially that she would be unable to deal with the least little setback. And she was too savvy to the garment business by now to delude herself into thinking there would be no setbacks. So Kathy decided it was in her best interests to set a boundary on how much she was willing to use of her paycheck to finance anything: a loan or whatever else. In the short run, the decision was painful for Kathy. She wanted her shop so badly she could almost taste it! In the long run, it was a wise decision, for Kathy found another way to finance her Dream that did not endanger her financial well-being.

It will do you no good to get almost to your Dream, only to blow it by setting insufficient boundaries for yourself. Then you really will have to start from scratch, which although certainly doable, is taking a more difficult path than is necessary.

For the most part, people aren't too resistant to running a systems check on how they are doing in terms of a Winner's approach to their Dream. Most of us start to resist systems checking when it comes to looking at our negative approaches. It's not much fun, admittedly, to sit there figuring out if yes, indeedy, you have been indulging in a serious pity party. However, bear in mind that if you weed out an ineffective approach right when it first appears, you'll do little if any damage to the successful pursuit of your Dream. If you let an ineffective approach grow, you may find your Dream increasingly difficult to manifest.

*Am I wanting to know too many of the answers ahead of time? Am I looking for certainty rather than access to resources?*

For many of us, it is a natural tendency to want to set in cement anything good that comes along. Faced with the Unknown of the Future, we attach ourselves to whatever is known and try very hard to extend the Known as far as possible into the Future. For example, almost as soon as May was successful in placing her exercise program with three of the local hospitals, she began to worry about whether or not the hospitals would renew her contracts. What May was forgetting is that she didn't get her original contracts by seeking certainty, she got her original contracts by being courageous, proactive, and generally adopting a Winner's approach.

"But shouldn't she try to keep the contracts she has?" you ask, confused, "that only makes good sense." Of course May should follow good business procedure in renewing her current contracts. But the nature of the

Future is such that those hospitals may or may not have funds for May's program in the coming years, they may or may not continue to specialize in cancer recovery, they may not even continue as hospitals, but be transformed into hospices or other facilities. By running her systems check, May realized that she was overly invested in seeking certainty, and neglecting to explore other resources so that her Dream would continue whether or not these particular contracts were renewed.

Your access to other resources, which allows you to continually renew and expand your Dream, is what will help assure your sense of safety and security in face of the Unknown. Your security lies in how you approach the Unknown, not in how any one situation turns out.

*Do I care enough about my Dream? Do I care enough about the different parts of my Dream? Am I thinking for myself, feeling for myself, making my own decisions?*

The day you stop caring deeply about your Dream and its fulfillment is the day to reconsider whether that is the Dream for you. If you do not care enough about your Dream, you will not have what it takes to fulfill it. Run a periodic check on the different aspects of your Dream and evaluate which parts still matter deeply to you and which don't. Ask yourself if there are fears in the way that are making it difficult for you to be passionate about your Dream. Make sure you are thinking through concerns and issues for yourself, weighing pros and cons, and coming to decisions that feel right to you.

*Am I taking others points of view into account? Am I refusing to see any other possibilities but the ones I come up with?*

Keep a close watch on your self-righteousness. Make sure you always leave room for other opinions, other approaches. Look to see if there's an area where you feel stubborn, then make sure you're being stubborn because you've considered different options and have adopted yours because it fits the situation best, not because it's "yours."

*Am I pointing the finger? Am I expending energy in blaming myself and others rather than getting on with seeking a solution?*

Tying yourself to the past by belaboring who did what to whom will only drag you down. Especially after a crisis or failure (yes, failures do happen on the way to success), check to see if you're guilt tripping yourself or others. As best you can, take as much responsibility (not blame!) as possible for resolving the crisis or failure and assuring a different outcome in the future.

*How's my pity quotient? Am I feeling sorry for myself at some level? Am I silently cursing the world for not appreciating me at my "true worth?" Am I feeling woeful and mistreated?*

When things aren't going too well is when we're most likely to fall back on self-pity. Especially when you bump up against repeated obstacles or it feels like nothing is working, run a self-pity and martyr check to make sure those attitudes aren't rapidly growing inside you. If you find you are feeling self-pity or martyred, give yourself 20 minutes to really get into it: moan, groan, cry, have a fit (privately and appropriately), whatever it takes. Then release it. Remind yourself of what you do have going for you by reviewing your list of "who I am" qualities (Chapter 2), and if right now no one is appreciating you, then appreciate yourself. Value yourself. And turn yourself forward into the Future from where new appreciation can come.

*Have I been angry lately? Am I hanging on to my anger? Do I feel rageful? Am I harboring bitterness or resentment? Am I being defensive?*

When you run a check on the status of your anger, separate out the anger that motivates you from the anger that, once felt, serves no purpose. Anger is a normal human reaction to slights and hurts; it's the way we say "I don't like that!" to ourselves, and "Back off!" to others. In terms of creating your Future success, make sure you aren't hanging on to your anger once it's filled its purpose, either as a reaction or as a motivator. If you touch base with your emotions from time to time, you can work with whatever anger is still dwelling within you, and avoid its developing into rage, bitterness, or resentment. Also check for any feelings of envy or jealousy, which also can lead to bitterness, resentment, or rage. Since everybody's path into the Future is different, some people may achieve success more quickly or fully than you do. To feel a flash of envy or jealousy is understandable, but to indulge yourself in nurturing those feelings gets in the way of your success. Feel them, release them, and move on.

Run a check on your level of defensiveness. If you find yourself defending or justifying your choices out of knee-jerk reactivity, make an effort to say less and listen more.

## Maintaining Winning Attitudes

There's a saying in psychology that "under stress, we regress." You will find that it's easiest to maintain winning attitudes when things are going well. Most of us don't tend to fall into negative attitudes until things are going badly. As much as you will feel justified when things are going poorly to get rageful, defensive, martyred, close-minded, and so forth, that's the very time when you must resist such defeatist attitudes the most, and the most important time to run a systems check on your attitudes. Winners are those who are able to rise above when they are in crisis, to believe in themselves and their abilities in spite of apparent failure. Keep your attitudes in winning shape at all times.

Sometimes an attitude or other adjustment just isn't enough. Sometimes you need to change your Dreams entirely.

## BE WILLING TO DREAM NEW DREAMS

Being willing to dream new Dreams answers an important question: *Is this still the Dream for me? Does this Dream fit the person I have become?* Just as the snake sheds old skin, so must we shed old Dreams when they have outlived their usefulness or their delight. Part of wisdom is knowing when to hold on and when to let go.

If you have accomplished your Dream, it may be time to start dreaming a new one. Because we are living so much longer, it is highly likely that any one given individual will have ample opportunity to pursue a number

---

### WINNER'S CIRCLE

Gary Jones found his Dream at 17. He was going to be a puppeteer. And in 1974, Jones succeeded with his Dream, touring the Unites States with a 15-person troupe and an astonishing cast of puppets. By 1984, however, Jones felt that too much of his work was about raising money, and too little about the joy of puppets, so he moved to Los Angeles to work with children. The 1992 Los Angeles riots gave the 49-year-old Jones a new Dream, one that fits his love of children and of puppets and his belief in the teaching power of puppets. Awarded an Arts Recovery Grant that year to help children overcome the emotional consequences of the riots, Jones went about his puppeteering-with-a-mission, and since then has developed a highly successful program in which he uses puppets and group discussion to teach children about AIDS and its prevention, drug abuse, and conflict resolution. Dreams are meant to pull you into a positive Future. Jones had the wisdom to see when his Dream was no longer doing that, and the courage to create a new Dream that would.[3]

of Dreams in his or her lifetime. Continuing to be successful in the future
means being willing to go on to new Dreams when it is time. "How will I
know it is time?" you ask. When your Dream no longer pulls you forward,
I reply. When it simply keeps you in place. Then it is time to Dream a new
Dream, to once again, pull you forward.

For example, the "empty nest syndrome," well known to many
moms, represents that painful transition point between a Dream fulfilled
(the children are raised and out of the home) and a new Dream as yet
undiscovered. The "empty nest syndrome" comes up only fleetingly for
moms who have looked ahead, who realize that one Dream is ending and
have created a new one even as the old is just on the verge of completion.

Not only do our Dreams, once fulfilled, cease to be our anchor to the
Future, but we ourselves literally outgrow them. You are not an inert, stagnant mass. You are a living growing being, all of your vital parts—your
mind, heart, body, and soul—change from your first breath to your last.
You outgrow your Dreams as you change. Once out of high school, for example, you've outgrown your dream of being a prom queen or high
school football hero (hopefully). You create a new Dream to pull you forward, and if you can't find that new Dream for yourself, life often seems
unfocused and joyless.

For example, a young woman had a Dream of being a recording artist,
which kept her firmly turned toward the Future and brought her a considerable measure of success. However, even as she was becoming successful as a recording artist, she found that she really didn't like being a
recording artist as much as she had envisioned. She didn't enjoy the public side of a recording artist's life—she didn't enjoy the touring or the live
appearances. She took some time off and rethought her Dream. She realized she had outgrown her Dream, that she was no longer the person she
had been when she first created it. It was now pulling her into a Future she
didn't want! The young woman had become more inward, more spiritu-
ally oriented, and needed a Dream that reflected her inner reality more accurately. She decided to explore the possibility of becoming a choir
director, and found that it fit well with who she had become. Once she had
chosen her new Dream, this young woman was once again pulled successfully into a Future she desired.

Being willing to change your Dreams doesn't mean abandoning your
Dreams because they are challenging! That's called giving up. Try not to
change your Dream when you're in the midst of a crisis. It's too hard to
think straight then. Resolve the crisis first, then take some think time.

Change your Dreams when they are not pulling you into *any* Future, or into a Future you no longer desire.

## HOW TO USE FLEXIBILITY TO CONTINUALLY CREATE AND RE-CREATE YOUR SUCCESS

The ability to bend, to be flexible, to adjust and change may seem at odds with the passionate resolve Winners have in realizing their Dreams. Yet it is the ability to hold to your Dream with steadfast and enthusiastic focus while adjusting your course as often as is necessary that assures your success. However, whimsical change, change just for the sake of changing, or poorly thought out change will sabotage a Dream. Let the following steps guide you to the type of *productive* assessment and willingness to change that will bring your Dream more and more fully into your life.

### *Personal Success Log 8: Your Flexibility*

*Step #1: Periodically Evaluate Where You Are Relative to Your Dream*

You can't know if you need to make a change if you don't assess where you are relative to where you want to be. Make a regular appointment with yourself to sit down and evaluate your current position. As always, be honest with yourself. Glossing over reality isn't the way to acheive a Dream.

*Step #2: Actively Seek and Welcome Feedback*

The more you know about where you stand in the eyes of those you serve or interact with, the better you will be able to succeed. Be brave! It is far better to find out if you just might be going along in a less-than-wonderful direction early on, rather than waiting until a crisis is upon you that lets you know in no uncertain terms that you are woefully out of touch with your success. Feedback is essential to the success of any venture.

*Step #3: Be Willing to Change*

Use your evaluation and the feedback you've received to help you make the necessary adjustments to keep you firmly on track toward your success. Change is just change. It is not failure. On the contrary, the willingness to change after honest assessment is one of the surest ways to make your Dream a reality.

### Step #4: Run Systems Checks on Your Beliefs and Attitudes

You are an ever-changing entity, and along with the mental, physical, and emotional changes you experience come changes in your beliefs and attitudes. Don't assume that because you believed something once, you still do or still want to. As you change, so should your beliefs. Take the time to review your beliefs every so often and make sure your beliefs have kept pace with your changing experience of the world.

Attitudes change also. Review your attitudes and make sure you're still adopting Winner's attitudes. Don't keep any unwanted negativity hanging around, jamming up the works.

### Step #5: Be Willing to Dream New Dreams

It is wonderful to achieve a Dream. It is also a little sad, for a Dream is what kept your sights high, your success moving in the right direction. Heal your sadness by dreaming new Dreams, lifting your sights ever higher, ever more in the direction of what satisfies you.

Don't be afraid to change a Dream should that Dream cease to serve you well. You answer to no one but yourself! Even if you've told everyone what your Dream was, and fear they will be very disappointed in you if you change your Dream, too bad! If that Dream no longer pulls you into the Future you desire, it's time to let it go and dream a new one. Your life is your own. Create Dreams that speak to you, now and through the whole of your life—Dream on!

### NOTES

1. Samantha Miller, Amy Laughinghouse, "Brush Work," *People Magazine,* April 13, 1998, pp. 67–68.
2. Samantha Miller, Joseph V. Tirella, "Into The Night," *People Magazine,* August 24, 1998, pp. 90–97.
3. Alex Tresniowski, Paula Yoo, Marilyn Anderson, "Puppet Power," *People Magazine,* June 15, 1998, pp. 121–122.

# CHAPTER NINE

## WHERE ARE THEY NOW?

### *Once a Winner, Always a Winner?*

A year and a half after Paul, May, Kathy, and Jim had completed their sessions with me, I invited each of them to come to my office for a follow-up session. I was curious. How had their lives unfolded? Had they been able to transform their Dreams into successful realities? How did their Futures appear to them now?

I started with the question: "What's going on with you now? Where are you in your life relative to where you wanted to be?"

PAUL

"Where am I in my life?" Paul repeated my question to him, as he sat, musing. "A heck of a lot better off than I was a year ago, that's for sure. One of my consulting clients turned into a 'full-time part-time' job. A young company on its way up—I just love working with them. They're growing by leaps and bounds, and my experience really helps them manage their growth so it doesn't overwhelm them. That's very rewarding. And that job pays the mortgage and the basics. Then I have freelance clients, clients that come and go as I do projects for them." "You've done a terrific job of turning your life around positively," I said, pleased for Paul and his obvious success.

He nodded, acknowledging my praise. "My wife's happy about it too, Dr. Noelle. You remember how I was worried she wouldn't like my doing consulting work because of the hours?" I nodded, "Sure, I remember." "Well, we made some agreements—no work on Sundays and a long weekend together every other month. It works out well. She's happy and I'm more relaxed. The funny thing is, our time together has become more valuable—something I never anticipated," Paul said. "We plan ahead for the long weekends, and somehow that's spiced up our marriage." I was pleased and surprised. "That's great, Paul, what a nice side benefit." "Yeah," Paul replied. "Now my wife's getting enthused about creating her own Future. She's looking into a mail order business for some crafts items she and a girlfriend make," he said grinning. "Winning is contagious, Paul," I replied. "You see one person becoming successful and you realize, 'Heck, I could do that too!'"

"But the really terrific thing," Paul said, continuing, "is my chat room." "Your chat room?" I asked, wanting to know more. "Mm-hm. The little chat room I started on the Internet is just great. It's no big deal—just a feature on my home page—but it really fills a need for me. I start discussions on it—all related to growing a business, of course—and I get all sorts of ideas and feedback from people on what is needed by new companies now. I get to brainstorm possible solutions with people, throw out ideas, see what happens. It's a very grassroots sort of thing. Then I take that information to my consulting clients so it helps them. Plus within the 'chats' I get to help people out with my expertise, so it's very soul-satisfying. And once in a while the chat room even generates business, through leads and referrals."

"In a weird way," Paul said as he shifted positions in his chair, "I feel I have the best of both worlds now. The young company provides me with a regular job I go to two and a half days a week, week in, week out. I like the stability of that." I nodded, knowing how much regular work contributed to Paul's sense of security. "Meanwhile," Paul continued, "since I'm constantly developing new leads and working with new clients on new projects, I don't feel so scared; all my eggs are not in one basket. Given my experience, relying on one company for my livelihood would absolutely terrify me," Paul confided. "Good point," I said, agreeing. "And the chat room makes me feel engaged in the world, involved in what's going on—I really enjoy it," Paul said. "So things are good."

"More than good," I replied, "it sounds like things are going very well for you, Paul. You've done a terrific job of transforming what appeared to be a dismal Future into a successful one. But I'm puzzled about something," I said gently, not wanting to burst his bubble. "Why don't you sound happy about it? What's going on?"

Paul sighed. "Trust you to catch me on it," he said, shaking his head. "I should be happy, Dr. Noelle, everything is going well. But what sticks in my craw is—I still fight my old demons. I don't know if that'll ever change. And that really bothers me," Paul said ruefully. I looked at him quizzically. "Which 'old demons'?" I asked. "My tendency to get depressed," Paul said, looking down as he shook his head. "Whenever things slow down, or there's a lull in how much work is coming in—I get depressed, I start going 'in and down.' You know—inside myself and down into the dumps," Paul continued, looking at me once again as he spoke. I nodded, remembering how valiantly Paul had worked to pull himself out of the muck of despair.

"Some mornings when I wake up," Paul continued, "I lie there, looking up at the ceiling and go 'Why me, God? What happened?' My self-pity mode. I long for the 'good old days'—which I guess weren't really all that good, since I could get bumped so easily!" Paul commented wryly. "I get scared," he admitted. "I find myself asking: Can I do it? Can I attract the clients I need?" Paul stopped, rubbed his face with his hands, sighed again and then said, "Oh, don't get me wrong, Dr. Noelle, I get over it. I use all those affirmations and inner quality lists stuck up on my mirror; I remind myself of my Dream, of all the resources I have. And it works. I get myself looking 'out and ahead' once again—out to the world around me and ahead to possibilities. I just find it so darn depressing that I still can get so down if things aren't going full speed ahead 100 percent of the time." "So you get depressed about getting depressed," I said, teasing him but telling the truth all the same.

## LEARNING TO TRUST SUCCESS

"Yeah, that's a good way to put it," Paul said, chuckling. I sat quietly thinking for a moment. "You know what the only thing I think is missing for you now, Paul?" I asked. He shook his head, "No, what?" "Trust," I replied. "Trust that you can do it. That no matter what happens, you can create a successful Future for yourself. Because that is what you are doing, isn't it?" "Yes," Paul said slowly. "You just don't trust that you can do it," I said, "so that's your missing piece. That's the realization you need to slowly bring yourself to. Trust yourself." "So simple and yet so hard!" Paul murmured, almost to himself. "Perhaps," I replied, "but essential if you are to keep succeeding. And all trust takes is a willingness to own your accomplishments. Not to become arrogant, not to show someone else up, but to truly let it sink in that you—little old you—can and do succeed. That you—just as you are, warts and all—have what it takes: the beliefs, the inner qualities, the attitudes, the Dream, and the access to resources that make for a solid and successful Future."

For Paul has indeed transformed himself into a Winner. Now all he has to do is let that sink in. It's important, even as you seek to create a more beautiful life for yourself, that you take the time to cherish those successes you've already accomplished. Success feeds on success. Even as you allow yourself, in the privacy of your heart, to fully own and enjoy your success, you encourage yourself to create more success. Gratitude, so important in sustaining any good thing, is important to give to yourself as well.

MAY

"How am I doing? All told, very well, thank you," May said, answering my question. "Although some things, Dr. Noelle, never change," May said, her nose screwing up with distaste. "Thomas's father is still a dead-beat. I'm still scared from time to time. I'm still prone to panic attacks. But what I do with it now is different," she continued, relaxing as she settled herself comfortably in her chair. "I belong to a panic disorders support group, I meditate regularly, I use deep breathing to help me when I get 'the flutters,'" May said, putting her hand over her heart. "I'm a lot nicer to myself. I take time to look on my accomplishments from time to time and remind myself 'I did this!' That helps me maintain my self-confidence."

I nodded, smiling to myself. May was demonstrating a true Winner's approach to life in which denial and negativity have no place. Instead, the focus is on working with and appreciating who you are. "And how about your Dream?" I asked. "Are you working with hospitals, creating your exercise groups?"

"Uh-huh," May replied, "but I am letting go of teaching the exercise groups myself as a primary focus." I was surprised. May had seemed so dedicated to her exercise program for people either in hospital or recovering from severe illnesses such as cancer. "A lot of things are shifting and changing for me," May continued, explaining, "many new and different things are happening." "Like what?" I asked, intrigued.

"Well, as I worked with patients and people who were recuperating from surgeries, chemotherapy, and the like," May replied, "I noticed how uncomfortable many of them seemed in their clothes. And how much of the time, the clothes they wore didn't seem right for people with special needs of various types. My old pattern-making mind got working and I started designing comfortable walk-about and exercise gear for people with special needs, both in the hospital and out. You know, clothes with soft textures for damaged or fragile skin, velcro closures, designs to accommodate prosthetics, colostomy bags, special needs. However," May said, stopping in the midst of her story, "and this is where I've really changed, Dr. Noelle, you will be very proud of me—I'm only creating the designs as rough sketches. I've found a pattern maker who translates my designs into patterns and makes those for me. That way, I protect myself from stress and overwork and I protect my time with my son." "In other words," I said, "you remember what is important to you and set appropriate boundaries." "You got it," May said. "You're right, May, I am very impressed, and very proud of the wonderful work you've done with yourself," I said. May smiled. "I don't know where I'm going with this," she continued, "all I know is that nothing is impossible now. Whether this 'special needs' line of clothing will become a business for me or something I do for a company or what, I don't know, but I'm willing to follow it through and find out." I couldn't believe my ears. Was this the same woman who was terrified of taking any chances at all with anything? What an inspiring transformation!

"I'm even thinking about taking a class in nutrition," May said, continuing. "I've found that helping people heal, helping them grow strong and healthy, is really my Dream, not just my exercise program, and I'm beginning to recognize that I may fulfill my Dream in a lot of different ways, both throughout my work life and in my retirement. And I may never really retire, in the sense of 'do nothing.' I've gotten somewhat addicted to following my creative urges, my impulses, asking myself, 'Hmm—wonder what that would do, how this would help?' and following through to see what the answer is."

## STAYING OPEN TO NEW POSSIBILITIES

Being willing to remain open to the infinity of possibilities ahead is truly a Winner's perspective. "I never knew the world was this interesting! I never knew there were so many ways in which I could contribute," is how May puts it. Her curiosity, and her willingness to discover the myriad ways in which she can fulfill her larger Dream of helping people heal are key to her continuing success. Added to these are May's willingness to pursue new workable choices as they pull her forward, letting go of what no longer does. It's important to let go of Dreams and choices as we outgrow them and discover new compelling ones.

"I'm less worried about making money," May continued, "not that I have a fortune now or anything like that. It just seems like if I don't panic, and sit down and either brainstorm with somebody, or read books, or meditate, somehow I can figure out what I need to do to be making money in a way that pleases me." "That's new," I commented, pleasantly surprised. "And it feels a lot better," May said. "For example, with the exercise programs at the hospital? Well, I proposed to the hospital that they help fund a training program that could teach other people how to do what I do. I worked out a deal with them that they would match whatever funds I came up with. Not that I had any idea how I would do that. But I knew I could find people to help me figure it out—and I did! So now I'm fundraising, and it's happening. Once the program is in place, I won't have to work as many hours. I'll be making more money doing less. And I'll be able to 'spread the word' out that much further. It makes me feel really good, Dr. Noelle."

## USING WINNER'S RESOURCES

May stopped, running her hand through her hair, staring out my window for a moment before she spoke again. "I never knew I could do any of this, Dr. Noelle," she said. "I never knew how much imagination and curiosity could contribute to normal work. I always thought that was for artists. Not for regular people like me. And I never knew you could do what your heart calls you to. I always thought you'd go broke following your Dreams. But that's what I'm using to make a living! My Dreams, my imagination, my curiosity—and realizing that I'm not alone. That if I don't know how to do something or where to find something I need, there's always other people somewhere who do. All I have to do is find them. They'll help me from there. It's a whole different life, Dr. Noelle," May said. "Yes," I said, agreeing, deeply moved by what May was saying, "it really is."

People are amazing. I am constantly astounded at what happens when people get a taste of what winning is all about. Given just a little leg up, a boost into discovering their own value, their own Dreams, some ideas about what resources there are and how to find them, what attitudes and beliefs serve them and which don't—people just take off! I look upon the people I've worked with, with awe. They always go so much further than I would ever have predicted.

## NOT EVERYBODY SUCCEEDS: WHO DOESN'T MAKE IT?

Are there people who fall by the wayside? Yes. From time to time, someone can't give up an attitude or a belief that holds them back; someone can't get used to the idea that no one is going to do it for them. And yes, those people stay stuck in a rut, carrying their misery and loathing with them wherever they go, ending up in a dark and joyless place. But fortunately, these are few. Most people, given half a chance, can't wait to get on the winning side. Most people, shown *how* to do it, pick up and move into a Future filled with success and joy. Do they stumble and fall? Yes. Do they get scared and freak out? Yes. Does that stop them? No! Because once you've seen what the Future really holds, once you realize the wonder of the life you can create, nothing will hold you back for very long.

KATHY

"You're not going to believe what I've been up to, Dr. Noelle," Kathy said dramatically, tossing her hair in her inimitable style. "What?" I asked, enjoying her obvious pleasure at whatever it was she was about to disclose. "I'm on the Web—me! I have a Web site, and I'm actually making money selling Kathy's Korner on the Web!" I was astounded. Kathy, recalcitrant "don't talk to me about computers" Kathy, selling on the World Wide Web? Now there was a switch. "What happened?" I asked. "How did this come about?"

"Oh, my!" Kathy said excitedly, "it's a long story." I nodded. I didn't care if it was a long story, I wanted to hear it. "Well, you know I was sort of stuck treading water with 'Kathy's Korner' at the shop." Kathy started, smoothing out her skirt and getting herself comfortably installed on the couch. "Mostly because it was going so well, except it wasn't what I really wanted. And when we last talked, you'd encouraged me to keep seeking my Dream, of having my own store, even though I'd been around and around looking for financing and couldn't find any." "I remember," I told her. "And we talked about different ways of getting financing," Kathy said. "Right," I replied. "Well," Kathy continued, "I started thinking about the 'accessory party' idea you and I had talked about, and I thought that would be a good place to start. It was. A really good place," Kathy said, smiling broadly, "it took off like gangbusters. I used my list of contacts from 'the biz' and soon, instead of having accessory parties, I was giving 'personal shopper' parties. I would find out ahead of time what the guests were interested in, style-wise, along with their sizes, and I'd bring over outfits with mix and match possibilities, accessories, the whole nine yards. It went so well, I cut back on my hours at the shop, and hired an assistant!" Kathy laughed, "A couple of years ago I could barely pay the rent, and here I am, with an employee! Part-time still, but heck—an employee of my very own. And with the way the parties are going, I should be able to drop my salesgirl position entirely within another six months or so and just keep up 'Kathy's Korner Comes A-Calling.'"

## No Longer a Bugaboo: Age Becomes Valuable and Profitable

"The best thing is, Dr. Noelle," Kathy continued, hardly pausing for a breath, "is that my age, you know—that thing I feared and hated—my age is what's making my parties so successful." "How?" I asked, delighted but not understanding. "I very deliberately targeted my parties to my age group and older," Kathy said. "I realized that since most fashion isn't geared to mature women, it's hard for us to find upbeat, trendy clothes that don't look ridiculous on us, or don't fit a 50- to 70-year-old or older body. I did my research and I found designers and ready-to-wear lines that both look good on and fit that age group. I approached these manufacturers, told them what I was doing, and persuaded them to let me demonstrate their clothes and sell on consignment. It's great! And that's also why I had to hire an assistant. Too much to lug around." I was thrilled. How creative! How like a Winner! Kathy took what she had considered a depressing downside, her age, and turned it into an upside, the very core of her success.

Kathy stopped talking as if finished, and sat there beaming. But I wanted the full story. "What about the Web, the Internet?" I asked, still waiting for that particularly beguiling piece of information. "Oh, the Web!" Kathy said, "of course. Well, that's my assistant's fault. Or his doing, I should say. Because it's turned out to be an awfully good thing." I nodded, waiting eagerly for the rest. "Kim—that's my assistant's name—Kim is real good on the Net. He suggested that anything you do in the real world, you can do in the virtual world. Meaning on the Internet. Since I was doing well with the clothes I was representing at the parties, why not approach the same manufacturers and see if they would back me and create a Web site where I did 'personal shopping' for women on the Web? And that's what I did. I remembered what you said about resources and figured I didn't have to know about the Web to be able to use it. Although I am learning now," Kathy confided a little sheepishly, "I mean, it only seems normal to learn a little something considering I'm on the thing." "And how's your Web site doing?" I asked. "So far, so good," Kathy replied, knocking on the table next to her for luck. "That's great, Kathy," I said wholeheartedly, "I am very happy for you." Kathy nodded, "Thanks."

## All You Need Is Enough

Winners are good at recognizing that all they need is enough—enough of the answers, enough of the resources to get them where they want to go—not perfection, not having to have all the answers, just enough. Kathy recognized that she didn't need to know all about the Internet in order to profit by it, and that freed her up to use it to her benefit. Kathy's power came not from wealth, position, or fame, but from her creativity, her ability to see the possibilities in the world right around her. That really is where your power comes from, from what's inside you, not from what's outside you.

Kathy sat quietly for a while, reflecting, and then said, "It didn't come by itself, though, Dr. Noelle. I had to keep myself moving forward. My tendency is to wait for something to happen." Kathy sighed, "I have had to realize over and over that I'm the only one that can make things happen. No one and nothing else will do it for me. Now, when nothing is moving forward and I find I've been sitting on my thumbs, I talk to myself. I look at myself in the mirror and talk to myself. I remind myself of what my Dream is and why it's important, why I deserve it. Then I go over my qualities and my resources. And that gets me back on track."

Knowing yourself—knowing what propels you forward into success and what holds you back—is vital to your ability to succeed and keep succeeding.

### JIM

Jim looked well, as he walked into my office and shook my hand. "How are you doing?" I asked, after I greeted him. "How have things turned out for you?

"Well, things have pretty much settled into a routine for me," Jim said, easing himself into the chair he'd spent so much time in many months ago. "In the winter, I do my Mr. Fix-It up and down the state, and in the summer, I'm strictly a tour guide. Don't have time for fixing in the summer." Jim smiled, "I'll tell ya, Doc, I'm having a good time. Do you know my little Gazette there, the one my nephew was running off on the local high school mimeo machine? Well, it's become a regular item here. They don't let me run it off the mimeo any more—one of the travel agencies has it printed up nice. But it's the same Gazette," Jim said proudly. He stretched his legs out in front of him, grimacing as he did so. "Your back still bothers you?" I asked. "Somewhat, depends on the weather," he replied, "but nothing like it used to. I sleep better, too." "That's nice," I said. Jim nodded in agreement as he settled himself back into his chair.

"So anyway, Doc," Jim continued, "I've got some news." "Oh?" I said, wondering where 'Mr. Negativity Jim' had disappeared to and marveling at the easily conversational, confident new Jim in front of me. "Yeah," Jim said, "I've got me a radio gig," he announced proudly. "A radio gig?" I asked, surprised. "It's from the 'secret scandals' thing I do on my tours. The local radio called up and said they'd like to do a 'secret scandals minute' a couple of times a week, and I said 'Heck, yes!' Beats being on the CB, I'll tell you that," Jim said, a big grin crinkling up his eyes. "And you know where I get the scandals, Doc?" "No, I don't," I replied, "tell me." "From my Mr. Fix-It stops!" Jim said. "Doesn't that just beat all?" he exclaimed happily, cracking himself up. "It's that resource thing you talked about, Doc—just about everybody knows a story or two, all you have to do is ask! Especially at the old folks home where I do odd jobs, and the county facilities where people have worked for a long time. And since they know I'm going to listen, people kind of save up their stories for when I come by. Works out great. It's a good life, Doc," Jim concluded, "it's a good life. I make enough to live OK and put some aside for later. I got enough people around so I'm not lonely hardly ever. But most of all, I know how I did it and how I could do it again if I had to."

## CREATING YOUR SUCCESS KNOWINGLY

And that's the real key to success in the Future. Jim's "good life" wasn't the stuff of happenstance or luck; Jim created his good life deliberately, one step at a time. Knowing how he did it gives Jim the critical assurance that if need be, he can do it again.

Just because the Future is Unknown, how to create success in the Future doesn't have to be unknown. Knowing you can create success for yourself over and over and over again regardless of how your world changes transforms a potentially terrifying Unknown into an exciting realm of positive possibilities.

There is no one "answer" for anybody in the Future. There are any number of "answers" that change and shift as society, technology, and how we live continue to change and shift. For example, information may come from sources we don't even conceive of yet—just as the World Wide Web was a complete unknown some 20 years ago—but information and the willingness to avail yourself of it will always be important to success. That's why a Winner's resources are process-oriented rather than content-driven. Information and imagination, for example, are available to you regardless of how that information is packaged, or what uses you'll put your imagination to.

## CONCLUSION

The Future lies before us, tantalizingly Unknown, scary and exciting at the same time. Every breath you take moves you inexorably—like it or not—into that Future. Be the Winner you were always meant to be. Use the eight steps set forth in this book to help you make that Future a wonderful one, replete with opportunity, fulfillment, and prosperity. Let the exceptional people who serve as dynamite examples throughout the book inspire you. Create the success and joy that is yours for the taking, in your bright and shining Future.

# RECOMMENDED READING

Batten, Joe D. *Building a Total Quality Culture*. California: Crisp Publications, 1993.

Batten, Joe D., and Mark Victor Hansen. *The Master Motivator: Secrets of Inspiring Leadership*. Florida: Health Communications, 1995.

Branden, Nathaniel. *Taking Responsibility*. New York: Fireside, 1997.

Caissy, Gail. *Unlock the Fear: How to Open Yourself Up to Face and Accept Change*. New York: Insight Books, 1998.

Cameron, Julia. *The Artist's Way*. New York: Tarcher/Perigee, 1992.

Covey, Stephen R. *The 7 Habits of Highly Effective People*. New York: Fireside, 1990.

Dychtwald, Ken, and Joe Flower. *Age Wave*. New York: Bantam Books, 1990.

Judy, Richard W., Carol D'Amico, and Gary L. Geipel. *Workforce 2020*. Indiana: Hudson Institute, 1997.

Naisbeth, John, and Patricia Aburdene. *Megatrends 2000*. New York: Avon, 1990.

New York Times. *The Downsizing of America*. New York: Times Books, 1996.

Reeve, Christopher. *Still Me*. New York: Random House, 1998.

Robbins, Anthony. *Awaken the Giant Within*. New York: Fireside, 1992.

Sheehy, Gail. *New Passages*. New York: Ballantine, 1995.

Siegel, Bernie S., M.D. *Love, Medicine and Miracles*. New York: Harper & Row, 1986.

# Index